Dr. Kurt Koch · The Revival in Indonesia

D1059842

2951 4861

NCMC
BV
3777
.I5
K5813
1970

The Revival in Indonesia

Dr. Kurt Koch

Kregel Publications
525 Eastern Ave S. E., Grand Rapids,
49503 Michigan, USA

Printed in Western Germany by
St.-Johannis-Druckerei C. Schweickhardt
Lahr-Dinglingen (Baden)   11247/1970

TRANSLATOR'S PREFACE

When we think of the miracles recorded in the Bible, we often overlook the other side of these events. We rejoice to hear of Peter's deliverance from jail, but fail to remember that James had just been killed with the sword. We are thrilled that Paul raised Eutychus from the dead, but hardly notice that he left Trophimus ill at Miletus.

The same God who spoke to Moses through a burning bush and who delivered Daniel from the mouth of the lions, was the God who allowed Jonathan to die at the side of Saul, and who let Jeremiah languish in a pit.

The words of Jesus are still very true today, "There were many lepers in Israel in the time of the prophet Elisha; and none of them was cleansed, but Naaman the Syrian."

"Teacher, we wish to see a sign from you," is the cry of many a heart, but it is a cry which has led many into the errors of extremism and the dangers of occultism. "If they do not hear Moses and the prophets, neither will they be convinced if someone should rise from the dead," said Jesus.

We must remember that man looks on the outward appearance, and that the human race is more impressed by the tinsel of sight, than by the imperishable jewel of faith and love. We forget so easily that the priceless miracle of conversion, which continues to occur in both Manchester and Morocco, and in the East and in the West, is incomparably greater than the mere raising of a body from the dead.

Yes, the God of the Bible is still alive today; the current events in Indonesia testify to this fact. Let us therefore rejoice with our brethren and sisters in this distant land, but having rejoiced, let us remember that it is not miracles that God requires of us, but obedience, and that we "do justice, and love kindness, and walk humbly with the Lord our God."

Translator

P. S. Many of the names of the people mentioned in this book have been altered at their own request.

6

CONTENTS

Part Two — Asia's Great Opportunity

8

INDONESIA

There are principally three countries today on which the attention of the world is focussed.

The first of these is Israel which stands at the very centre of world events. It can almost certainly be said that this, the smallest nation in the world, has the greatest history. We shall not be discussing this here, however, since we have already done so in my book 'Der Kommende' (The Coming One).

The next country which most occupies world opinion, is Vietnam. In this pit of fire the future of Asia will be decided; and the prospects from the Western point of view are not good.

The third country, which is much discussed today in Christian circles, is Indonesia. What is the reason for the unusual interest centring around this land? Let us leave the question open for the moment and look first of all at Indonesia's religious history.

I. THE HISTORICAL DEVELOPMENT OF INDONESIA

Whoever wishes to understand the present must first acquaint himself with the past.

As a land-bridge between two continents, the island world of Indonesia has not had an insignificant history.

Fossils found there relate her to Peking man, and this ancient Asian link has in many instances extended into the economic and cultural history of the country.

The rock inscriptions, dating back 3,000 years, have not yet all been deciphered, and they still await close scientific investigation.

The religious situation in Indonesia is also very interesting. The country has been penetrated by four different streams of thought, and these have added their various influences to the animism which developed simultaneously in the area.

In the first and second centuries Indian traders brought Hinduism to the country. It was these traders who conveyed the famous Indonesian sandalwood to the West. Thus Europe was to have this aromatic wood before it knew anything about the country of its origin. The Hindu religion and culture developed during the 6th to the 14th centuries into a powerful kingdom, and the roots of the present-day Indonesian language lie in this Hindu culture.

In the 6th, 7th and 8th centuries Hinduism became overlapped by Buddhism. Once again it was Indian importers who brought the new religion into the country. In building their temple at Borobudur the Buddhists erected a holy place on Java, which was at the same time the site of the most sacred Hindu shrine, Prambana. And so the two great Indian religions lived side by side on Java in peaceful coexistence.

Then in the 12th and 13th centuries came the epoch of Islam, which gained its first foothold at Atjeh in northern Sumatra. The Islamic kingdom that came into being in 1205 under Sultan John Sjah was to last until 1903. These religions were to afford the Dutch colonial lords many bitter struggles, including a number in our own century.

Whoever reads the prophets of the Old Testament finds that they frequently mention the islands or coastlands of the sea. The visionary gaze of these men of God reached out far beyond their own land (Is. 66:19).

Were these islands to be neglected then by the One who said, "Go into all the world and preach the gospel to every creature"?

The first messengers of Christ to arrive there may have possibly even come during the time of the early Christian fathers. It is not to be totally dismissed that even the apostle Thomas, who worked in India, crossed over to Indonesia with the Indian traders. In any case, we know that missionaries in the Mar-Thomas Church, named after him, worked in Indonesia.

The next real proof of missionary work in the area was confirmed by some painstaking and detailed evaluation of historical documents: Christians from Persia brought the gospel to Indonesia in the years 671 to 679. But after this it remained in darkness for a long time. These were the centuries during which the Christian Church in the Western world slowly lost its missionary strength. Gradually the candlestick of Rome was pushed aside, and the spiritual impetus shifted into central and northern Europe. One only has to think back to the missionary efforts of the Germanic peoples, to the Cluniac reform, and to the forerunners of the Reformation: Wycliffe, Hus, and Savonarola, for the evidence of this fact. At that time practically nothing was known of Indonesia.

This, however, was soon altered when merchants sailed to the ports of India and learned of the island world to the east. Following the epoch-making discovery of Columbus, the world became filled with a tremendous craze for discovery. At the same time the seafaring nations were seeking to increase their trade.

In 1511 the Portuguese conquered the Moluccas, causing

the Moslems to withdraw under pressure to the south. Catholics among the Portuguese occupation forces founded the first Catholic church in the Moluccas in 1522.

Not long after this the missionary Francis Xevarius came over from India. Although he only worked in Indonesia from 1546 to 1547, his influence was so great, that ever since he has borne the nickname: Apostle to the Indonesians.

The 16th century also saw the beginning of Dutch colonial power in Indonesia. The Indonesian Christians were not exactly pleased when the Dutch banned missionary work in northern and southern Sumatra and on Bali. The reason for this was a fear that the natives might rebel and leave the work on the plantations. The ban on Bali will be treated in more detail later.

The foundation of the Protestant Church in the Dutch East Indies is regarded today with mixed feelings by the believers there. The pastors were state officials receiving their pay from the government. It was similar to the time of Constantine the Great — anyone who wanted to get on in life became a Christian in order to achieve his goal. Thus a Christian church came into being in Indonesia which had basically freed itself neither from the heathen nor from the Hindu traditions.

Besides the Dutch State Church, however, following the labours of various Christian missionaries various other localized churches came into being on Java, Bali, Celebes, Borneo, Sanghir, Nias, Sumatra, Sumba, and New Guinea, — to mention but a few of the more important ones. In East Java the formation of an Indonesian church was very much linked with the name of a faithful German watchmaker, brother Endo. A Christian from Russia, brother Coolen, should also be mentioned in this respect.

In the 20th century, as the era of decolonization was born, the might of the Dutch colonial powers gradually crumbled. In Indonesia a movement founded in 1908, the Resurgence of Asia, gained ground. This trend underlined the Indonesian peoples' struggle for independence.

In the Second World War Indonesia was occupied for three and a half years by the Japanese. After their withdrawal, Indonesia proclaimed its independence on August 17th 1945 and set up a constitution, the so-called Pantja Sila. The constitution, however, could not be enforced at once for the Dutch refused to recognize their independence. This resulted in a war of liberation which lasted for more than four years. Under pressure from the U.N.O., and especially from the Americans, the Dutch gave in and finally left the country in 1950.

Yet the country was still not able to relax. The next enemy came from within, from among its own people. First the power of colonialism had had to be broken. Now there followed a battle against an even greater enemy of the Indonesian people.

II. INDONESIA'S TRIBUTE OF BLOOD

By means of an attempted coup d'état on October 1st 1965, Indonesia underwent a radical change in its history. There are revolutions of various dimensions in some corner or other of the world practically every day of the year. Amid present world events, however, they are hardly ever noticed. And yet the circumstances in Indonesia are somewhat exceptional. Here, events have taken place whose course has been of crucial importance in the political development of East Asia.

It was known for years that the former President, Sukarno, had communist sympathies. When, on September 1st 1963, the eastern part of New Guinea came under Indonesian administration, the missionaries foresaw the great difficulties that might soon be facing them in their work.

The premonition was not unfounded. Communist influence grew in the country. What was the final result to be? The outcome was completely different from what the Communists had expected.

The Planned Massacre

On the 1st of October 1965 the Communists had intended to take control of the country. The first objective was to remove the general staff. The Communists had their own officers ready and waiting to take their places.

In Djakarta alone six generals were arrested during the first Communist onslaught. They were dealt with in accordance with the usual Communist practice in Asia. Their eyes were partially gouged out and the mutilated victims were then made to run naked among some Communist trained women who hacked at the unfortunate men with their knives until the generals finally succumbed to their tortures.

However, at least two of the military hierarchy in Djakarta escaped. The first of these was Suharto. His child had been dangerously ill in hospital and so he had sat at its bedside all night. When the Communists had searched for him at his home, they had been unable to find him.

This one small slip was enough to frustrate the thoroughly planned revolution of the Communists. Suharto was the head of the strategic reserve. He immediately alerted his men, and in their first retaliatory action they obtained control of Djakarta Radio.

Humanly speaking, this action saved the lives of the Christians and the missionaries in the country. The Communists were in fact waiting by their radio-sets all over the country for orders from Djakarta to attack. But the orders did not come and the revolution faltered at the very outset.

Suharto's counter-action brought to light lists of those who had been blacklisted by the Communists. These contained the names of every single political opponent the Communists had in the country.

The religious list contained the names of all the Moslem priests and teachers, together with all the Catholic priests and Protestant missionaries. The Christian communities in Indonesia would have been eliminated by this one blow, had God granted the revolution success.

The second general to escape the Communist assault was Natsution, the former Defence Minister. His deliverance, just like that of Suharto, is a miracle in the minds of the Indonesians.

When the Communists had forced their way into his house, Natsution was ready to give himself up. His wife, however, pulled him back. The first bullet missed him, hitting his small daughter instead, who had just rushed out of the bedroom into the corridor. She later died.

Natsution fled through the back-door. His wife ran with him to the garden wall. Climbing on her shoulders he reached the neighbouring grounds, which belonged to a foreign embassy. The two guard-dogs miraculously allowed him to pass and he was able to escape. Meanwhile, back in his house, another act of Christian love was being played out. Natsution's adjutant was a Christian officer. In order to cover his chief's retreat, when the Communists demanded, "Are you Natsution?", he replied, "Yes, I am." With that he was immediately shot.

Christians may possibly ask, whether he should have lied or not. Whatever the case, the adjutant acted as he did in order to save the life of his superior officer, and this act of practical Christian love will probably be valued more highly in eternity than the act of adhering to some inflexible doctrinal outlook.

The Terrible Retaliation

The horrible manner in which the generals had been mutilated aroused the anger of the Indonesians. In addition to this, another incident, which was later shamefully hushed up, provoked the revulsion of the whole nation. The Communist women, besides the other atrocities they had committed, had actually raped the generals while they had been bound. And then, last but not least, the mortal danger which had threatened the Moslem priests caused a public outcry. After all, nine tenths of the Indonesian population is Moslem.

The subsequent retaliation to which the Moslems were driven, actually occasioned the deaths of more people than have currently died in the Vietnam war. A wave of anti-Communism spread through the whole country. At night, the people, moved by revenge, broke into the houses of the Communists and other suspects and murdered all the men they could find. This wave of murder cost something in the region of a million lives in the months of October, November, and December 1965. The West was kept completely uninformed as to the extent of these brutal retaliatory steps. Just for once the Communists received the treatment they had intended to inflict on others.

The aftermath of this series of murders was horrific. In many villages in East Java not a single man remained alive. Nearby mass graves were dug in which the thousands of murdered Communists were thrown.

Imagine the sorrow that has come upon these families: children deprived of their fathers, and wives of their husbands! This is surely the only place in the world where the Communists have had to suffer what they have inflicted on others in Russia, Red China, Cuba and elsewhere for decades.

The Suffering of the Christians

The Moslems contented themselves mainly with "liquidating" their political enemies, but as in other parts of the world like Eastern Nigeria and the Southern Sudan, they took the opportunity to attack the Christians as well.

For example, a Christian family in a Moslem village tried to alleviate the sorrow of the wives of the murdered men. But this was just what the Moslems were waiting for. "We have proof," they said, "that the Christians are in league with the Communists." Going to the house they killed the husband, and forced his wife to cook for them each day and even wash their bloodstained clothes.

The persecuted Communists often sought refuge among the Christians who frequently came to their aid. This of course provoked the Moslems who repeatedly claimed, "The Christians and Communists are working together." Thus in many areas the persecution of the Communists widened to include a persecution of the Christians as well.

Yet the Lord watched over his children. A missionary from Borneo, who lived through the confusion on the island, gave me a report concerning his own district. He said, "Amid all the bloody persecutions and frightful atrocities, one could still see God's power at work, for none of the 300 Christians in the area were killed. The Lord didn't allow one hair of their head to be harmed."

Another missionary working on a different island reported, "When the murdering began, a young Communist teacher went and sought refuge within the Christian community. While he was with them, they showed him the way to Christ. He continued to come each day to the Christians who prayed with him regularly. Although he had been driven there by fear originally, he later testified that he had in fact accepted the Lord as his Saviour.

"Later, an informer reported this to the Moslems. Going to the church where the teacher used to sleep at night, they lay in wait for him, and one morning they dragged him outside and beheaded him in front of the church. The Moslems then turned to the Christians, 'This is further proof that you are really all Communists.' After some discussion the Moslem leaders decided to slaughter the entire Christian population in the district; but God intervened. A company of soldiers arrived from a nearby garrison and undertook to protect the Christians for several months until the troubles were over." — I have had the opportunity of visiting this community personally.

The military intervention in this instance was quite remarkable. The government troops usually took little notice of the murders that were taking place. The only questions they asked were, "Who should we fight for? Which side is more in the right? If the Communists had triumphed, everything would have been reversed."

This strange Moslem lust for shedding blood has often been a source of much anxiety to the Christians. A Chinese Christian on the island of Java once said to me, "We're a thorn in the flesh to the Moslems in three ways: firstly, they don't like our race; secondly, they're jealous of us, because the Chinese work harder than them and are therefore more successful in business; and thirdly, they hate us simply because we are Christians."

I have witnessed this same tense relationship in all the countries of the Far East. Towns and countries with a strong Chinese element tend to expand more rapidly than the surrounding areas. This is the main reason why Malaysia and Singapore have experienced such a strong economic upsurge. In both these countries at least 50 % of the population is Chinese.

Looking into the future, conflicts are almost bound to arise, and in some cases they can be seen appearing on the horizon already. For example, the Christians wanted to build a church in a suburb of Djakarta. The population of the area, however, consists largely of Moslems, and they soon found ways and means of hindering the construction of the church.

Similarly a Christian doctor told me of how he had bought a large plot of ground from a Moslem in order to build a Christian hospital on it. When the Moslem discovered what the intended building was to be, he cancelled the sale during the final stage of the legal settlement. The doctor lost several thousand American dollars as a result of this. Although he was legally in the right, he decided not to take the Moslem to court on account of what is written in 1 Corinthians chapter 6.

The Moslems will one day come into open conflict with the Christians. This is but a part of the picture facing the world before its end. The followers of Christ are to face greater and greater trials before the Lord comes in his glory and releases them from all their sorrows.

III. THE ECONOMY OF THE LAND

This book is founded upon several visits to Indonesia, and although the conditions of 1966 and 1967 do not necessarily continue to hold true today, the comparison is still worthwhile for it illustrates the growth that Indonesia is currently experiencing.

On my first two visits to the country I was immediately struck by the poverty of the general population. Djakarta, which at that time was a town of about three million inhabitants, apart from having a few buildings built for prestige purposes, proved to be nothing more than a conglomeration of bad roads, tumble-down shacks, gaudy colours, and undernourished people.

During periods of drought, starvation soon became evident in many places. I had previously had no idea that a situation like this ever existed in Indonesia. Usually when one speaks of hunger one thinks only of India.

During these early visits of mine to the country, I witnessed the almost daily demonstrations of groups of school-children and students. I found it difficult to tolerate them at first, for the incessant noise of their shouting gradually got on my nerves. However, I was struck by two things about these demonstrators which contrasted them sharply with the unruly mobs one often finds today in Europe and America. Firstly, the processions moved through the streets in perfect order. There was no violence of any kind. And secondly? Well, at the time, they really did have something to demonstrate about, which cannot be easily said for their counterparts in the West.

What motivated them? Their hunger! How come? For some weeks past the price of rice had gone up to 100 rupees a kilogram, which works out at about three shillings and sixpence in English money. This was roughly equivalent to the daily wage of a rickshaw driver or an ordinary factory worker; and on top of that, 1 kilogram of rice did not last long when one had a hungry family to feed.

As a result of this, in some districts one could find children walking the streets with distended stomachs and slowly dying of undernourishment.

The students and the schoolchildren whom I saw, were therefore justified in drawing people's attention to the problem. Whether this would do any good, however, is another question. One of the members of the government said in a speech, "If shouting would help to bring the price of rice down, then I would start shouting louder than anyone."

What is basically the root of this problem? Is Indonesia capable of feeding its own population? Well, in theory the answer is yes, for the surface area is capable of supporting not only the present population of 110 million but also a three or fourfold increase in this population.

The country is in fact extremely large and consists of about 3,000 separate islands stretching almost 4,000 miles from tip to tail. The land, too, is very fertile and is only in need of cultivation.

This, however, was one of the many problems which had yet to be overcome. There was a complete lack of any systematic plan to clear the ground and make it arable. How easy it would be to transform the mountain slopes into rich rice terraces. It is only a matter of collecting the rain during the rainy season. But instead of this, the water rushes down the hillsides to flood the villages below. While I was staying in Djakarta the water was standing in the streets sometimes to a depth of one and a half feet.

Because of insufficient exploitation of the land, rice has often had to be imported. In 1968, I was told, 600,000 tons were lacking. "From where do you import the rice then?" I wanted to know. "From India or other Far Eastern countries?" "No, they haven't got enough for themselves! The rice comes from America, but it's really too dear; and besides, we haven't the foreign exchange to buy it."

The result was that what rice they had, was sold at exorbitant prices. So while the rich people hoarded it, the poor were unable to afford the price and were left to find other ways of filling their stomachs. An importer told me, "We are already buying pig-food from the United States and mixing it with the bread."

Yet Indonesia does not need to go hungry. It is a rich country. As regards minerals and mineral resources, it is considered to be about the third richest country in the world.

What use are natural resources, however, if they are not exploited? Industrialization was as much in the doldrums as agriculture. There was a lack of specialists, and even where they existed, they were unable to obtain the posts for which they were most suited.

The reins of the country were in the hands of the senior military officers. Indonesia was a military state. That meant that all the important posts, instead of being occupied by the specialists for the job, were held by high-ranking officers in the army.

What does a general know about agriculture or mining? Usually nothing. To have proved oneself on the parade ground or at gunnery does not automatically qualify one to plan the economy of a country.

"The army has literally ruined the country economically," I was told again and again. People pointed to the fact that senior officers had taken over as directors of the former well-established Dutch firms. The results had been disastrous. In 1967 alone 2,000 importing firms had gone into liquidation. The situation needed to be taken in hand quickly.

Wandering through the shabby shopping centre of Djakarta I saw many empty shelves in the shops. The shopkeepers were unable to buy up stock for they lacked the capital. The counters were therefore filled with goods of a very inferior quality.

That was the picture in the first few years following the end of the general strike. The question now is, whether or not the government has been able to clear up all these troubles. My most recent visit shows clearly that the problems facing Indonesia have now been tackled both shrewdly and effectively.

As early as the end of 1968 the government began to reinstate specialists in all positions of responsibility. Then, on the 1st of April 1969 a five-year plan for the country was introduced. The price of rice dropped so dramatically that it fell to a quarter of the 1967 level. No longer did they have to import American pig-food to mix with their bread. The shops are again full of goods. The country has been able to overcome the stalemate in its economy.

It would be wrong to listen to the propaganda the Communists put out concerning Indonesia today. Just think instead what the country would have been like under Communist rule. It would have been a case of organized mass-misery, as it is in almost every Communist country in the world.

There are three essential factors which one must recognize when attempting to assess the political and economic features of Indonesia. These are:

1. In the first place the army prevented the country collapsing under a Communist assault. For this the whole of the Far East should be thankful.

24

2. The government must be allowed time to build up the economy. The twenty or so years since the Dutch left the country is hardly enough time for it to have developed into a thriving economic community, particularly since in many respects it was deliberately held in check before that time.

3. A people who gained their independence only two decades ago must learn first of all to consolidate and to preserve the freedoms they have won. One cannot achieve the impossible. Did either the United States or Switzerland evolve into what they are today in the space of a few short years?

However, in its brief period of independence Indonesia has achieved a great deal. It has already carved out a name for itself in the free world, and today it is rapidly improving and consolidating its own economic position.

If you Want to Despair, Go by Air

What does this proverb mean? With humour in their voices the Indonesians use these words to describe the unreliability of their own airline, an unreliability we were able to taste for ourselves. There were about 80 of us waiting together in Djakarta to fly to East Java in order to take part in the conference soon to be held there; but we were simply unable to move. For days we just had to sit around and wait. It was a great test of our patience, and yet it became a blessing to me too.

While we were waiting there, I made a number of new contacts. One of the first people I started talking to was the Rev. Ward, the vice-president of 'World Vision'. He had heard me speak once in California. In an attempt to catch another plane, he had taken a taxi and made a journey lasting 30 hours — you could see the exhaustion written on his face. Yet instead of complaining, his only words were, "Well, disappointment means His appointment!" It was a wonderful attitude to take. In spite of the trouble he had been forced to endure through the inefficiency of others, not one word of complaint passed his lips. This missionary was certainly several classes higher than myself in the school of God.

The Bible and life have often taught me the lesson that God transforms our times of despair into hidden blessings. In this respect many of the stories of the Old Testament have been of great profit to me.

Consider, for example, the story of Joseph in Genesis chapters 37 to 50. Joseph was first of all thrown into a pit by his brothers, and then sold to some Midianite traders. Imagine the anguish and homesickness he went through. Yet this affliction, or rather this crime of Joseph's brothers, was transformed after many years into a great blessing by God. When the famine came, Joseph was able to save both his father and brothers, and in this way he became part of God's great plan of salvation for mankind, for through their sojourn in Egypt the children of Israel were destined to become the nation of God's choice.

The almost unbearable delay which I owed to the Indonesian airline GERUDA, brought with it many surprises. The only reason I describe these, is to illustrate God's kindness to us in the fact that he hides a blessing within every disappointment we meet in his service.

As my companion introduced me by my surname to an Australian who was waiting with us, the man immediately exclaimed, "Dr. *Kurt* Koch? I heard you speak some years ago in a Baptist church in Australia."

Half an hour later I was to meet another Australian. Introducing myself merely by the name Koch, he replied, "I've got some books by a Dr. Koch of Germany. They've helped me a lot in my work. Do you know him at all?" Did I know him? Only too well! You can imagine his surprise. He at once invited me to come to his church in Melbourne to speak there at various meetings, and the most encouraging thing was that I was actually able to fit these meetings into my Australian tour.

The best experience of all was the last one. For years now I have been on the trail of Bakth Singh. At the moment he is India's most well-known evangelist. No fewer than 300 new churches have been founded as a result of his ministry. In many large towns he has held mass meetings involving thousands of people, without any recourse to American advertising methods.

I had tried unsuccessfully to meet him on each occasion I had toured India. And now here we were facing one another on a morning which had been filled with so much irritation and disappointment. We sat talking together for a few hours, since he was waiting for the same aeroplane as myself.

It was a really wonderful occasion. As I asked him about himself, he told me a part of the story of his conversion. In the end he said, "Let's find somewhere quiet where we can pray together." My new friend from Melbourne was still with me, and so, finding a place somewhere apart, the three of us were able to forget the problems surrounding us for about half an hour. Bakth Singh had also been badly affected by the delay. He should have been speaking at the same conference in East Java to which I was going, and although he was 65 years old, he was also forced to make the 18 hour train journey when we found that we were unable to travel by air.

The fellowship I enjoyed with this brother in Christ over a period of 14 days was a great blessing to me. When we finally parted, he invited me to go to Hyderabad to speak there sometime. I intend to follow up this invitation within the next few months.

The English proverb was therefore fulfilled. Without the failure of the airline to supply us with a flight, I would never have been granted this wonderful opportunity of fellowship with the many missionaries who found themselves with me at Djakarta airport waiting for a plane.

What the devil breaks and ruins, God remakes and moulds into blessing.

IV. BALI, ISLAND OF THE DEVIL

Scenically, Bali is a pearl among the Indonesian islands. To embrace the beauty and wonders of this island in a single account is practically an impossibility.

The first thing I was able to enjoy from my cheap and extremely primitive hotel was the beach. The waves played on the sand some 40 yards away from my terrace. Daily they would drive ashore the hosts of mussels, starfish and other creatures which the local inhabitants immediately collected as the tide ebbed, thanking the ocean for its freely given gifts.

Beyond the shore, about 200 yards out, the surf boils night and day around the coral reef. It is an ill-advised bather who trusts himself to this seething of the elements. A young German doctor paid for his foolhardiness with his life by being subsequently swept out to sea and drowned. His room had been only two doors away from mine.

On the far side of the bay one could identify no less than three volcanoes. The largest of them, the 12,000 feet high Agung, was actually active during my stay.

Bali has inherited many names from its visitors. Some tourists dubbed it 'the Island of Paradise,' and others 'the Gem of the Tropics'. When Nehru visited Bali in 1954, he christened it, 'Morning of the World'.

Pulau Dewata — Isle of the Gods — is what the Indonesians call this island. They should know best. But who are these gods? Certainly none from the Old and New Testaments. Bearing in mind the island's local name, as the missionaries became familiar with the practices of the inhabitants, they renamed it, 'the Island of the Devil'.

The nickname, 'Island of the Devil', acts as a kind of challenge. We must explain what it really means.

The ancient tribal religion of the Balinese is a poly-theistic form of nature worship. They have their moun-tain-gods, river-gods, lake-gods, sacred trees, and holy places. In short, they visualize the whole of nature as possessing a soul.

Over the rice-fields the rice-goddess Devi Sri holds sway. Every cemetery, rock, hill and cavern has a spirit of its own. About 40 miles northeast of Denpasar, 2,000 wild buffalo still live in a vast cemetery, venerated as sacred beasts. No one is allowed to kill them. They are regarded as incarnate spirits of the dead natives buried in this extensive graveyard.

After the introduction of firstly Hinduism and later Buddhism into the country, together with the animism which already existed there, the Balinese temples soon began to express this religious syncretism. Beside the various gods of nature one finds the Indian gods Siva, Brahma and Vishnu.

The problems arising from this religious mixture have been solved by the Balinese with a certain amount of cunning. Whereas Buddha teaches men not to kill, the old Balinese nature-gods demand sacrifices of blood. How could this dilemma be resolved? Very easily! The animals were left to kill each other.

This is one of the reasons lying behind the terrible cock-fights. Next to the temple of Taman Ajun is a gigantic hall where this very popular form of entertain-ment takes place. The cockerels are fed well before the fights. Their owners massage their necks for weeks on end in order to strengthen the muscles. They also buy fetishes from magicians to try to make their cockerels win. And then thousands gather to see the awful spectacle.

The contest continues until one of the birds is dead. The next pair is then brought on to fight.

By means of these cock-fights both the Indian and the Balinese gods are satisfied. The inhabitants of the island kill no animals. The cockerels do this instead. And so the nature-gods have their blood-sacrifices.

These contests, however, have another side to them. A distinguished visitor asked a district governor, 'Why don't you do away with these grotesque shows? It's a blot on your culture." The Balinese replied, "There's a terrible struggle going on inside every native of Bali. We need a kind of release. The cock-fights are merely a safety-valve. If we didn't have these cock-fights, we would probably turn to worse things still. So the lesser evil keeps a greater one at bay."

The Balinese know of other compromises arising from the blending of their nature religion with the religions of India. For thousands of years the 'dog-dish' has featured on the gourmet's menu. What's more, the meal is really only fit for dogs since the numerous stray dogs in the area feed predominantly on human excrement. They act in a way like toilet disposal units. But Buddhism forbids the killing and eating of animals! The Balinese therefore redeems himself before slaughtering an animal by offering a prayer to his god, asking for forgiveness, and in addition, promising a small portion of the meat as an offering: "You'll get some of it as well!" He then enjoys the dog in peace, if enjoys is the right word!

Temples and Dances

The Taman-Ajun temple, which I mentioned earlier, is a real curiosity. The Balinese themselves call this temple 'the Hotel of the Gods'. An excellent term. Until coming here I had not realized that even gods can go away on holiday. One automatically recalls the comment of Elijah

(1 Kings 18, 27), who annoyed the prophets of Baal by saying, "Shout louder, perhaps your god has gone away."

But this is apparently exactly what the Balinese gods do! There islanders believe that they meet together once a year for an annual conference. Some have a long way to travel, others come from the immediate vicinity. Before they come together in Bali's largest temple, Besaki, they first spend the night in the Taman-Ajun temple, the common rendez-vous point. They then go on to their conference at Besakih, which is situated on the slopes of the volcano, Agung. During the eruption of the volcano in 1963 part of this temple was destroyed. However, as the gods have so far made no approaches to the West for aid, the temple has still to be repaired. Elijah's jest in 1 Kings 18 still applies.

Famous dances are performed on Bali in connection with the temple feasts.

First of all there is the fire-dance. The dancers are put into a trance by a priest. A fire is lit in front of the temple. Each dancer is then persuaded that he is a horse and is being hunted by a tiger. He begins to tremble. Next the priest persuades him that his only means of escape is through the fire. With this the hypnotized dancer rushes through the fire. The sequence is repeated several times in the presence of an enthusiastic audience. When the dancer is taken out of his trance by the priest, although he is completely covered in sweat and still shows all the signs of terror on his face, his legs and feet show no signs of being burnt at all.

Another dance is even more famous: the knife-dance. This is Bali's greatest attraction which draws thousands of tourists to the island every year.

The Balinese calendar has ten months, each of 35 days. New Year's Day and other festivals therefore tend to wander somewhat. Two of these festivals, celebrated rather like fêtes in the West, are called Galungan and Kunigan.

The greatest and most important festival, however, is Melis. As a part of this major festival, sacrifices are brought to the seashore. The sacrifice takes place before the tide comes in. It is quite remarkable how after the offering of the sacrificial gifts a great flood-tide comes in and engulfs them all. The Balinese maintain that this shows that the gods have come to accept the offerings. In fact it is really just a quirk of nature, since the tide normally comes in much more gradually. Only at the time of Melis is there a flood-tide like this.

When the sacrificing has ended, the natives begin to dance. As they do so they commence to enact an ancient mythological story. The aim is to kill a witch named Rangda. She, however, manages to escape from her enemies. The men therefore turn their swords against themselves but as they do this, a friendly god comes to their aid and the points of their blades are prevented from piercing their flesh. The mythological implication of this test is that although the dancer intending to slay the evil witch, Rangda, has his blade turned against himself by her magical powers, the avenger of evil is nevertheless protected. Behind this display therefore, one finds the concept of the triumph of good over evil. Basically the dances are all trance-induced. Trance-phenomena like this can be observed all over the Far East. I have had ample opportunity of witnessing events like this for myself, since the proceedings often take place out in the open. But although it is easy to get caught up in a crowd which is gathering to watch such a spectacle, I have never yet deliberately gone out of my way to watch one, since I feel a Christian should avoid such heathen rites if at all possible.

The Magical War

From time to time in other books of mine I have mentioned magical duels. When I arrived in Bali in March

1968 and called at a ministers' convention, they said to me, "You've arrived just at the right time. There's a magical war going on in Bali at this present moment."

One of the pastors explained to me what was taking place. There have been magical wars on Bali as far back as one can remember. These matters are usually, however, kept strictly secret. The tourists know nothing of them. The terrible battles only become publicly known when Balinese natives who have been involved in them are converted to Christianity and confess their secret sins. One finds that all the magicians on the island, and there are quite a number, are intimately involved in these affairs.

On Bali, just as in Tibet, there are a number of teachers of magic. Each of these has his own followers or pupils, and when the pupils have reached a certain stage in their training, contests are held, aimed at testing and strengthening the magical powers of the individuals involved. These magical 'Olymics' are a 'peaceful' form of combat.

The situation is immediately altered, however, when two of the combatants 'fall out' with one another. The duel that often results can end with the death of one of the magicians. The fights, however, are not fought with conventional weapons, but with mental powers. They squat beneath haunted trees maybe a mile or so apart and fight with their magical powers.

Should such a duel spread to the circle of friends of those involved, then a magical war can ensue.

The magical war in March 1968 took the following course. A magician ordered a cup of coffee in a small Balinese restaurant. The owner of the restaurant, himself a magician, poured some poison into the coffee. The customer noticed this and challenged the owner to a duel. Calling their friends to their aid, the two rival factions took up their stand over a mile apart. The signal for the battle to commence consisted of two lights coming together from the east and the west. When the villagers saw them, they recognized them to be magical lights.

The magical wars are nearly always limited to about one month's duration. The magicians fight during the night and sleep during the day. Normally they send the weaker participants into battle first. When I received this report from the local minister, he added, "Six or seven people have already died magically in the battle." Towards the end of the conflict, the two chief combatants finally fight each other personally. The war ends when the weaker magician succumbs and dies.

I have often been asked if a magical war is not really a sign that the devil is divided against himself. No! When two boxers fight the stronger also wins, yet both men remain boxers and therefore belong to the same professional group.

Before I left Bali, I tried to learn a little more about these magical wars from an old Balinese native. He was astonished that I knew anything about them at all and asked, "How did you get to know about these ancient Balinese matters? They are usually carefully concealed from tourists, and we never reveal our secrets to strangers." I could discover nothing more from him during the time of our short conversation together.

Demonic Possession on Bali

It will be of interest to philosophers of religion, to parapsychologists and to Christian ministers that there are various forms of possession on Bali. In no other country on earth have I come across so many different distinctions. This again throws some light on this so-called 'Island of the Devil'.

First of all, there are certain expressions in Balinese which have no ethical meaning at all, but simply refer to the actual state of possession. Such terms include Kepangloh, Krangsukan, Kerauhan. These three words are merely used to describe an inexplicable state that comes upon a person.

Another expression, Daratan, comes from the Balinese word darat meaning earth, and describes a type of possession caused through earth spirits.

Kerasukan is used to describe the kind of possession where a person is overwhelmed by a power outside himself. 'An invisible harness' is slipped over the victim.

The term Kemidjilan comes from the high-Balinese word Midjil, meaning apparition. This form of possession is linked with the experiencing of hallucinations.

The word Bebainan originates from the expression Bebei, meaning the unredeemed soul, or little demon. People plagued by this form of possession are controlled. Balinese specialists are able even to distinguish between different types of sickness arising from possession. That is more than the sceptical psychiatrists of the West have yet achieved. I was amazed by the psychiatric knowledge of the islanders, who can explain for example the difference between Bebainan possession and St. Vitus's Dance. I have never heard of any Western psychiatrist who could do the same, and yet Western scientists often put on such an air of superiority that one would think they have a monopoly of all knowledge.

Among the most interesting phenomena of possession is one which is described as Sanghgang tutut. This refers to a piece of wood that has the power to protect a person. This is really an animistic form of possession. Since in the minds of the natives inanimate material possesses a soul, it can itself be possessed. From the point of view of religious history, this is of course a question of pantheism, but it also crops up on the perimeter of Christian culture. The psychiatrist Dr. Lechler has said that not only people, but also houses can be possessed. No less a person than Prof. Jung from Zurich held the same opinion. However, he did not dare to air his views publicly. The reason for this was his fear of being regarded by his associates as being out of his mind. This he confessed once in a private conversation in Männedorf. He did, however, write the foreword to Dr. F. Moser's book called 'Spuk' (Ghosts). And so phenomena like these which the West usually tries to push aside, are very familiar to the natives of Bali.

The above-mentioned types of possession are by no means the only forms known on Bali. This itself is an indication that possession and demons are part and parcel of the daily round of the island.

How should we as Christians or missionaries begin to tackle a problem like this? We can only breathe a sigh of relief that in Christ all these things are both surmounted and surmountable. The power of his redemption and the efficacy of his blood which was shed for us are sufficient to break every demonic ban that we may meet. Naturally, every Christian and minister has reason to be glad if God spares him from having to wrestle directly with problems like these. But whoever is called upon to heal the souls of those who are occultly oppressed, must know something about the battle involved. We cannot regard the mentally ill as being possessed, nor the possessed as being mentally ill. The continual errors made in this respect are found to a frightening extent not only among psychiatrists, but also among ministers. And such errors lead to both incorrect and extremely inappropriate treatments.

Another factor that sheds a ray of light on the whole situation in Bali is the doctors' finding that 85 % of all the sick on the island are neurotic. Is this not the other side to all the trance-induced, magical and demonic phenomena which occur on the island?

Christianity on Bali

Considering the circumstances we have just outlined, we need not be surprised that up till now Christianity has made little progress on Bali. Of the two million inhabitants, 6,000 are Protestant Christians and 4,000 Catholic.

It must also be taken into account that an unhappy combination has taken place between Christianity and the other local religions. Thus, not only have Hinduism and nature worship united with one another, but also Christianity and the magical practices of the island. It has even reached the point where there are so-called Christian magicians.

But let us first hear something of the development of the Christian Church on Bali. I received my information from several ministers living in the area.

In the history of Dutch colonialism, Bali was the last large island that the Dutch occupied. Until the turn of the century, eight kings had shared the government of the island between them. The son-in-law of the chairman of the royal council was my interpreter. He is actually a Christian.

Since these eight kings had opposed the Dutch and carried on protracted struggles against them, the Dutch failed for a long time to take over full control of the island, although they had already been in Indonesia for 300 years.

In the second half of the 19th century a Catholic Missionary settled in Bali. He succeeded in winning a Balinese for Christ. This first Christian, however, later apostatized and promptly killed the Catholic missionary. The king in whose area the murderer lived, desiring to please the Dutch, handed him over to be judged by their law. The colonialists, caring little about a trial, had the murderer shot. The Balinese were angered by this apparently arbitrary treatment. The king told the Dutch, "We do not condemn a person without first giving him a hearing." On account of this injustice, opposition flared up. As a result about 170 Dutch people were murdered by the Balinese. The Queen of the Netherlands reacted so strongly to this uprising, that she signed a decree forbidding any missionary from settling on Bali.

As this decree was never revoked, a Christian church was not founded on Bali until 1929 when a handful of missionaries from East Java came to Bali secretly and passed the Christian message on from mouth to mouth.

This method of evangelism was not as inept as one might have thought, since the Hindu religion on Bali had always centred on individual families. In this way each family has its own praying-place and sacrificial shrine.

Progress towards the foundation of a Christian church could not be halted, in spite of the ban. Even some of the Dutch colonial officials looked favourably upon Christianity, in defiance of the existing decree. And so in the 1930's a Christian church was formed. The Church on Bali is therefore still very young and in the first generation, so to speak. Today there are about 25 Balinese pastors on the island.

The Christian Church is faced with massive bulwarks in the dominantly heathen customs of the island. In 1963, however, an amazing opportunity was presented to the Christians. In that year Agung erupted and devastated twelve villages. 1,500 people perished. The Balinese were all the more shattered because their national shrine, the great Besakih temple, was also partly destroyed. Their faith in their gods was shaken, and they became wide open to the Christian message, especially as Christian aid in the form of practical gifts began to flow into the devastated area.

However, the Church did not use this extraordinary opportunity. So many gifts arrived that the organization of the still small body of Christians was at first unable to cope with them all. A whole year was needed before everything was sorted out. In the meantime the doors that had been open were closed again. The Christian Church on Bali had missed its great opportunity. The social work involved had left no time for preaching the gospel.

The Balinese church is not alone in this respect. It has its parallels in many American and European churches.

How often in our churches has welfare work stifled evangelistic effort. Concern for the body has pushed aside care for people's souls.

The Stronghold of Magic in the Church

The Balinese church has a character similar to that of many churches on other mission-fields. Christians who have come from a heathen background, or whose parents or grandparents are still tied to their heathen beliefs, are often caught up in magic. This I also found to be the case on Bali.

I have been able to speak in five different churches there altogether. When I warned about witchcraft, excited questions followed. One church elder said to me, "What should we do when we are bitten by a snake? There are no doctors for miles around. The witch-doctors are the only ones who can save us from dying. Why shouldn't we as Christians go to the Hindu magician in a case like this?" In replying to the church elder I said, "Have you never read in Mark 16 : 17 that the Lord Jesus can also heal snake-bites? And have you never heard of the story where Paul was bitten by a snake on Malta and survived?" The elder did not reply. I went on, "How can we as Christians go to a heathen sorcerer? We can only do this if we trust the devil more than God. Yet if God wouldn't help me after I had been bitten by a poisonous snake, I would still rather die than go to the devil for help."

I then recounted to the congregation some examples of missionaries who had been bitten by poisonous snakes and who had survived. One such example concerned the experience of a missionary in Brazil who was bitten by a very poisonous snake, the sukkru. The Indians present at the time had told the missionary, "You are finished. There's no cure for this bite." The missionary's sight was

39

already beginning to fail. His foot swelled up to the size of an elephant's. The Indians carried him to the hut. There they watched over the missionary who had already become unconscious. After some minutes the unfortunate man regained consciousness, and in that moment cried out, "Lord Jesus, your promises!" He then fell unconscious again. But the power of the poison had been broken. Instead of dying, the missionary, after lying in a coma for a long time, recovered. There were no after-effects.

I recounted this story to the Balinese church. However, the elder had further questions. He explained, "We have a man here who although he isn't a magician has a white stone with which he heals the sick. When I was ill, I asked this healer for his white stone, but since I was a Christian, he wouldn't give it to me, even though I kept on imploring him for it. Why would it have been wrong to have used the stone if it really did possess healing powers?" I replied, "Be glad that you didn't get hold of the stone. Its effects also belong to the realm of witchcraft, even if it is only a matter of suggestion."

But I was not able to convince the native elder. However, at least the others were no longer likely to resort to the power of the Hindu sorcerers again. It is lamentable that most of the native pastors discern no evil in these things and give their congregations no clear direction on the matter of occult contacts.

At a Balinese ministers' convention, one pastor even claimed that his mediumistic powers were given him by God. His grandfather had been a clever and much-feared magician. Both he and his father had inherited the grandfather's magical abilities. And these occult powers were supposed to be God-given! A complete confusion of spirits! Yet these are the men who preside over the local church.

Another elder declared quite openly in the overcrowded church, "I still have my old fetishes and charms at home;

but they can't do any harm to me because I don't believe in them any more." I referred the man to Acts 19 : 19 where the Ephesians brought out all their fetishes, threw them into a heap and burnt them. I advised him to likewise destroy all his occult objects, because they would without doubt represent a strain and a bad influence on both himself and his family. But I could not convince him either.

Can we still wonder that the Church on Bali has not yet experienced a revival similar to that on other of the Indonesian islands? Magic is always a bulwark which acts against the gospel. We can see this all the more clearly in the fact that in the revival on Timor and elsewhere, the movement always began with the people recognizing their sins of witchcraft, and bringing their charms and fetishes out and destroying them.

And yet the situation on this 'island of the devil' is not completely black. There are a few 'first fruits' which show that the Lord Jesus desires to begin a work on Bali too.

In Denpasar I made fleeting visits to both a college and an orphanage. I was quite moved by the sight of the young boys of seventeen and eighteen there. I told them that it was at their age that I had first found the Lord Jesus. As I left, they begged me if possible to come back soon and tell them more. This request encouraged me greatly and so a few days later I returned to give them a series of talks on the Christian faith. It was obvious that these young Balinese wanted to hear more about Jesus.

In another village after talking for a while with a Christian, he told me, "Until a short time ago I was a Hindu. Since I have started to follow the Lord Jesus, I have been persecuted a great deal. My fellow villagers plague me in every conceivable way. My wife can no longer fetch water from the public well, and I was threatened and told that I wouldn't be able to be buried in the village graveyard since I had, as they said, cut myself off from the village community." I tried to encourage him as a brother. Anyone who becomes a Christian in a heathen environment must reckon with persecution. That is even true in our 'Christian' churches in the West.

In East Java I met another young Christian from Bali. He told me his story. In 1962 a missionary had arrived on Bali with a team of Christians to work there for a while. Some young boys had found the Lord Jesus at the time. Three of them are today at a Bible school in East Java. One of these, my informant, reported that he was no longer able to enter his parents' house now that he was a Christian. His parents are still heathen in belief and are not prepared to tolerate his decision. And so the Bible school has become his home now.

But Bali can boast of more first fruits than those we have just mentioned. There are a number of Christians scattered about here and there who have been able to escape from the bondage of their forefathers' occultism. These are admittedly few, but one of them is Pastor Joseph, who actually organized my lecture-tour on the island.

These Christians, who are so much in the minority, are really Christ's vanguards on this island. There is no need to despair. The Lord Jesus has always built his kingdom upon a 'few'. If these individual vanguards of Christ remain faithful, then their number will not remain small. For even this stronghold of darkness — this paradise of demons — can become the island of Christ.

V. JOHN SUNG

No one seeking to write about the current revival in Indonesia should overlook the work of the two evangelists who, during the past 30 years, have held many large-scale revival meetings in Java. These are the two apostles of God, John Sung and Andrew Gih. They were friends who worked together originally but then developed their individual evangelistic methods. Both came from China, and both saw the extension of their work into the countries bordering their own land. Among the Chinese in Indonesia today there are many genuine Christians who still trace the renewal of their faith back to the evangelistic missions of these two men. In Djakarta, Dr. Toah told me that these two Chinese evangelists had brought more of the Chinese to Christ than all the foreign missionaries put together. Let us hear first about John Sung, who began his work in Java before Andrew Gih.

The Little Pastor

Without going into boring biographical details, some picture should be given of the time in which the life and work of John Sung took place. The lamp of this exceptional man burnt for barely 43 years; from 1901 to 1944. God gave to him a fulness of power that I have not observed in any other evangelist of our century. This is no exaggeration, but my firm personal belief.

Being born and bred in Hinghwa, John was present as a nine-year-old boy when the revival broke out in the Hinghwa church. Although only a small boy at the time, he broke down in tears and experienced a definite conversion.

Right from the start, prayer was the spiritual high-point of John's life. When in those early years his father was critically ill and had almost been given up as lost by his family, John's despairing mother, who in her anguish could no longer pray, told him, "John, go to your room and pray for father. God listens to prayer." John had thrown himself down on his knees and prayed ardently for his father's life. As a result, in spite of all the doctor's expectations, he soon recovered. This was the second great answer to prayer in the life of this young warrior of the Lord.

In the Hinghwa revival John's father became the leading pastor in the town and was soon weighed down with the work. He appointed lay-preachers whom he used on a rota system to preach in the surrounding villages. John soon took his place among these messengers of Christ, although he was by far the youngest of them all. He was therefore already giving conscientiously prepared sermons at the age of fourteen. Whenever his father was unable to take a service due to the pressure of his work, John readily stood in for him. The congregations loved to listen to him preach on account of his vivid style of delivery. At the time old established Christians were already thinking, "What will become of this young child?"

As in the life of every man of God, the planning and guiding hand of the Lord can be seen in the life of John Sung. As a schoolboy, John had already aroused much attention by his flair for studying and his unflagging industry. Thus it is hardly surprising that this zealous young man soon set his sights on a university education. However, since China had been going through much unrest since 1919, he began to think of entering an American university.

But severe obstacles stood in the way of this plan. Who would pay for the journey? Who would stand guarantor for his stay in the United States? And most difficult of all, John had a typical Chinese infection of the eyelids, which would automatically bar his access to America! As a fourth stumbling-block his own father was opposed to his ideas of travelling. Four formidable hindrances!

Could anything be impossible to God? John resorted to prayer. This was his proven course of action at such times. The Lord gave him his answer in the form of a letter. An American missionary lady, who knew nothing of his scheme, wrote to encourage him to study in the U.S.A. saying that she would stand as guarantor for his visit there. Overjoyed, John showed the letter to his father and asked, "Isn't this God's answer?" Following this breakthrough John received so many gifts of money from various sources that he was not only able to pay for his fare but had a considerable sum left over to help finance his start in the new country. Help came from an unexpected source for the infection of his eye-lids. While he was having a haircut, the barber noticed the infection and offered to clear out the inside of the lid with a sliver of bone, and afterwards to wash it. John agreed to this. The painful process was undertaken several times until the infection was completely cleared. Finally, his father gave his consent also. This was the work of the 'Great Architect' who in his mercy always enables his apostles and children to reach their goals.

The Crisis

The new life in America was anything but easy. Delicate health, a continual lack of money, and an unavoidable operation were subjects for much prayer. The American missionary too, had unfortunately not kept her promise. It has often been a cause of great vexation to many believers, that promises are treated so lightly in American circles. For John it meant that he clung all the more closely to the promises of the Bible.

In spite of these tremendous hardships, John achieved breath-taking progress as a student. In three years he completed a curriculum intended to take five. Moreover, he was consistently among the top students. Besides receiving the prizes for Physics and Chemistry, he was awarded the gold medal for that year. When he finally received his degree, newspapers carried glowing reports on the gifted Chinaman. Three universities tried to woo him. The world-famous Harvard University offered him

1,000 dollars a year if he would enrol there, a sum of money which would be worth at least four times as much today. John, however, plumped for the more modest offer made by Ohio State University.

At this point the knowledge-hungry student applied himself to obtaining his M. Sc. and Ph. D. in chemistry. Since, at that time, German chemistry was at the forefront, John thought of learning the language in order to have access to German scientific writings. During his vacation he flung himself into the unfamiliar language, and in two months mastered it so well that he was able to translate a hefty chemistry textbook into English. The professor who checked the translation thought he must have been studying the German language for years. What another man might have taken two years to do, John Sung had managed in two months. Once again, his achievement caused a great stir. He was showered with awards and invitations. During this time, Peking University became aware of its successful compatriot and offered him a professorship. However, the invitation which most attracted John came from Germany, where the services of this extraordinarily gifted chemist were much sought. A scientific team offered him a research post with unusually favourable financial conditions.

Dr. Sung, as he was now called, prayed a great deal about his future path. In reply, the Lord referred him to the words of Matthew 16 : 26, "What does it profit a man if he gains the whole world and yet forfeits his soul?" His thoughts returned to his original plan and vow. He had only intended to study in America temporarily and then return to China as a preacher of the gospel. So he decided to go and study theology at a theological seminary for a while. In this way he arrived — certainly guided by God — at the Union Theological Seminary in New York, known for its liberal teaching.

And so began his final preparation for the service that lay ahead for him in preaching the kingdom of God.

But the schooling was to bring him completely to his knees.

The main cause of this was the rationalistic theology taught in the college. Every problem concerned with the Bible was discussed in the light of human reason. Only that which could stand up to the scrutiny of logical thought was accepted as being worthy of belief. Belief in Christ suffering for the propitiation of our sins; belief in miracles; the resurrection; the ascension and the second coming: all these were rejected as unscientific. Served with this diet, Dr. Sung soon lost his former faith and he came face to face with the most critical inner crisis of his life. He said to himself, "Everything that I have believed in till now has been taken away from me. I cannot go on living in this state. Either I end my life, or, through the Holy Spirit, God must give me another way to live."

Again God heard the cry of his heart. During the night of February 10th, 1926 the Lord came to him. Breaking down under his burden of sin, Dr. Sung cried to the Lord, praying and weeping till midnight. Suddenly he heard a voice saying, "My son, your sins are forgiven." At this his soul was filled with light. Even though it was still night, reaching for his Bible, he began to read the Gospels in a way he had never done before.

The next morning, all the scholars and students noticed the transformation; and Dr. Sung made no secret of his new experience. Wherever possible he bore witness to the Lord Jesus and his abrupt manner soon began to cause something of a stir. Ever since childhood he had been a person of clear-cut and radical decisions.

Describing his theological books as books of demons, he burned them and dedicated himself exclusively to the study of the Bible and to prayer. His liberal teachers were so shocked by his brusque manner and his condemnation of their brand of theology, that they begged him to submit himself to a psychiatric examination.

This is typical! First of all these rationalists destroy

the faith of a person, then, when that person denuded of all security finds the Lord Jesus, he is looked upon as mentally ill and packed off to a psychiatric clinic. I sincerely hope that in spite of their theology, these modern theologians may have realized their mistake and come to the Lord Jesus Christ to be saved. I should like to see their faces one day when they at last realize that through their theology they have been serving the devil's interests on earth.

In the story of Joseph he says: "You meant evil against me; but God meant it for good." (Genesis 50:20). This is how it was in the case of Dr. Sung. What the Union Theological Seminary contrived was also part of the purposes of God.

Dr. Sung was advised to rest for six weeks and he agreed, although only after some protest. However, when he asked to be permitted to return to the seminary after the six weeks had expired, it was made clear to him that he would have to stay away longer. His old fiery temper flared up, "I've been deceived. I'm not mentally ill, though my heart might well have been damaged by the miserable theological fare I was served with at the seminary." This energetic outburst led the psychiatrist to transfer him to a ward for violent patients. It was one of the worst experiences in Sung's life, to have to spend his days and nights in a ward of dangerous, fighting, swearing maniacs.

He asked the Lord what it all meant. The answer came, "All things work together for good to them that love God." Then Dr. Sung received yet another personal message from the Lord. He was told, "You must endure this treatment for 193 days. In this way you will learn to bear the cross and to walk the pathway of obedience to Golgotha."

With this, John Sung was content. He knew it was the will of the Lord, and that all he had to do was wait. The psychiatrist allowed him to return to his original private room. There Dr. Sung had time to pray and to read the Bible. He avidly read many chapters each day. Later he commented, "That was really my theological training." Altogether, he read the Bible through 40 times during this period of enforced rest. He told no one of the Lord's promise that he was to spend 193 days at the clinic, but after exactly 193 days he was discharged. This was proof that it really had been a message from the Lord, and not his own imagination. Dr. Sung was now finally armed for his evangelistic work in China.

We frequently come across periods of quietness like this in the lives of the special instruments of the Lord. Joseph was two years in prison. Moses spent 40 preparatory years in Midian; Elijah was allowed to hide by the brook Cherith; Jeremiah found himself in prison and later in a pit; John the Baptist sat in the mountain fortress of Machaerus; Paul was two years in Arabia; Luther was at Wartburg until his time had come.

These times of solitude are part of God's schooling.

The Wesley of China

The Union Theological Seminary had long since removed the name of Dr. Sung from its roll of students. They had wanted nothing more to do with him since his burning of their books. But John's thoughts were now set on China, and on the 4th October 1927 he set sail from Seattle for Shanghai.

When Dr. Sung arrived back in his homeland, and was united with his family whom he had not seen for the past seven years, he found there was one remaining hurdle for him to take. His father said to him, "Son, I have always been a poor preacher. I hope that you will now take a post at a university here and help to pay for the education of your younger brothers." John had feared this might happen. All the same he replied to his father, "My life is dedicated to the spreading of the gospel. I am dead to the world and to myself. I can take no other path." And so his course in life was fixed.

Then, in May 1928, Dr. Sung met Andrew Gih for the first time. Both men realized that their lives were following similar paths. For both of them it was a case of being completely surrendered to the Lord for the task of spreading the gospel wherever his Spirit led.

At first the two men worked together as a team with Andrew Gih sometimes acting as interpreter to Dr. Sung in districts where the dialect was unknown to him.

Dr. Sung's first meeting with the so-called 'Tongues Movement' proved to be both significant and informative. It was in the port of Tsingtau that he had to deal with the question of the gifts of the Spirit. The 'charismatic movement' within this port, with its ever changing population, was very strong. Its followers claimed that the fulness of the Holy Spirit would manifest itself in outward signs such as tongues, spiritual songs, visions and dreams. Dr. Sung was drawn into a heated argument over this problem. He became so confused, however, that he decided not to preach but to listen to Andrew Gih instead. Praying earnestly for clarification, the Lord soon granted him his request.

Andrew Gih was preaching on John 4 at the time, and talking about the living water which Jesus offered the woman of Samaria. The answer came just like a revelation. Later John said, "The blessing of God and the fulness of the Holy Spirit do not consist in our searching for fulfilment in strange tongues and other outward manifestations, but in becoming purified streams, through which the living waters of the Holy Spirit can flow to the thirsty souls around us."

From that moment on Dr. Sung preached with a new power. Often he prayed, "Lord, purify and mould me in such a way that the living waters may pour forth like the torrents of Niagara."

Wherever he went there was a spiritual revival: men

acknowledged their sins, enemies were reconciled, stolen goods were returned, students and scholars begged their teachers for forgiveness, and the teachers themselves confessed their own sins. Best of all, after each missionary campaign, teams were formed to carry the gospel to the outlying villages. Sometimes, following a single campaign, 60 to 100 of these teams would be formed overnight.

Dr. Sung was a master at illustrating his messages. When he preached once that sin must be pulled out by the roots, he went to the pots of plants around the platform and tore the flowers out one by one crying, "Now they can't grow again. Sin must be torn out in the same way."

One day he was speaking on Romans 6:23 which reads, "The wages of sin is death." Having a small coffin and a number of stones brought on to the platform, he exclaimed, "The coffin represents death. The stones symbolize sins." Dr. Sung thereupon started naming some sins, and for each one, he threw a fresh stone into the coffin. The evangelist then explained what it all meant: "Every man carries a coffin and as the coffin fills with stones and becomes too heavy, the bearer is gradually crushed."

On other occasions he used the following illustration when speaking of the pastors and their congregations. He would have a helper bring a small charcoal stove on to the platform. Next he would order some small pieces of charcoal to be thrown into the fire, together with one large piece. Ten minutes later he would ask his assistant, "What can you see?" The reply would come, "The small pieces are glowing already, but the large piece isn't even red yet." Dr. Sung would then sum up this message. "The small pieces of charcoal are like the people in the congregation and the large piece is like the pastor. The pastors always take longest to catch fire." One can imagine that an example like this did not always endear him to the ministers of the churches. And yet at the end of his missionary efforts, these same men would have to acknowledge that the church attendances had usually doubled or even trebled.

In the course of his preaching, Dr. Sung often received the gift of prophecy. Once he pointed to an individual in a crowd of over a thousand and said, "You're a hypocrite, mend your ways." The person he was addressing was a church elder who thought that the pastor must have complained about him to Dr. Sung. The next day therefore, the elder sat in a completely different part of the large hall. In the middle of his sermon, the evangelist once again pointed towards the elder and said, "You're a hypocrite." When Dr. Sung had said this to him a third time, the elder decided to murder the pastor. He invited him to a meal at his house. The minister, however, was forewarned, yet in spite of the warning, this faithful brother went to visit the elder. As he entered his house, the man came straight at him with a long knife, and in his fury raised his arm for the fatal blow. Reacting almost instinctively, the pastor fell to his knees and cried, "Lord, save this elder!" The knife went over his head into the wall. The blade broke. At that instant the spirit of repentance came upon the elder. Falling on his knees beside the pastor, he begged him for forgiveness and surrendered his life to Christ. Such was the outcome of the drastic pronouncement of the evangelist.

In the short period of time from 1931 to 1935, Dr. Sung became one of the leading figures in China. The Christians nicknamed him 'the Ice-Breaker'. In a journal of the National Christian Council, Dr. Sung was placed at the top of the list of the six most well-known Christian personalities in China. This country, with its many millions of inhabitants, had never before possessed an evangelist of such power. For this reason he was described by many as the 'Wesley of China'.

Christianity in the West, and indeed throughout the world, is marked by all manner of deficiencies. The number of conversions is small and there are pastors and ministers who, for 40 years or more sometimes, have never experienced a single case of confession of sin or conversion to Christ. Of course, conversions are basically the work of the Holy Spirit. Nevertheless, He usually uses men as His instruments.

The lack of conversions means that there are too few young men and women offering themselves to the Lord to do his work both at home and overseas.

A further deficiency is the lack of money which is always evident in Christian work. Consequently, the Church is constantly begging and collecting. The Bible too, is read so little that men know less and less about the God to whom all the treasures of this world belong.

What was the situation regarding Dr. Sung?

Let us take as an example his three missionary campaigns in the towns of Taipeh, Taitschung and Taiwan on the island of Formosa. At the end of the three campaigns, none of which were undertaken with the massive present day American style of organization, 5,000 people acknowledged that they had found the Lord Jesus Christ as their Saviour. 460 young people offered themselves for missionary service. 4,000 dollars came in freewill offerings, plus many gold rings and other precious jewellery. Dr. Sung took none of the money for himself. The gifts were used for the maintenance of the lay-evangelists and not for lining his own pockets. Just how indifferent he was to money is illustrated by the following incident.

A wealthy business man visited him and brought him a large sum of money. Dr. Sung did not know the man, and looking intently at his benefactor, he finally said,

"The Lord does not want your tainted money. He wants your soul." Thereupon he threw the large sum of money at the man's feet and refused to accept it.

Wherever the Holy Spirit holds sway, the most important thing is the salvation of men, and not the accumulation of bank-notes. Jesus said, "Seek first the Kingdom of God and His righteousness and the rest will be added to you as well."

Pioneer Work in Indonesia

This brief biography of Dr. Sung is given here for two reasons. First of all Christians in the West, to whom this man is often still unknown, should be able to share in the glory revealed by the Lord in his short evangelistic life. Secondly, one should realize that the present revival is not the first time that Indonesia has heard an authoritative gospel message. The waves of revival stirred by Dr. Sung were just as strong as the present ones. The only reason they were not so widespread was because Dr. Sung only lingered for a few weeks in Indonesia. It must also be remembered that it was the Chinese who were predominantly gripped by the work of this pioneer.

Altogether, Dr. Sung came to Indonesia four times. In 1935 he evangelized the Chinese church in Medan in northern Sumatra. This community was revitalized by his ministry.

In 1936 the evangelist came to Sarawak in the northern part of Borneo. In the British as well as in the Indonesian part of the island, there are large Chinese settlements. The campaign took place in Sibu (Sarawak). In the course of the ten-day mission, nearly 1,600 Chinese found their way to Christ, and more than 100 offered themselves for active service in God's kingdom. In addition to this, 116 teams were formed to go out into the villages to carry the fire of the gospel further. If one considers that a European evangelist often works for forty years before seeing results similar to those of this ten-day campaign by Dr. Sung, one will soon realize that evangelists in the West are in a very impoverished state. The work of the teams, who constantly maintained their witness despite the later occupation by the Japanese, is significant. Their work never faltered even amidst the confusion of war.

Dr. Sung's third visit was to the island of Java in January 1939. In September of the same year he visited the island again, later holding further missions on Celebes and the Moluccas. We must say more about this, in order to learn of God's exceptional grace towards Indonesia.

The Total Claim of the Gospel

The reputation of Dr. Sung as a great evangelist had already reached Java before his own arrival. Nevertheless, the people who gathered in Surabaja for his first meeting were quite amazed by the small, thin man dressed in a cheap Chinese tunic who stood before them. They had pictured the Wesley of China very differently. However, one sermon was enough to make them reconsider their hasty first impressions. Everything about this unprepossessing man was energy and power.

On the very first evening they were to know for themselves what claims he made in the name of God. Speaking to his audience he said, "I have 22 messages to give to you this week. This means that I must hold three meetings every day at which you must all be present, otherwise you will fail to discover what God's message is for you."

A whisper went round the church, "What's going to happen? Must we stay away from work and be at the church the whole day?" The pastors warned John not to be too demanding. Dr. Sung persisted. He was right. His addresses communicated such power that it was no longer necessary to urge the people to attend the meetings. The

Chinese shopkeepers closed their shops and came to listen to the evangelist preach. They hung notices on their shop doors, "Closed for the week — Missionary Campaign".

The revival spread still further. The school-children stopped attending school. They too, sat the whole day listening to Dr. Sung, and the teachers did the same.

Yet in John Sung's eyes, even this was not enough! Although the meetings lasted altogether about eight hours a day, the evangelist urged the young people, "Do not think that following Jesus is only a matter of being uplifted inside. There are millions who do not know the Lord Jesus. Go out and take the gospel to them." The young people formed themselves into the usual teams of three. Then going out into the streets and into all the bars which they had formerly frequented, they spread the glorious message of the gospel. During the days that followed, many were able to report the blessing which God had granted in their work.

The pattern which was to shape the current revival in Indonesia, can already been seen emerging: teamwork.

Those who attended the missionary addresses in Surabaja certainly had no spare time of their own. From morning till night they were absorbed in listening to the gospel preached and in organizing the evangelistic bands.

What was the life and work of the evangelist who made such total demands like?

He was usually up by 5 a. m. to read and pray for several hours. Then, as was the case in Surabaja, at 9 a.m. he held a meeting for the sick which lasted for an hour. Following this came his three daily messages, each lasting at least two hours. Also there were the letters he had to answer. Since he often had to preach throughout the day, there was little time for the work of personal counselling. He therefore encouraged his listeners to write to him and tell him their needs. He also asked the newly converted for a photograph so that he would always be able to remember them in his prayers. It was often after midnight when he finally finished writing, and this now left only a few hours for sleep before the next day began.

Even when a week of evangelizing was over, there was no pause for rest. He literally preached for four weeks every month. The only free days he had were those he spent in travelling.

Preaching

Dr. Sung did not usually base his sermon on a theme or a text, but rather preached his way through the Bible, verse by verse. His approach to each passage, however, was so varied, that one can compare him with Spurgeon. His preaching was the expression of his own private study of the Bible. We have already heard of how he burned all his theological books in America and called them 'books of demons'. Ever since that time the Bible had taken first place in his life, and he made a habit of reading at least ten or eleven chapters on his knees every day, conscientiously writing up in his diary the thoughts which the Spirit of God would bring to his mind while he read.

His sermon on 1 Corinthians 13 remained indelibly stamped on the minds of his audience in Surabaja. He illustrated how in his own life he had become more and more proud as a result of his swift ascent to fame in America, but how Jesus in His love, had ever remained close by his side. What an abyss lies between our pride and His patient waiting; our arrogance and His humility; our vanity and His simplicity; our greed and His self-denial; our suspicion of others and His faith in the sinner; our self-righteous smugness towards those who fall and His concern for the fallen. Yet although we deserved the cross, the Son of God in His perfect love and humility bore the shame on our account.

The message of Dr. Sung struck home at the conscience of the audience. Their wills were moved and thousands were converted. Even today, 30 years later, the effects of his first missionary campaign in Java have not been erased. Many of the Chinese have remained faithful followers of the Lord ever since that time.

The Laying on of Hands

We enter now into a very controversial area. Praying under the laying on of hands is abused in three different ways.

First of all the Church abuses the New Testament's direction to lay hands on the sick (James 5:14; Mark 16:17f) by failing through unbelief to make use of this God-given means of grace.

The next abuse is found among extremist groups who lay hands on people both hastily and indiscriminately.

Then thirdly, certain spiritists and sorcerers adopt this practice, performing various types of magic under the laying on of hands.

In view of this, has any Christian still the courage to pray for a person under the laying on of hands? Is there in fact a correct use of the laying on of hands today? The answer is yes; a scriptural one.

But what is the scriptural practice like? Dr. Sung gives the answer. At his first meeting for the sick in Surabaja he read James 5:14 and went on, "I come to you as an elder of the Church. I come in the name of the Lord and not in any name of my own. I have no magical powers within my hands; so don't expect anything from me but only from the One who stands by me and whose servant I am."

The thing that is often forgotten in Christian circles today, was at the forefront of Dr. Sung's mind. He explained that he could not lay hands on an unconverted person. Whoever had not confessed all his known sins could not expect help from prayer under the laying on of hands.

Dr. Sung also encouraged the sick to realize that healing

depended on the will of the Lord. He said, "I cannot guarantee that all the sick among you will be healed. Even the Lord Jesus did not heal all the sick. He was not always allowed by his Father to heal the sick of his day. How much less then his servants!"

After these introductory remarks the sick were then brought up to Dr. Sung on the large platform one by one. As they knelt he anointed them each with oil in the name of the Lord and prayed with them.

That same afternoon a praise meeting was held in which those who had been healed gave their testimonies. Many had been cured of serious illnesses. A missionary wrote later, "Blind people received their sight, the lame walked, the dumb spoke, the ears of the deaf were opened; and best of all, the cures have lasted." So it was not just a case of auto-suggestion.

What was even more striking than the healing of the sick, though, was the fact that many of these people experienced a fresh infilling of the Spirit of God during this anointing and laying on of hands. It was the story of the Acts of the Apostles all over again.

That which has already been said must be underlined again. Dr. Sung cannot in any way be included among the ranks of the extremists of today. His ministry was sober and faithful, and clearly biblically based. He was opposed to all fanaticism. He rejected tongues, dreams, visions and a life of exaggerated emotionality. In God's kingdom we need no ecstatic experiences but need rather to be completely purified channels for the water of life. Such was the standpoint of a man, who, unlike most other evangelists, was involved in a continually increasing fulness of the Holy Spirit. Indeed, those upon whom he laid hands were even able to receive this fulness for themselves.

Thus it is not only possible to speak of the work of the Holy Spirit in fanatical terms, but also in a sober and biblical sense. Therefore a person who rejects extremism is still a long way away from rejecting the fulness of the Holy Spirit as well. In fact the contrary is probably the case, for extremism hinders the work of God's Spirit within us more than anything else.

The Volcano Among Volcanoes

On leaving Surabaja, Dr. Sung promised to make a return visit soon. The Indonesians had won his heart. He was to keep his promise in August and September of the same year.

He began his second missionary tour of Java with a campaign in Djakarta. The whole Chinese community was stirred. No one wanted to miss hearing the preacher, whose reputation was filling the Chinese-speaking world. Before the week was out, 900 people had repented and surrendered their lives to Christ.

The next stage of his tour took Dr. Sung across the waist of Java, among the volcanoes. He was in his element! Meanwhile in Surabaja preparations were being made to receive the eagerly awaited guest.

2,000 volunteers declared their readiness to assist with the campaign. The co-operation of every Christian church had been enlisted, including even those which had remained so critically aloof during the first mission. Above all, the youth were full of expectancy. Dr. Sung had become their champion, their model. In the largest square in the town a makeshift hall had been erected. A gigantic roof of palm-leaves gave protection against sun and rain, but there was still far too little room.

During the course of the week 5,000 people streamed in daily to hear the evangelist speak. Thousands would take their places at 8 a.m. in order to obtain a seat, and would remain there until 11 p. m. at night when the last of the three or four meetings finally ended. I have never known in my own experience of such a campaign, not even with Billy Graham, where people have endured some ten to fifteen hours of preaching the Word of God each day, for ten solid days on end. Only the Holy Spirit could have brought this about. Mere advertising and even the best possible organization cannot create such a response and hunger after the Word.

The Bible Society's local depot in Surabaja had soon sold out of all its Bibles and New Testaments in spite of the stocks it had set aside especially for the campaign. The 5,000 hymn books were similarly quickly sold out and a new edition had to be printed as quickly as possible.

Dr. Sung preached at length on the Gospel of Mark and it served the purpose of preparing the newly organized evangelistic teams for their task. The final result of the ten-day campaign in this respect, was the foundation of another 500 of these bands, which subsequently swarmed across the whole of Java spreading the gospel message.

One of Dr. Sung's interpreters, a pastor from Malang, said, "There was nothing remarkable about the preaching style of Dr. Sung. His repertoire of sermons was not large; his presentation occasionally childlike, but a great power radiated from him, and as his interpreter, I could feel the effects of it upon myself."

It almost sounds trite to say it, yet the comparison is justified; Dr. Sung preached among the volcanoes of Java and was a man who was built in the same mould. He once said of himself; "There are many people better than I! For exposition of the Scriptures I am not equal to Watchman Nee! As a preacher I am not up to Wang Ming-tao! As a writer I cannot compare with Marcus Cheng! But in one matter I surpass them all; that is in serving God with every fibre of my body and every ounce of my strength." Did not Paul write something similar? "I have laboured more abundantly than all of them." (I Corinthians 15:10).

In what way could the same be said of Dr. Sung? After having already heard something of his daily routine, we must realize a little the extent to which his labours drained him of all his strength.

For a long time his friends had been aware that he was ill. They advised him to seek medical treatment. He answered, "I havn't the time. I must preach the gospel." During John's last meeting in Surabaja the pain in his hip became so unbearable that he could no longer stand in the pulpit to preach. Having a stool fetched for him, he knelt down and preached on his knees. He said later, "The pains only ceased while I preached or prayed. As soon as I had finished they returned."

Surabaja was the climax of Dr. Sung's work in Indonesia. How the Christians and Malays had hung on to his every word! When he left the town on September 30th 1939, hundreds stood singing on the quay to see him off. Some Catholic missionaries on the boat looked at the quayside in astonishment when they saw the crowds of people gathering. They wondered what important person would appear. But the only person who came was a little inconspicuous Chinaman bent under the pain of his sick body.

Naturally, many well-meaning voices will arise and ask, "Why didn't he spare himself? Why didn't he take Paul's advice about bodily health being profitable a little? Why did he simply make a martyr of himself?"

The answers are not difficult to find. It is true that these objections apply to every worker in the kingdom of God, but is there any sense in saying to an active volcano, "Would you please stop sending up clouds of smoke and ashes into the sky; and no more lava please!" A volcano would never obey instructions like these! Yet Dr. Sung was a volcano by nature.

The Prophet

John Sung would not be restrained, and this too was certainly part of God's plan for his life. In retrospect, this can be said with absolute certainty.

This man of God was continuously under the impression that he had to hurry: "I have so little time." And surely, this was true, for in his forty-third year he returned home to be with his Lord.

In regard to world politics, too, there was little time left. In Surabaja he said, "Wars and times of persecution will come upon you." How literally these words were fulfilled! Indonesia was occupied for two years by the Japanese. Then came the struggle for independence against the Dutch, followed later by the bloody conflict with the Communists, which cost about a million people their lives. On top of all the chaos caused by war came the persecution of the Christians in Sumatra, East Java, and other areas of this great archipelago.

Not least of all, Dr. Sung felt that the second coming of Christ was near. He continually preached this fact and endeavoured to prepare Christians to be ready to meet their Lord.

Dr. Sung's last message to the Church, which he gave shortly after his tour of Indonesia was, "The work of the future is to be the work of prayer." It was almost prophetic.

As a Chinaman God had shown him that in China, and little by little all over the world, the doors were closing. In China today the doors are already closed, and other countries are quickly following suit. Under the coming anti-Christ the wave of persecution will surely grow.

Driven from within by the Lord, and accounting his own life as nothing, John Sung burnt himself out in the service of his Coming King. Indeed he had always hoped that he would die in the pulpit.

Apart from this prophetic side of his life, there is one last human issue which can be mentioned. The Lord had to teach his servant a final lesson; the art of suffering. Following a medical examination in Shanghai, the doctors discovered tuberculosis of the lungs, and cancer. An unending schooling in pain and agony, combined with three operations followed.

Dr. Sung understood that this was God's way. He said, "God must melt my stubborn temperament in the crucible of pain." And this is just what happened. In his suffering he lost his often harsh manner and instead became patient, compassionate, warm.

Seeing death approaching, he said one day, "The Lord Jesus is waiting outside the door to collect me." And so it was. Within a few hours of uttering these his last words to his wife, he was translated into the Heavenly Kingdom.

VI. ANDREW GIH

I have stumbled across the tracks of this much blessed evangelist many times in my life; in Hongkong and Singapore, in Formosa and Los Angeles. Next to Dr. Sung, he is one of the most prominent Chinese evangelists of this century. At the time of the writing of this book, he is 68 years old and passing the evening of his life in California. In order to be able to understand the power of his ministry, we will first hear something of the experiences he had in his missionary work.

The Bandit

At the time of the first Communist disturbances in West Shantung, a bandit by the name of Wang was engaged in his usual habits of raiding, kidnapping and blackmail. One day, coming to a village in the hope of finding some spoil, he was suddenly confronted with a large crowd of people. "What's happening here?" he asked. He received no reply, but instead heard a man talking at the front. It was Gih, and he had just begun to read the story of the prodigal son from Luke 15, "And he took his journey into a far country, and there he squandered his property in loose living." Wang was astonished and wondered, "How did this man know my story?"

The bandit listened now all the more attentively, and when the evangelist summoned the people to come forward and to repent, he went forward with them. At that moment the criminal was changed into a disciple of Christ.

His transformation bore instant fruit. He went home, knelt before his wife and begged her forgiveness. Then searching out his aged parents, he asked them to forgive him too. His next journey took him to the pastor of the district in which he lived. He became a loyal member of the congregation there and used every opportunity to testify of his new found faith to his former friends. When they jeered and made fun of him he calmly stood his ground, which was proof enough that his nature had been changed.

However, on another occasion one of his former colleagues, while making fun of him, said, "If a gangster can preach the gospel, then this bloke Jesus must also . . ." — He didn't get any further. Wang was on him in a moment and bit off one of his ears. Spitting it out he wiped the blood from his mouth. He then said quietly, "You can insult me as much as you like, but you're not going to insult Jesus while I'm around." The wounded man withdrew, vowing revenge.

Wang went to the pastor and recounted the incident to him. He was convinced that he had done the right thing. The pastor then read to him the story of Peter who had struck off the ear of the high priest's servant, and he added, "You have done exactly the same. When Peter was filled with the Holy Spirit later on, he no longer acted like that." Wang repented and asked God to fill him with the Holy Spirit.

Here we see already an indication of the blessing that rested upon the work of Andrew Gih; but he still had a long way to go. Let us now hear something of the way in which his ministry developed.

Andrew's Conversion

Buddhism was the religious background of Andrew's parental home. The family, however, was only nominally Buddhist. They were just about as concerned with Buddha as nominal Christians are with Christ.

It was curiosity that one day led Andrew to visit a Buddhist temple, but the monstrous idols and dreadful pictures illustrating hell completely revolted him.

His next goal was a Roman Catholic church. When he went in, he was still wearing his straw hat, but someone quickly took it off his head! Andrew was annoyed by this and determined never again to visit a Christian church.

However, God's hand can already be seen at work in his life. Andrew's friends started studying English, and this made him want to master the language as well; but he could find no place to study. In the end he reluctantly decided to attend the Bethlehem Mission School in Shanghai. He made up his mind though, that he would under no circumstances become entangled in the religion of the foreigners.

A morning service was held at the Mission School every day, and Andrew avoided it with the excuse, "I live too far away and can't get to the school on time." At the Mission the English language was taught through the Bible, and in this way Andrew's knowledge of the book grew.

Most of the students were convinced Christians, and because of this they often challenged Andrew. "Do you believe that God created the world?" one of the girl students once asked him. "No," replied Andrew. "Then where do we come from?" another student butted in. "From our parents, of course," Andrew answered flatly. "And where did the first parents come from?" "From lower forms of life," Andrew replied again. "Why do apes still exist then? Why didn't they also develop into human beings long ago?" Andrew was baffled and annoyed at the same time. However, the Christians gave him no peace and they prayed for him continually.

One day, the teachers at the Bethlehem Mission invited the students to a missionary meeting. To make it more convenient for the students, the school offered them an evening meal. Since the Chinese are brought up to be very courteous, Andrew felt obliged to stay.

That evening was to be the turning point in Andrew Gih's life. There awoke in him a strong awareness of his own sinfulness. That night he could not sleep; he struggled with his sin, until he finally cried out, "God, have mercy on me, a sinner!" At that moment the peace of God came into his life. He was certain that God had taken possession of him. The next day he immediately made his experience known to the Christians and non-Christians alike. "Becoming a Christian is the best thing a person can do."

The Open Door

From the start, Andrew was a man of prayer. He would lay hold of every possible promise he could find in the Bible. Thus it was a great encouragement to him when the Lord gave him the verse: "Behold, I have set before you an open door which no man can shut" (Revelation 3:8).

Relying on this promise, he set out to find a job. He had to help his mother to keep the family, since his father had died a number of years before. At that time, the main post-office in Shanghai had a hundred vacant posts. However, the number of applicants ran into thousands. Moreover, only those who knew English were accepted and Andrew was only a beginner in the language. Many of the other applicants had, in fact, already been abroad

67

to English-speaking countries. Andrew resorted to prayer. He was given a post.

Tears ran down his mother's cheeks when he brought home his first wage packet. "Son," she said, "I haven't had so much money in my hands since your father died."

Yet Andrew did not want to be a post-office employee all his life. One night he had a dream. He saw an old man ringing the bell for church. Suddenly, whilst he was still ringing the bell, he was attacked by a lion and killed. Andrew then heard a voice saying, "Who will take his place?" On hearing the question, he awoke, and he knew straight away what his answer must be.

With a heavy heart, he told his mother that he felt himself called to God's service. She began to weep and said, "Then I shall have to do my weaving until midnight again so that I can feed the other children." How this answer pierced his heart. The Lord, however, directed him to the verse: "He who does not leave mother, wife, children for my sake is not worthy to be my disciple."

Andrew applied to become a Bible student at the Bethlehem Mission. He received a small grant, half of which he shared with his mother. The half he retained for himself, though, was not really sufficient for his clothing and shoes, so he had to go about very poorly dressed.

His inner life was the exact opposite of his outward appearance. His heart burned for Jesus. Every evening he was out and about in the streets and on the outskirts of the town preaching the gospel to the people he met. Since he had no money for the bus, he went everywhere on foot. During the rainy season, he often waded knee-deep in water. This resulted in him catching a very heavy cold from which he could not seem to recover. He prayed and the Lord answered him through Isaiah 43:2: "When you pass through the waters, I will be with you; and through the rivers, they shall not overwhelm you."

In spite of a stubborn cough, he carried on preaching.

During the holidays he and a friend undertook an evangelistic tour. They had been away for three months in a southern province when Andrew began to spit blood. At the beginning of one of the evening meetings, he coughed up so much blood that he filled his handkerchief with it. His friend sent him to bed but Andrew could not rest. When he heard the singing from his room and the time for the sermon approached, he slipped back into the church. Going to the pulpit he began to preach. Within three months he had preached away his tuberculosis of the lungs. Later, he realized that it was wrong to be so reckless with his health. We have a responsibility towards our bodies as well. However, the Lord had shown him mercy.

Andrew depended on the Lord completely for his personal needs. One day he prayed to God for some money for a pair of shoes. He received the answer quickly. A friend brought him two Chinese dollars which, at that time, was just enough to buy a pair of shoes. Shortly afterwards, Andrew received another visitor, this time a young man who had not long been converted. This new Christian was in a desperate situation as he had given up his former dishonest occupation after his conversion. He asked Andrew for help, having already had to sell some clothing simply to buy rice. Andrew prayed to God for money for his brother in Christ. A voice then encouraged him, "Why do you ask? You have two dollars. Give those to him." After a little hesitation he complied, and gave his poverty-stricken brother the money. Some days later the Lord paid him back with an interest of 1,400 %. He was given 30 dollars!

Once after an evening meeting, Andrew stayed behind in the church to pray for the people who had just attended the service. Suddenly a commotion developed outside and he heard a threatening voice start shouting, "Beat the swine up." Immediately some of the Christians rushed back into the church to be at Andrew's side. Kneeling with him, they began to pray. A mob armed with clubs pushed their way into the church, but on hearing the Christians praying for them, they drew back speechless. The Lord had stood guard over his servant.

Endued with Power

Although Andrew had already had some wonderful experiences with his Lord, he still sometimes felt a lack of authority in his life. As a result, when he was listening to an evangelist preaching once and heard the invitation to go out to the front, he got up and went out himself. The renewed humility before the Lord was richly rewarded. The presence of Jesus became for him a new and living reality. He wrote about it later, "I didn't experience any ecstacy or any holy laughter; I didn't speak in tongues or have a vision; and I didn't hear a voice. I simply surrendered my whole life completely to Jesus. In this way a new strength came into my life."

This new blessing bore fruit. Wherever the young evangelist went, the Lord allowed revival to follow.

For example, in one particular town in the province of Canton, the rector of the local college set himself against Andrew Gih's missionary campaign. Yet many of the students were converted. Finally, he too was won over. As John Sung had said, "The largest pieces of charcoal are the last to be set alight." At the end of the mission, the rector stood up and gave the following testimony:

"I was fortunate enough to be brought up in America. It was there that I was taught my modern theological views. When the young evangelist Gih began his work here, I was opposed to him. I claimed he was just playing on the emotions of the young people to get them excited. However, the message at the last meeting affected my conscience. I had to confess my sins, though I fought against doing so, and now I stand before you students whom I have been teaching for years. This morning, a young man of about your own age gave his message.

When he asked who wanted to decide for Christ, and you all made your decisions, it became clear to me that I lacked something in my life. My lengthy training has not made me capable of influencing you in the way this mission has done. Please, pray for me that I might be given what I need."

It was the same story in the next town. The students at a Bible school experienced a fresh and deep sanctification of their lives. Even the lecturers repented and sought the forgiveness of their sins. The girls of a senior girls' school remained in prayer in the church for hours until their teachers also came to Christ. All petty quarrels were pushed aside. The senior boys' school was likewise drawn into the revival. Boys who had been a problem at the school for years were converted. Their headmaster similarly repented of his sins. He stated publicly, "Because of my education I was an atheist. Now I have surrendered my life to Christ." Even pastors and other ministers of the gospel repented and confessed the slackness of their own work. Prayer groups sprang up everywhere, often with a membership of 50 to 60 people.

Andrew Gih gives us a wonderful example of how the message of the Holy Spirit can be preached without fanaticism. He once said, "Before we can start to speak of spiritual gifts, a person must have been born again and filled with the Holy Spirit. Only after this has happened does the Holy Spirit impart his gifts to men as and when and to whom he chooses." Another time he declared, "Anyone who is not filled with the Holy Spirit is powerless in God's service, and this is a terrible predicament to be in if we claim to be the followers of a victorious Lord. If all the Lord's servants were to be filled with the Holy Spirit, then the ailing Church would soon bear fruit and be transformed, and a world-wide revival, for which we all pray, would surely be the result."

In his addresses, Andrew Gih gave valuable advice concerning the theme 'being filled with the Spirit of God'. Some of his thoughts are worth repeating here.

"If the Christian Church is going to pray for a revival, then it is only on the understanding that the Bible, being the Word of God, stands at the central point. First of all you must read the Bible, emphasize the Bible, teach the Bible, preach the Bible, revere the Bible and practise the Bible, before you can expect to be filled with the Spirit of God." Is this the situation today at our theological faculties and among our Church leaders?

"The Holy Spirit changes everything. For example, on the road to Capernaum the disciples were arguing about which one of them was the greatest, but after Pentecost they were humble, and even Peter accepted Paul's rebuke without a murmur. In the same way, before Pentecost, Peter had run away from a young servant girl, whereas after Pentecost he stood up and faced the entire world."

With Christ's original followers it was a matter of saving souls, but today the emphasis seems to be on constitutions, social service, ecumenical links and things of a similar nature.

After being filled with the Holy Spirit, Peter and John were able to testify, "We cannot but speak of what we have seen and heard." Today, a pastor's job seems to end in the pulpit and Paul's encouragement to preach in and out of season is almost forgotten. This is why it was possible in one church in Java for the pastor to be dismissed because he went out and preached the gospel in the streets. The church justified itself by saying, "Preaching outside the church is against the constitution."

In order to receive the Holy Spirit, certain prerequisites are imperative: faith, prayer, obedience. Before his ascension, Jesus promised the disciples, "You shall receive power when the Holy Spirit has come upon you, and you shall be my witnesses" (Acts 1 : 8). The disciples returned and waited in Jerusalem. This was already a sign of their faith; and with one accord they devoted themselves to prayer.

Andrew's views on the gift of tongues are also significant. He said, "At his conversion Paul did not receive the gift of tongues at once. This only came later. At the revival in Samaria there was also no mention of the gift of tongues. Moreover, Jesus himself never spoke in tongues. There are today, however, believers who erroneously assume that the gift of tongues is the sole and essential evidence of someone being filled with the Holy Spirit. This is clearly contrary to the Scriptures. It should also be remembered that great men like Wesley, Moody, Spurgeon, General Booth and Hudson Taylor never possessed the gift of tongues, and yet they were all men who were filled with the Holy Spirit."

I personally, also find it very significant that Andrew Gih recognizes three different sources behind the gift of tongues. These I have described already in my booklet entitled 'The Strife of Tongues':

1. The gift of the Holy Spirit: Mark 16 : 17 f; Acts 10 : 44; Acts 19 : 6; 1 Cor. 12 : 14.
2. The fruit and expression of one's own soul: Jeremiah 23 : 16; "They speak visions of their own minds."
3. The demonic: Deuteronomy 13 : 1—5; "That prophet or that dreamer of dreams must be put to death, because he has taught rebellion against the Lord."

Today there are two extremes in the Christian Church. The one — predominantly the new rationalists — deny the existence of the Holy Spirit, and the other — predominantly the extremists — overdo the fifth article of the creed. Let us not forget that the task of the Holy Spirit is to glorify Christ. Jesus must stand at the centre of our creed. Any shift of emphasis leads to false teaching.

Andrew Gih was one of the forerunners of the revival in Indonesia. Of course, there is no direct connection between his work and the present revival. All the same, under Andrew Gih and John Sung, Indonesia experienced a clear presentation of the gospel.

In 1951 Andrew came to Indonesia for the first time. His work began in Bandung. The first fruits of his ministry came sooner than anticipated. A young man sought him out and asked him, "Please baptize my father. He is on his death-bed." Andrew was no longer able to get through to the dying man. The old man lay there with his eyes closed. He said to him, "The Lord Jesus came to this earth and died for you on the cross in order to take away your sins. Do you believe that?" An unintelligible grunt was the reply. Andrew went on, "If you believe in Christ and accept him as your Saviour, then he will carry you up to heaven. Do you want that?" Again an incomprehensible murmur. Next Andrew prayed, "Lord Jesus, I can only baptize this man on trust. Just grant that he says one more word of witness before he dies." The next day the old man was a little better and his son told him, "Father, yesterday Pastor Gih baptized you. Do you acknowledge the Lord Jesus and accept him?" The dying man replied, "Of course I accept him."

This was a good start. After the mission in Bandung came one in Surabaja. On the first evening 400 people came. Gradually, as the week progressed, the church was filled up, so much so, that in the end there were some 300 people left standing outside. Every evening between 30 and 200 people came forward and accepted Christ. Surabaja had not experienced such a revival since the days of Dr. Sung.

In addition to the ordinary preaching services, a healing meeting was held. During the mission, Andrew Gih was repeatedly asked to pray for sick people and to lay his hands on them. In the end he agreed to hold a meeting for the sick. He thought that perhaps a dozen people might come along. To his amazement 300 to 400 were present. Later, many testified that they had been healed.

One woman had suffered from a growth. Four doctors had advised an operation. However, since she had to look after another person who was sick, she was unable to go into hospital. Gih prayed with her. When she went to the hospital again for another examination, the doctors could find no sign of the growth. The Lord had touched her body and healed her.

At the senior girls' school in Surabaja there were four teachers. Three of these became Christians during the course of the mission. The fourth refused to attend the meetings. Towards the end of the week she heard that Andrew Gih came from Shanghai, where she herself had been born. This led her to go and hear him out of curiosity. She was gripped by what she heard and was converted the same night. That evening she experienced two miracles in her life. For twenty years she had suffered from a stomach complaint and had had to keep to a strict diet. Consequently she had grown very thin. After the meeting she stayed behind together with many others who were sick. After waiting for a long time on account of the great crowd, Gih prayed with her under the laying on of hands. She went home very late that night and felt extremely hungry. Having eaten her fill, she slept soundly and, from that time onwards, remained in the best of health. The Lord Jesus had saved her both physically and spiritually.

Andrew Gih concluded his work in Indonesia with a mission in Malang. Since 120 young people in a single evening decided for Christ, Andrew conceived the idea of founding a Bible school. Naturally, such an enterprise was fraught with many difficulties. He needed teachers, a site, and money to build the school. He took all these concerns to the Lord in his prayers. And the Lord responded. Of the £ 7,000 required for the building, three gifts amounting to £ 2,400 had come in during the first week. The first five teachers also came forward and offered their services. The Bible students themselves — the major problem in the Western world — were no cause for concern. They were already there waiting to be admitted.

In 1968 God allowed me to pay a personal visit to the towns affected by Andrew Gih. I was able to speak four times at the actual Bible school he founded. To date there are some 90 students studying there, and in the college he also founded there are 400 students.

This then completes our short biographies of the two Chinese evangelists who pioneered the present work in Indonesia. They were the two friends, John Sung and Andrew Gih.

Their work was predominantly among the Chinese, whereas the current revival largely involves the Malay population and the Moslems. God has therefore, in his mercy, reached out to the three distinct groups comprising the population of Indonesia. Without doubt, the Lord is working his purposes out among the Indonesian people.

The earlier pioneers of Christian missionary work have one by one lost their influence, although their organizations may still continue to exist today. The Lord chooses new instruments when the old ones are worn out. At present, it is Indonesia's turn to be used by God. In the millennium no doubt Israel's time will come as well. Nevertheless, Indonesia is probably the last country destined to carry the torch of the gospel before the second coming of Christ. The signs which support this claim are clear.

VII. QUESTIONS SURROUNDING THE REVIVAL IN INDONESIA

Over the years I have been fortunate enough to be able to visit a number of places which have been the centres of revival. This has encouraged me to read reports and books dealing with revival.

Almost every revival seems to display the same recurring biblical pattern. This runs as follows:

Firstly, God's Spirit blows where he wills. He is sovereign over his own actions. We cannot compel him to act. Trying to force God's hand by prayer usually leads off on a psychical sidetrack.

To say this, however, does not invalidate the biblical truth: "The kingdom of heaven suffers violence, and men of violence take it by force."

One finds, secondly, that every revival seems initially to provoke the anger of the Established Church. The comment of John Sung comes to mind again: "The large piece of charcoal is affected last." If the Church agrees with a spiritual movement from the very outset, there is reason to doubt the biblical nature of such a movement.

A revival is also characterized by people breaking down under the burden of their guilt, repenting and accepting Christ as their Saviour.

Every revival, too, has to contend with tributaries originating from the devil. Nominal Christians are often impressed by the activities of their own churches, and yet so often the words of the glorified Lord still apply, "I know where you dwell, where Satan's throne is." (Rev. 2 : 13).

Welfare work, social service, community action and theological study may be all well and good, but on the other hand they have very little to do with revival. Indeed they are often endowed with a catastrophic immunity to revivals. It is often in the very place where money and intellect abound that revivals are found to be absent.

The kingdom of God is characterized by other traits. God seeks to bless those who are humble and broken, and often esteems the illiterate more highly than the university professor. Water settles in the lowest place, and the water of life does likewise. God does not revere human greatness. The Spirit of God has little time for the attainments of human reason. God makes fools of the wise men of this world. We do well to remember what Paul wrote in this respect in 1 Corinthians 1. Herein lies the limitation of intelligence.

In a similar way the Spirit of God must not be confused with the psychological workings of the mind. This is the second great danger. That which originates in the organic or the psychical is just as incompatible with the Holy Spirit as the spirit and intellect of man. The false prophets of today should just for once read the words of Jeremiah 23, where God ascribes the many dreams, visions and prophecies of those who claimed to speak in his name, to the workings of their own subconscious mind. This is the basic trouble with extremism.

The Holy Spirit comes from God, not from the realms of the human intellect, nor from the realms of the organic, or the human psyche. How many are the dreadful short-circuits this confusion has already occasioned. This is one reason why revival seldom lasts for more than a couple of generations. One of my teachers pointed out to me many years ago the principle of totaliter aliter — completely otherwise! The Holy Spirit is so utterly different from our sinful nature that absolutely no parallels are possible. This is a completely different state of affairs to that depicted by Paul Tillich. As a theologian, he maintained, "What we understand by God or the Spirit of God is nothing more than the sum total of the outward manifestations of the good qualities within human beings." What an idea! The Holy Spirit is supposed to be dependent on man's understanding of himself. This is the basic trouble with modern theology.

If we wish to investigate a revival, we must be prepared to allow the Holy Spirit to be the Holy Spirit, and nothing else. We cannot compass him with our intellect. Even less should we relegate him to a mere expression of our subconscious mind. We must speak of the Holy Spirit in the way that the Scriptures describe him, and not according to what our own minds can grasp.

The Dangers of the Indonesian Revival

It may seem strange to speak of the dangers first, but our aim must be to preserve this wonderful gift of revival to Indonesia for as long as we can. I have already been to mission fields where revivals have died a natural death. They have been like dead volcanoes, yet people have often failed to recognize this fact. They have confused life with the mere activities of the flesh.

My heart, however, goes out to this tremendous gift which God has given to the Christians in Indonesia, and daily I remember in my prayers the friends I have made in that land. May the Lord be pleased to uphold through them this movement of his Spirit in the service of his Church throughout the world.

Personality cults are dangerous. When God calls and prepares his instruments they must never become more important than the Lord himself in the work that they are allowed to do. How easy it is for our hearts to swell with pride when the Lord deigns to use us. But did not God first anoint and choose king Saul before he later cast him on one side? As we then read the stories which are to follow, we must under no circumstances forget that the glory they reveal belongs to God, and not to men.

A second danger among many Christians at a time of revival is to sensationalize any stories they might hear. It was this that explained the sudden arrival of an American Pentecostal Christian on one of the islands. He wanted to take a native woman, who had been used

79

in a quite remarkable way, back to America to parade her triumphantly — as the Americans often do — before the Christians. Although the woman had been actually instrumental in the raising of the dead, the only effect that the offer had was to swell her pride and cause her to lose all the authority she had had.

Revivals can sometimes be 'visited to death', or 'reported to death', or even 'praised to death' by well-meaning missionaries and evangelists.

Why then do I write about it here? My missionary books are read by anything up to 40,000 people, and I would beg them all to pledge themselves to pray for this revival in Indonesia, that the fire which God has lit there will not go out.

The Indonesian revival faces two particular dangers, namely its being confused with two other religious streams.

It is flanked on the one side by a wave of mass baptisms among the Batak tribe, and on the other side by the tongues movement, which is currently causing concern throughout the Christian world, in spite of the claim made that it is a revival movement itself.

The mass baptisms that are taking place in Sumatra, particularly among the Karo Batak, can be traced to two sources. Spiritually speaking everything in Indonesia today is in a state of flux. From the psychological point of view there is no easy explanation for this. Just as the many Indonesian islands are washed by the waters of many seas, so too the present religious and spiritual situation of the islanders is affected by innumerable differing streams of thought.

One understandable reason for the wave of baptisms, however, is the present political situation in the country. Following the Communist uprising, the government has ordained that all citizens must belong to a religion. The only options that exist are Islam, Hinduism, and Christianity. Since the Moslems were responsible for the slaughter of the Communists, many Indonesians, wanting to give them a wide berth, have opted for Christianity instead. And so in 1966 and 1967 admission to the church by mass baptism began. This reached such a pitch that in the space of two months 10,000 islanders came forward to be baptised. There can be little talk of genuine spiritual rebirth in a situation like this.

These christenings, however, have both a good and a bad side. The danger consists in the Church finding itself being further diluted by these nominal Christian converts. The blessing consists in the great opportunity to reach all these people through the gospel. The Lord is able to build up his kingdom, even out of a 'semi-artificial' movement.

The tongues movement too, should not be confused with the genuine Indonesian revival. This world-wide psychic epidemic, founded upon the subconscious minds of religiously inclined people, is not a revival at all. But in making this statement those with genuine spiritual gifts have nothing to fear.

Just how dangerous tongues speakers can be to the revival is illustrated in the following incident. Once while the Bible School teachers in East Java were on holiday, their school was visited by a Pentecostal from Holland. He told the students that a person has only been truly filled with the Holy Spirit if he has spoken in tongues. He was just on the point of gaining a hearing among the students with his heretical ideas, when the teachers returned. One of the teachers' wives, realizing the situation quickly, confronted the man and said, "You're a false prophet." Soon after this he left and the danger was averted. The enemy had planned to try and ravage the flock while the shepherds had been away. The Lord, however, had prevented any damage being incurred.

The extent to which extremism and spiritism are related is illustrated in the following example. The Pentecostal evangelist we have just mentioned, went for a walk one day with one of the missionaries. Suddenly he said to his astonished companion, "You see those three birds over there? The middle one is a spirit. Watch closely what happens." The middle bird then flew towards the evangelist and disappeared into thin air. It was a clear example of spiritism. Yet this was supposed to be a sign of the baptism of the Holy Spirit. It was the Dutch evangelist's companion who actually recounted the incident to me.

There is one more danger which, although often overlooked, threatens every revival. An old believing minister in England who was present at the time of the Welsh revival said once, "Towards the end there was too much talk about the Holy Spirit, and not enough about the Lord Jesus." This is indeed a very real danger, when the accent is taken off the work of Christ and placed exclusively on the work of the Holy Spirit. Although our churches are guilty often of not emphasizing the Holy Spirit enough, during revivals on the other hand, Christians often go to the opposite extreme. The whole task of salvation was placed upon Christ by the Father. And Jesus said before the outpouring of the Holy Spirit, "The power of the Holy Spirit will come upon you, and you will be *my* witnesses."

VIII. A BIBLE SCHOOL IN EAST JAVA

The Bible School in East Java is still very young and therefore, so to speak, still in the period of its first love.

This young seedling was first planted in the soil of Indonesia in 1959. It began quite simply as a large family, with four teachers — among them David Simeon — and nine students. Within a year the number of students had grown to 17. The most well-known of these was Pak Elias of whom we shall hear more.

In 1961, one of the founder members left to join 'World Vision', because he felt called to concentrate more on social work among children.

When David Simeon therefore returned from his furlough — during which he had got married — the leadership of this young work was placed in his hands.

The work of the school expanded amazingly quickly. By 1967 the number of students alone had almost reached three figures, and many more were on the waiting list awaiting their turn for a place. This is indeed what happens when the Spirit of God begins to move.

Parallel with the swiftly increasing number of students went the erection of the many necessary buildings amidst a chain of miraculous circumstances. A former Dutch church which had earlier been completely destroyed, was so reconstructed that it looked like new. The main building in which the school became housed was also built at this time, mainly on gifts from the Indonesian Christians themselves.

Depth and Width

These are two of the key words which can be used to describe the development and growth of the Bible School. Had it been width without depth on the other hand, the result would have been shallowness.

Dr. Rachel, the matron of a hospital in central Java who has long had connections with the Bible School in East Java, told me some interesting facts. She has invited evangelistic teams from the school on a number of occasions to address her hospital and staff. She said to me, "We sensed at once and clearly saw the change it made in the character of our girls. Four of them decided to train for full-time service straight away. Then when they returned from the Bible School the change was even greater. They were willing to perform the most menial

83

of tasks, and were so honest and appreciative that we ourselves felt ashamed. The Spirit of Christ has literally imprinted himself upon them."

At the Bible School itself, the wind of revival has been blowing for a number of years. This was particularly illustrated in the spring of 1967. The teachers were having a great deal of difficulty with a number of the students, and were even considering whether or not they should be sent home. Then they began to pray. At once the deadlock between the teachers and students was broken, and the prayer meetings lasted deep into the night. Students came to the teachers begging their forgiveness, and in return the teachers confessed to the students that they too were in the wrong. One teacher told an assembled group of students, "I know that I'm very proud, so please pray for me." Everything that the Holy Spirit revealed was brought out into the open and put right.

Dr. Rachel, who had been partially able to share in this period of revival in the Bible School, told me about it herself, since I was unable to get much information from the actual teachers themselves. However, perhaps this is best, for not everything should be broadcast far and wide. These matters are neither to be sensationalized nor gossiped about by Christians. This would be the best way to quench the Spirit of God. Dr. Rachel went on to say, "During this time, as a spirit of cleansing was sweeping through the school, things began to happen which were very reminiscent of the time of Christ. Occult oppressions, often involving the third or fourth generation, were brought to light. One girl was possessed. A number of demons were driven out of her."

David Simeon said to me concerning this, "Up till then we only knew of these things from your books. Now we've been able to experience them for ourselves." I was pleased and grateful that my books had been used to prepare them. Sometimes a remark like this is a great encouragement amid the battles that constantly face one.

I find that I am often under fire from every side and in danger of losing courage and becoming tired.

Let us now listen once more to the words of Dr. Rachel, "If I had merely read or heard about things like this, then I should have doubted the reports. As it was, I was right in the middle of it all. Still more important to me than people's deliverance from the sins of sorcery was the fact that the fruits of the Holy Spirit became visible among the students. It could be seen, for example, that God had poured the Spirit of love into the heart of one Indonesian. Others were so broken that you could almost sense the humility in them afterwards. Another acknowledged his disobedience and openly asked to be forgiven. Not a single teacher or pupil remained untouched by the events. In addition to this, distinctions in status and rank became invisible. The students and teachers formed a single fellowship before God. The wind of God blew, and still blows, in this school. I'm not ashamed to admit that in this spiritual atmosphere I could hardly refrain from tears."

Now it is my turn to give my own impressions. I was in Indonesia for four weeks, two of them in East Java. What I experienced there impressed me more than anything else in my 39 years of following Christ, and God has allowed me to see a number of things in this time. My own spiritual life was so enriched, that since leaving there I have devoted three times as much time to prayer as I formerly did. On account of travelling a great deal, my memory has become like a huge map. Since my time in Indonesia, I daily wander across each continent praying for the people I know. It was brought forcibly home to me that through negligence in prayer I had become guilty, not only before God, but also before the people I should have served. We indeed only obtain what we seek on bended knees. Of course, I have always prayed regularly ever since I first learned to follow Christ, and this includes the spending of many nights in prayer. Yet all the same, since being stirred by the revival in Indonesia, I feel that

I am somewhat guilty. How different my life would have been, if I had only prayed more. How many wrong decisions would have been avoided if I had always remained faithful in prayer. I feel that I must now try to make up for where I have failed, if that is at all possible. For this reason, each day I travel from Alaska to Tierra del Fuego, from Scandinavia to Capetown. Then ranging along the coast of East Asia, I finally cross the vast expanse of the Pacific, touching all the islands as I go. What a help I find my travels in the past to be, for I feel at home practically everywhere I go. I have but one request, that God will forgive me for all my lukewarmness in prayer, and preserve in me all that I have received through visiting Indonesia.

It is part of the essence of Christianity that the Lord always leads his people from solitude to service. This can be seen in the Bible School in East Java.

A Bible school with no practical outlet soon gets bogged down in theory. The idea of evangelizing Indonesia therefore, became laid upon the hearts of the teachers and students alike. This was all the more justified, since the country has very few foreign missionaries within its borders. In spite of having a population of some 110 million people, Indonesia has only 2000 foreign missionaries.

For this reason the first task which presented itself to the school was the country's evangelization. To achieve this goal, fully trained students were sent out to work on the surrounding islands. One of the most outstanding events in this respect was when a tribe of poison mixers asked if a missionary could come and visit them too.

An even greater opportunity for practical service lies in the habit of the school, of training the students in the work of evangelization. To do this, each year the students are split up into teams and sent out to work on their own for two months. In June 1967, 17 such teams were organized, involving altogether 95 students, and these were sent out on a mission covering the whole of Indonesia.

It is worth noting the way in which the teachers decide where each team must work. For some days they pray together seeking to discover the will of the Lord. One of the clear indications of the guidance of the Holy Spirit is the agreement between the conclusions reached both by the teachers and the students. I have never experienced anything like this before. So often the missionaries who are sent out to the field find themselves unable to agree with the decisions of the leaders at home, which only serves to illustrate the lack of unity in the Spirit between those who lead and those who are sent. In East Java, however, the Christians continue to pray until there is clarity on every point. This too is a sign that this revival is sound and biblical.

The next step, as the field of their work widens, is the sending of missionaries to other countries. While I was at the Bible School in 1968, the subject of their prayers was the sending of missionaries to Thailand and Cambodia.

Yet even this, I feel, will not be the final step. Since the Western world is so steeped in the corrosive acid of rationalistic theology, it would not surprise me if Europe and America one day received missionaries from Indonesia. If the brothers in Indonesia retain their humility, this will surely take place.

Gradually, even the Established churches in Indonesia are ceasing their opposition to the Bible School. Many churches, among them Presbyterians, Methodists, Mennonites and other Protestant groups including the more moderate Pentecostals, are sending their young people to the school for instruction. This is another step forward. It is as if the Lord were standing on Mount Nebo and saying to the Christians, "There is Indonesia. Go over and possess the land!"

And this is what they have begun to do.

I had already left Indonesia and almost finished writing this book when, by God's grace, I received an additional account of the revival at the Bible School. The report came to me through two of the leaders teaching at the school and is far more revealing than my own account. Here I must express my extreme gratitude for this marvellous testimonial to the working of the Holy Spirit in this Indonesian Bible school.

> "When the Lord restored the fortunes of Zion,
> we were like those who dream.
> Then our mouth was filled with laughter,
> and our tongue with shouts of joy;
> then they said among the nations,
> 'The Lord has done great things for them.'
> The Lord had done great things for us;
> we are glad" (Psalm 126).

"Dear friends, our mouths are filled with laughter, and our tongues with praise. During the past few months we have had at times a foretaste of heaven. There has never been so much praise and thanksgiving, so much singing at the school before. Never before have the teachers and pupils been united by such a bond of love. The Lord has poured forth the early and the latter rain. Great things have happened among us and on nine other islands through the ministry of seventeen teams.

It all started with our becoming aware of our own unworthiness. For months we had been bitterly disappointed by the spiritual state of our school. A group of people began to pray for revival. Meanwhile, we were approaching the end of the school year. The 5th grade would soon be leaving us for good, and yet a number of the students were spiritually at a very low level. But then the Lord began to answer our prayers. He sent us two of his messengers. Their authoritative messages concerning the spiritual battle to be fought in the full armour of God, showed us how far away we were from our goal. Oh, how hungry and thirsty we were! How far we had wandered from the light! But nevertheless the Lord was still at work. Ten days later, Dan, our Indonesian fellow-worker, experienced a wonderful renewal in his life. The Holy Spirit aroused such a consciousness of sin within him that he wept bitterly for more than an hour. Afterwards the Lord filled this man, who in the past had often caused us a lot of heartache on account of his pride and criticism, with such a spirit of humility and love that he is now a completely different person. Whenever I see him now, praise and gratitude fills my heart for such a wonderful work of grace.

At last it was possible for the staff to pray together. We began on a Wednesday evening. The Lord humbled us so much that for the first time in our lives we began to weep before Him for our young people. And His reply was so unexpected! At the end of our first session of prayer, He poured out His Spirit in such a way that the darkness was brought into His light. When we arrived back home late that night, we found the girls already waiting for us at the door. One of them was demon possessed. In fact, she had been so all along. We had sometimes suspected it, but things had previously been so black that the evil spirits had easily been able to find their way into the Bible School. During that night and the ones that followed, we drove over fifty demons out of the girl in the name of Jesus. It was a life and death struggle. Over and over again the evil spirits attempted to drive her mad or force her to commit suicide. We were often at the limits of our physical and spiritual strength. But Jesus is a wonderful Saviour. The Lord taught us a lot during this struggle. All the evil spirits had to reveal their identity and their reason for possessing Hanna. Vast fields of occult practices were uncovered. Later, we discovered that not one of the pupils or teachers was uninvolved. Confessions consisting sometimes of a list of up to 200 sins of sorcery were not rare — and this at a Bible school, where the students were taught about the dangers of occultism! This just shows how the enemy can blind men's eyes! But it also reveals how penetrating the light of the Holy Spirit is — but I am jumping the gun.

After that first night we began to pray together every evening, and some students were renewed in the same wonderful way as Dan. Yet the real breakthrough only came when, on the Monday, we cancelled all work for the entire school and, according to Joel 2, called a day of fasting and prayer. After we teachers had bowed ourselves in tears at our failure, the Holy Spirit worked so mightily that many students were also convicted of their sins. By now the extent of the darkness was at last becoming visible, and the real battle began. We prayed every evening until late into the night. Nobody was aware of time any more. Further cases of possession came to light. Often the struggles went on into the early hours, because young boys and girls, overcome by sin, crowded round for counselling. During those weeks we didn't get much sleep, but the joy of the Lord was our strength. The work of the school proceeded, even though we had to drop everything on several occasions when the prayers of everyone were needed in difficult cases of possession. But even this was instructive. The final examinations for the 3rd and 5th grades drew near. However, the results were no worse than usual, despite the fact that so little time had been spent on revision. It was a triumph of love that the students were repeatedly prepared to leave their books, whenever it was a question of helping to deliver one of their oppressed brothers through prayer.

During those weeks the Lord gave us a deep insight into the reality of sin, inherited sin, the curse of God till the third and fourth generation, and occult oppression, and possession. What an abyss of darkness and need, and how dreadful and abhorrent the enemy! Yet also: how mighty the name of Jesus in destroying the strongholds of the enemy, and how invincible the power of his blood to wash away all sins and to answer all the accusations of the evil one! How wonderful is the perfect salvation which comes to us through Christ! Sometimes questions were raised: aren't things like God's curse on the occult practices of our forefathers automatically lifted when someone is born again in Christ? Aren't we belittling a person's salvation when we later try to loose him from these oppressions? The Lord gave us the answer to this by reminding us of the story of Lazarus. Although he received the gift of life from Jesus, he was unable to benefit from it properly until his grave-clothes had been removed. And Jesus left this task to the onlookers who had witnessed Lazarus' raising from the dead. We experienced this for ourselves in a very practical manner with some of our students. Many of them, in spite of being born again, had never really experienced the joy of their salvation or been able to fight effectively in their spiritual lives. However, once their 'grave-clothes' had been removed, they became both joyful and powerful witnesses to their Lord. We found that the task and the authority to loose people, which Jesus has given to all his disciples, was revealed to us in a completely fresh light. Maybe this is the answer to many of the problems facing churches and Christians throughout the world.

We were approaching the teams' valedictory service. In fact, the teams should have been decided long ago, and the necessary letters sent out to the churches involved. The Lord, however, had confounded every meeting at which we had endeavoured to settle these matters. Finally therefore we gave the students a free rein: "Wait for direct instructions from the Lord, and then let us know what they are!" A wonderful plan of the Lord was then revealed. The various calls — most of them conveyed through the Bible, although some by visions — never overlapped. What is more, He led us to districts which we would never have dared to tackle, because we would have been afraid to accept responsibility for our young people working there: the occult strongholds of the islands of Ambon and Sabu, the wild island of Mojo, the Islamic fortresses of Atjeh and Minangkabu, the impassable swamplands of the Sumatra provinces of Djambi and Riau, the moral quagmire of the port area of Djakarta, and the prostitutes of Surabaja. Some of the students were quite understandably a little fearful concerning the tasks the Lord had assigned them, and so, instead of telling us what the Lord had told them, they left the decision to us. However, in the two days of prayer preceding the Sunday when the teams were to be sent out, the Holy Spirit worked so mightily, that these young men and women broke down in tears and asked the Lord to forgive them, urging us at the same time to allow them to follow the Lord's call. How wonderfully the Lord responded! What promises he gave, what power in prayer! I wish you had been able to share in these two and a half days of prayer! We prayed continually with only a short pause for lunch and for supper from eight in the morning till ten or eleven at night — with no feeling of tiredness at all! At the same time, during the lunch periods and also at night, we were able to counsel the students to whom the Lord had directly revealed his will, and also the guests who, almost without exception, experienced the same spiritual blessing as we had earlier. Then came yet another climax: the Sunday of the valedictory service. If I remember correctly, the afternoon service lasted from 4.30 p. m. until about 9 p. m. What a joyful time! This was followed by a few hectic days preparing for the teams' departures. The Lord added material blessings to all the spiritual ones: blankets, rucksacks, bags and sandals for the teams, also chests of clothing from Germany and crispbread from the German army which was marvellously light and nutritious. Two days before the departure of the first team, we received a batch of portable record players. In addition we had been able a few weeks previously, by means of a gift earmarked for literature, to obtain a large number of tracts, John's Gospels and New Testaments. Finally, we received enough monetary gifts to start all the teams on their journeys. The fact that no team set out with enough money to cover all their daily requirements and their return fare, did not deter anybody. They all knew that they could depend on Matthew 6:33. Please praise and give thanks, and pray with us."

Let us now hear of the victories which God accomplished.

IX. JESUS AMONG THE MOSLEMS

Reuben's life is a testimony to how the Lord honours his Word: "God chose what is low and despised in the world, even things that are not, to bring to nothing things that are" (1 Cor. 1:26 f).

On applying to be accepted at the Bible School in East Java he received the reply: wait another year! Since he could not just sit around doing nothing for a year, he applied for a job at the Post Office and was accepted.

A year later he made a second application to the Bible School. He was told this time that if he wanted to, he could be employed as a gardener. He accepted, but continued to persevere in prayer. Four months later he made a third application and was finally granted a place.

However, as the course proceeded, it became clear that the new student was not very gifted. In spite of working very hard, he found that he could only retain a very little. One day his tutor called him and asked, "What are we going to do with you? You're not really getting anywhere with the work." Reuben replied humbly, "If you think I'm not good enough, then I must give it up." Back in his room, however, he threw himself on his knees and prayed, "Lord Jesus, you have called me. Please, get me through the course." Next day his tutor summoned him again and instead of expelling him, encouraged him to carry on with his studies. This was again a sign of the consistency of the Holy Spirit's guidance. Reuben in his simple faith was sure that he had to see the course through.

The time came for the examination. The young student, in spite of his lack of ability, studied day and night. But nothing stuck. Then, the night before the examination, the Lord spoke to him and said, "Just read the following sections." Reuben obeyed. Next day the questions covered the exact passages he had read the night before, and as a result, he passed. It was quite wonderful the way the Lord had 'cheated' at His own Bible School, but although He may do this, we must never follow suit.

Reuben, however, was so honest that afterwards he admitted to his teachers, "The night before the Lord Jesus told me which sections you would examine me on. That's how I passed." The teachers, though, were content to leave things as they were.

With regards to his ministry, in spite of Reuben's lack of natural gifts, the picture was very different. I have visited a number of countries in both Africa and Asia under the sway of the Moslems, and have seen the many very real problems facing the Christians in these areas. So let us see how Reuben fared.

He was sent by the school to a Moslem village in East Java. There was only one single Christian family in the village, and even they were only nominal in their faith. When Reuben visited them, they would have nothing to do with either him or his work.

The young missionary was not to be discouraged, however. Sleeping out in the open, he used the streets as his pulpit. When he asked the Lord to supply him with his daily needs, he was not disappointed, and it was not long before he was receiving invitations from the Moslems themselves to eat with them and to spend the nights at their homes. What the Christians had failed to do the Moslems did for this faithful servant of the Lord.

At the end of the first year, 100 Moslems had already been converted, and the young brother had now a congregation of his own. By this time too, the single family of Christians had been stirred and had opened their house to him. He was afterwards able to meet with them and to pray with them each day.

The Moslems were annoyed about Reuben's missionary successes. During the second year they banded together, and one day about 60 men came to the Christians' house, armed with long knives. The Christians could do nothing more than kneel and ask for the Lord's protection. At that moment they heard a siren, and a police car sped up the road to make a routine check. Quickly hiding their knives, the Moslems made off as fast as possible. The Lord had been at hand in their hour of need.

Some weeks later 60 more Moslems had come to Christ. It was as if the wave of persecution had borne fruit. By the end of the second year the simple native brother's congregation had grown to include 200 converted Moslems. And all this was the fruit of the labours of one ungifted brother in Christ! "God chose what is foolish in the world to shame the wise, God chose what is weak in the world to shame the strong."

X. IN THE KORAN'S STRONGHOLD

In my English Bible I have often come across the expressions: a broken spirit and a broken heart. We find these words recorded, for example, in Psalm 51:17, "The sacrifice acceptable to God is a broken spirit; a broken and contrite heart, O God, thou wilt not despise." These words imply a spiritual situation in which a person no longer resists the will of God, but counting himself as nothing, allows God to use him in which ever way he chooses. This is more easily said than done, and few indeed are the Christians whom the Lord can lead thus far. Knowing my own rebellious heart, I find it difficult to write about this at all.

In Indonesia, however, I saw this attitude demonstrated clearly in the life of one young believer. His name is Dan. Although coming from a heathen family, some years after his birth his parents adopted Christianity as their faith. They then had all the children baptised. Little Dan, however, experienced no change in his inner life, and subsequently sin took the upper hand.

Then, during a mission in 1957 he was converted. Immediately he felt himself called to the service of the Lord. He applied to the Bible School in East Java and was accepted there. On completing his initial studies, he took the ministers' training course and then remained at the Bible School as a teacher.

As time went on, however, he felt that he lacked authority in his life. It was then that Roy Hession and William Nagenda visited East Java. These two men of God were used by the Lord to impart a new blessing to the students and staff of the Bible School. After they had left, the young teacher was greatly exercised concerning the theme of walking in the light.

However, he still felt that there was something wrong in his own life. One day God opened his eyes. He was still carrying upon himself the occult sins of his parents and forebears. In no other sphere are the effects upon the third and fourth generation so evident as in the realm of sorcery. This was the background to his oppression and lack of spiritual power. He confessed his sins and became free.

As we have already mentioned, during the revival that came to the Bible School, Dan was so filled with the Holy Spirit that he became a model to the students, teachers, and visitors alike. In my own contact with him I found his life a blessing too.

Following his deliverance, Dan became the Lord's chosen instrument for Atjeh. This district lies in the extreme north of Sumatra and is known to be one of the most fanatical strongholds of the Moslems. It was here that the Dutch had to face the longest resistance to their occupation of Sumatra and Indonesia. Not until 1903 was this opposition finally overcome.

During the prayer meetings at the Bible School it became clear to Dan that he should visit Atjeh with a team. Christians in the West will be unable to imagine the difficulties that were involved.

A distance of several thousand miles! An area unexplored by Christians! No one to take care of the team when it arrived! No contacts! Dan did not even have a single address to which he could turn for help. And on top of all this, very little money.

It was therefore a uniquely hazardous enterprise which confronted Dan. Even stronger resistance came when one of the students had a vision in which he saw the whole venture ending in failure. However, the other Christians soon realized that this was a vision from the devil, designed to stop the whole campaign. The incident shows that the devil can also occasion visions, even during a revival. Indeed, right in the midst of times of great blessing, the enemy is for ever very active.

With eyes directed towards the Lord, the mission was begun. Six students, among them Dan, set off as a team to carry the light of the gospel into the darkest depths of Sumatra.

Their financial provision was ridiculously small. They had between them a total of 35,000 rupees which at that time was worth about £100. What use was this to six men who intended to cover some 6,000 miles on a journey lasting two months?

Yet they carried more than just this meagre sum of

money with them. The most valuable treasure they possessed was the Bible with its countless promises which assured them that God was true.

They were able to experience this already on the journey by rail from Surabaja to Djakarta. As the train set out they began to sing together and to talk to the other passengers. One woman listened to them attentively. Finally they became tired. After all, it is an eighteen-hour train journey, which thanks to the 'well-organized' airline, I myself once had to enjoy. The other members of the team settled down to sleep. Dan, remaining awake, continued in prayer. As they came to a station, the woman who had listened so attentively, got up. Just before alighting from the train, she handed Dan a small parcel wrapped in newspaper. She added, "This comes to you from the Lord." Dan asked her name. She replied, "That's of no importance. The Lord Jesus wants to give you this." She then vanished into the crowd of people on the platform.

Dan wanted to share his joy with the others. Arousing them out of sleep he recounted to them what had happened. As he finished he said, "You see, God has fulfilled his promise yet again: 'He gives to his beloved in sleep'." He then opened the parcel and found 500 rupees, worth about £1 10s, in it. It was not a very large sum, but it was nevertheless a sign from the Lord that he would provide for them. Together they thanked God for the encouraging gift.

After the long journey by rail and the final crossing to Sumatra, the team stepped ashore with the words, "In the name of the Lord we enter this mission field." About 100 years earlier another missionary had used almost exactly the same words. He was Nommensen, the apostle to the Batak. He had called out, "I begin a battle here which the Lord Jesus has already won long ago." In this we see that the original pioneering spirit of Christians is not dead. The team, however, was not aiming to reach the Batak, but the Moslems of Atjeh.

The team did not know at first where it ought to go. Before deciding what to do therefore, they prayed, literally asking the Lord to show them the direction they should take. As it was raining heavily, the young men looked for a place where they could spend the night, seeking the Lord's will in this matter too. Finding their way to a cheap hotel, they discovered that it was situated opposite a Christian church. Moreover, they met a man who turned out to be one of the elders of the church.

But there were still more wonderful things to come. That same day a pastor arrived back at the airport by plane. On meeting the team he told them, "I was on my way to Java to find a pastor for this church. However, since it was raining so heavily, the plane was unable to land and we had to turn back. So here I am without having had any success."

On hearing the man's story, Dan again sensed the Lord's guidance in his heart. "That's not true," he replied, "the Lord has arranged everything. You couldn't find a pastor, because that pastor is already here. You can have one of these young Christians. They are all fully trained, and one of them can stay here as pastor." And so it happened. Who could still doubt that the Lord was their guide? How wonderfully everything fitted into place, and all without previous contact, and without any planning at all. This was indeed guidance!

In the same way as He arranged where they should go, the Lord also settled their problems of transport and provisions.

As the team started to give their testimonies and to preach in one of the villages, the Holy Spirit stirred the heart of an influential man who was the manager of an oil company. Although the man was a Moslem, he placed a car at the team's disposal which they were able to use free of charge while they stayed and moved about in the area.

The young Christians were even more deeply moved when the president of the oil company, who was also a Moslem, presented them with a gift of 5,000 rupees — about £ 15. In this way the enemies of the cross became the servants of the crucified Lord. God will surely not overlook these deeds on the day of judgement. How many Christians will be put to shame by the generosity of Moslems like these!

The team had some quite strange and marvellous experiences with regards to their daily provisions. They had needed 200,000 rupees to cover the expenses for the two months' campaign, and yet they had only set out with 35,000 rupees. Nevertheless, when they returned home they brought a total of 80,000 rupees with them, in spite of the fact that they had been working among Moslems and materialistic nominal Christians. Mathematics like this is difficult to explain. It is not the sort that one is taught in our universities today. This type of higher mathematics only exists in the school of the One who bears the name Wonderful.

Darkness

The pathway the team trod, however, was not always filled with light. The area in which they found themselves was indeed a stronghold of the Koran.

The young messengers of Christ had arranged to speak one day in a certain village but when it had begun to rain, they had been forced to abandon their intended visit. — Rainstorms in the tropics can be much severer than in European countries. — They were quite disappointed at first. However, they later discovered that under the instigation of a well-known Moslem leader a group of armed Moslems had planned to kill all the members of the team. The Lord had thus protected them. What to us is a disappointment, is not always a misfortune; the Lord so often hides a blessing in times like these.

The numerous nominal Christians were also a great hindrance to Dan and his friends. They discovered to their great surprise that there were some 14,000 registered Christians living in the area. This they noted down with a view to later evangelistic work.

These nominal Christians quite often turned their backs on the team. But this was not really surprising since most of them were in the habit of visiting the local sorcerer whenever they needed help, and besides, a large number of them kept fetishes in their homes.

Whenever the team was rejected, they would ask the Lord, "Where shall we go?" They thought to themselves that no areas were closed to them as long as Christ's words, "I am the door," remained true.

Their dependence was on God alone. At the beginning of each new day they would ask God, as they prayed and read the Bible, "Lord, where shall we go today?" They never started out until they were sure what the Lord's will was.

Dan told me, "It was often difficult to discover what God's plans were. We would therefore continue to pray and to fast until we could recognize his will. Once, when every door seemed to be closed, we had to travel 50 miles until another place opened up for us to work in. We felt as if we were being accompanied by pillars of fire and smoke. It was a good thing that we had all surrendered ourselves completely to the Lord during the revival at our Bible school. Otherwise our mission in Atjeh would have been a failure."

The Fruit

In the end this evangelistic missionary campaign was a great triumph for the gospel. Hundreds were converted. The natives brought their fetishes and occult objects out of their houses to be burned. They confessed their sins and accepted the Lord Jesus. 36 young people offered themselves for active missionary service. They wanted to go to Malaysia, another stronghold of the Moslems. Others felt called to India. Both these countries are in fact nearer to Atjeh than their own capital, which lies some 1,200 miles away from the northern tip of Sumatra. Today some of the young Christians from Atjeh are already at the Bible School in East Java. I have met them there myself.

What a blessing it was that Dan had recognized the oppression he had carried as a result of the occult practices of his ancestors, and that by the grace of God he had been delivered. In this way he was able to help loosen the bonds of others. The authority to loose men in the name of the Lord (Matthew 18 : 18) is only given to those who have experienced this release for themselves.

The two months of the campaign bore much fruit. "By this my Father is glorified, that you bear much fruit, and so prove to be my disciples" (John 15 : 8).

The Lord had fulfilled his word in the work of this team.

At the Bible School I met pastors who had experienced a renewal of both their own faith and that of their congregations through the ministry of the team.

XI. AMONG THE POISON MIXERS

We shall now visit the area to the extreme south of Sumatra, although we shall not be leaving this 1,000 mile long island itself.

As we have already heard, the Dutch prohibited missionary work in these parts, because they feared the unrest it might cause. Today, however, the area has become the stage for the greatest revival ever known among Moslems. The story has no parallel in the history of Christian missions.

When God decides to work, he chooses the instruments which are most suitable for his purposes. In this case they were not Christians, but Moslems. Now let us hear their story.

Abram, Chief of the Poison Mixers

Under Sukarno, the former president of Indonesia, the Communists had many great successes in the land. And so it was that in 1963 Abram, as a tribal chief, received an invitation to attend a Communist educational course. The political course ended around Christmas time. On the day of his departure, Abram saw a car with the word 'Indjil', meaning gospel, written on it. He watched the car with interest. The word intrigued him for he recognized its meaning from the Arabic. As he came to the place where the car was parked, he heard the words of a Christmas sermon coming to him through the open window of a Christian meeting house. He had never heard the gospel before, but in spite of his interest he remained outside, not daring to go into the room.

The sermon's message remained in his mind. Back home with his tribe, he told the people the story of Bethlehem instead of the latest Communist revelations. Without realizing it, and in spite of the fact that he was still a Moslem, Abram became the first Christian missionary to his tribe. Because the men wanted to hear more of this Christ-child, Abram promptly sent a letter to the following address: Indjil, Bengkulen. Despite the complete inadequacy of the address, the letter still arrived, whereas even properly addressed letters often fail to reach their destination in the Far East.

After this, a number of Christians from various places took an interest in Abram's tribe, the members of which were much-feared on account of their renowned poison mixing. The first to arrive was a Christian official from Bengkulen, and he was later followed by a student from the East Java Bible School, who was staying in Palembang at the time. Finally Pak Elias visited the tribe. I will not repeat the story here since I have already described the events in my book 'Name über alle Namen Jesus'. The result was, that a remarkable revival broke out, although Abram himself did not make a decision to follow Christ for a long time. He feared the dangerous reaction it might bring forth from his tribe. Only when several hundred of them had become Christians already, did he himself take the decisive step.

The ways of God are often strange. Cyrus, the heathen king of the Persians was called 'the servant of God'. Abram, the Moslem chief, brought the first Christian message to his Moslem tribe. The Word of the Lord does not return void. Luther once said, "Even if a priest is a rogue, his word will not lose its effect."

Timothy

The next witness to the gospel we can mention besides Pak Elias, is Timothy. Like many others, he too was a convinced Moslem before his conversion. Studying at Jogdjakarta University he decided that he wanted to become a teacher. Driven by his extreme fanaticism he became the leader of a Mohammedan youth-group, and through it carried out all kinds of acts of terrorism against the Christians. Once, together with his friends, he smashed the windows of a Christian church and those of the Protestant minister's house nearby.

The minister, however, did nothing about these attacks. This annoyed young Timothy who finally visited the pastor and asked him why he did not retaliate. The pastor explained to him, "God loves you and therefore we love you too. Christians don't repay evil with evil!"

Afterwards the young Moslem leader could get no peace. Buying himself a Bible, he began to study the principles of the Christian faith. He wanted to be in the position to refute both the Bible and the Christians' beliefs.

But the result did not turn out as he expected. Timothy was converted. Giving up his Mohammedan name, he adopted a Christian one instead. This caused a great stir among his circle of friends, since Moslems find it very difficult to tolerate the conversion of one of their number to Christianity.

All attempts to change his mind failed. Giving up his studies, he decided to read theology instead. At first he considered enrolling at the theological seminary in Djakarta, but when he heard that the college was steeped in modern theology, and that it questioned most of the basic truths of the Bible, he became disconcerted. Had he given up his life's ambition and heaped upon himself the scorn of his parents and friends, just to have his hard-won faith taken away from him again? He started to ask himself, "What kind of Christianity is this? This isn't what I've exchanged my former beliefs for!" And so he began to seek out Christians who had faith in what the Bible said. His search was not in vain.

Timothy came into contact with the Bible School in East Java and thereupon enrolled. When his training was at an end, he felt with his teachers that he should work among the Moslems in Sumatra. His subsequent ministry there has been greatly blessed. I have met him now on several occasions and we have become good friends. He stands high on my prayer list for Sumatra.

The following incidents are just a few which illustrate the work of this brave young soldier of the cross. One day Timothy met a 90-year-old mosque servant. The young pastor asked him, "Do you realize that when you die you'll go to hell?" The old man replied, "Yes, I know that, but if you know the way to heaven then show it to me." Timothy showed this aged Moslem the way to Christ. The man accepted the Lord Jesus as his saviour and was thereby saved.

Another time Timothy fell into conversation with a Moslem priest. As a former Moslem himself and student of the Koran, Timothy was able to show the man the differences between the Christian faith and belief in Allah. He told the priest, "The Koran tells us nothing about becoming children of God. The Bible promises us, however, 'See what love the Father has given to us, that we should be called children of God' (1 John 3 : 1). What's more, the Koran gives us no assurance of forgiveness, no certainty of eternal life. But the Bible on the other hand tells us, 'He who believes in the Son has eternal life' (John 3 : 36). Then again, Paul tells us (Eph. 1 : 7), 'In Christ we have redemption through his blood, the forgiveness of our trespasses, according to the riches of his grace.'" The priest became thoughtful, and then the thing which no missionary can accomplish — the conversion of a Moslem priest — took place through the working of the Holy Spirit. Tearing off his Moslem robe, the priest threw it down at the entrance to the mosque. Afterwards, learning to follow Jesus, he was even elected to be an elder of the local Christian church.

> Thou art the Truth — Thy Word alone
> True wisdom can impart.
> Thou only canst inform the mind,
> And purify the heart.

Christophorus

I was to meet Christophorus at the conference which was held at the Bible School in East Java. However, when he had only just arrived, he received a telegram recalling him immediately to Sumatra. The Moslems had once again concocted a murderous plan against the Christians.

Christophorus is Timothy's younger helper in his work among the tribe of poison mixers, and similarly received his training at the Bible School. Already his ministry has proved to be a particular success.

One day he received an invitation to dinner. Without suspecting anything he accepted, but after the meal he was overcome by some terrible stomach pains. His so-called hosts had mixed some poison with his food which in any normal circumstances would have proved lethal.

Christophorus lay in bed. For three days he suffered from terrible burning pains in his stomach and lungs. He cried to his Lord without ceasing. After three days the crisis was past. The Moslems were amazed that the poison had failed to kill him. They began to say after this, "You have to be careful with Christians. Their God always helps them."

The actual result of this abortive attempt to kill Christophorus was that a number of Moslem families were converted. This, however, did not include the poisoners themselves.

Every converted Moslem must be prepared for death each day. He must live in a state of being continually ready to die. This is a very sobering yet wholesome lesson for those who become Christians in the area.

In the end God won the actual poison mixers to himself too. He employs many ways and means to achieve his goals.

For example, a Christian prayed with a Moslem priest who was mentally ill, and as a result the man was cured and subsequently became a Christian. This angered the Moslem Governor, since the converted man had been a Moslem priest for 38 years. He sent soldiers to arrest him, and under threats of torture the priest was asked, "Why did you become a Christian?" He replied, "I was mentally ill, and the Lord Jesus made me well; so I'm going to stay with him." Almost miraculously the priest suffered no harm at all, but was allowed to go home in peace. On other occasions, however, Moslems who have become Christians have often been beaten up by the soldiers or even sent to prison on the spot.

God has used Moslem children as his instruments too. Pastor Christophorus once taught some children the chorus, "The blood of the Lamb cleanses you, making your whole life new." The following Friday, the Moslem Sabbath, the children began to march up and down outside the mosque during one of the services singing their song. Christophorus was rather alarmed by this and went outside to try and stop them. However, when he saw that the son of the Moslem priest was taking part too, he decided not to interfere. In many cases parents are being pointed to Christ through the witness of their own children.

At another Moslem service the Christians were coming heavily under attack. Fearing the worst, the believers met together to pray. But the result was very different from what they had expected. As the Moslem priest was inciting the Moslems to attack the Christians, one of the men in the mosque suddenly left and went straight to Pastor Christophorus' home. "I want to become a Christian," he told the pastor. Christophorus hesitated a little, for he feared a trap. The Moslem went on, "You don't believe me. Look, there's some pork. Give it to me and I'll eat it. That should convince you." To eat pork for the Moslems is absolutely taboo. When he had eaten some, he added, "Now give me some for my family. We are all leaving the mosque and coming to the Lord Jesus instead." And this is exactly what happened. The whole family was converted. This was God's reply to the baiting of the priest and the prayers of His children.

When another Moslem named Uzza was converted, he brought all his family and neighbours to Christ at the same time. Not long after this the Moslems had him imprisoned. One night his wife suddenly came running to the Christians, crying, "Our rice field is on fire. It must be our persecutors again. Come and help me put out the fire."

The Christians hurried to her aid, for the rice was just ready for harvesting. However, the task was hopeless since, as a result of the drought, there was no water in the neighbourhood at all. The only thing the Christians could do was to fall on their knees and pray to the Lord for help. And then the miracle happened. In next to no time, immediately after their prayer, the Lord sent rain, although at that time of the year it generally never rained at all. The fire was soon quenched and the harvest was saved. As a result of the miracle two other families in the district were saved. The persecution had again served to extend the kingdom of God.

Near to Pastor Christophorus lived a certain Moslem family. Christophorus had prayed and wept a great deal for them. One morning the wife came to see him and said, "We all want to become Christians." "What made you decide this?" Christophorus asked. "Last night," the woman replied, "I had a dream in which I was told that my family and I were to become Christians."

There are many sorcerers among the Moslems. In fact, the majority of the priests, instead of basing their authority upon the Koran, use their magic powers instead. In the course of his preaching Christophorus one day came face to face with three sorcerers. As he talked with them, he showed them the way to Christ and subsequently two of the men were converted. The third sorcerer, however, was quite rich and did not want to forsake his possessions. When Christophorus visited him later, he pointed him to the words, "What shall it profit a man if he gains the whole world and yet forfeits his life?" The sorcerer, however, resisted and continued to reject Christ. Nine days later, with no warning at all, he suddenly collapsed and died.

The gospel continues its onward march. Neither poison, nor threats, nor attempted assassinations can hinder the work of the Spirit of God. How wonderfully this is illustrated in Indonesia today! Moreover, every event proceeds without recourse to the fanaticism or extremism which is so often used by people who desire to simulate revival.

During recent years many of the Christians on Sumatra have been imprisoned for their faith. Yet even here the will of the Lord can be discerned, for through their imprisonment Christians have often escaped the frequent attempts which are made on their lives. On top of this, many of the other prisoners and warders have been converted through their testimony in the jails.

One of the most well-known people to be sent to prison was the former director of a Moslem mission. He had been converted at one of Pak Elias' open-air meetings. When he had later been baptised, his former supporters had begun to suspect his political motives and had had him put in jail. Undeterred, the converted man led another four Moslems to Christ, baptising three of them while they were still with him in prison. The fourth, after his release, walked over 25 miles to find a Christian church in which to be baptised, and in this way confirmed through his actions the things he had heard and learnt while in jail.

The revival among the Moslems is like a modern Acts of the Apostles. The Holy Spirit is really working, and the Lord Jesus continues to glorify his own name. Yet at the same time the revival is a time of persecution, an epoch of demonic attacks. But this is part and parcel of the Christian faith.

The Moslems use everything at their disposal. They creep into the Christians' closed meetings in order to spy on them. They forge documentary evidence against them. They send the police and the army, and have the Christians arrested and put in jail. They use poison and arson, or whatever else is at hand. The Christians are treated as outcasts, and are dismissed from their posts to keep the government offices 'clean'. And if a Moslem ever becomes a Christian, he immediately loses his job.

Yet in spite of everything the Lord is still on the throne: "His kingdom lasts for ever."

Notwithstanding these pressures, the church of converted Moslems is steadily being established. Today the number of Christians who were formerly Moslems and enemies of the cross of Christ is already about 1,400. Since 1965 they have even had their own Bible school which is attended now by some 30 young members of the tribe of poison mixers. Instead of practising their former art, they are today preaching the gospel of Christ.

XII. A UNIVERSITY LECTURER BECOMES A CHRISTIAN

While I was in Indonesia I had the pleasure of meeting a Christian lawyer by the name of Mr. Tamba. He is a competent and confident member of the Batak tribe, yet in spite of the fact that the Batak are a very proud people, Mr. Tamba had entered the school of Christ where all that is esteemed by man is brought low. He kindly gave me permission to publish this brief account of his testimony. May the Lord use it to speak to those who find themselves in a similar situation. Now let us listen to Mr. Tamba himself.

"The name of the Lord Jesus Christ be praised for the great love he showed me when I was allowed to find my way to him. I wrote the date, the 10th August 1967, down in my Bible. It was my spiritual birthday, the day of my conversion in a church in Palembang, Sumatra.

I was and still am a member of the Batak Church, which I believe is the largest church in Indonesia. Before I found the Lord Jesus as my Saviour I was a very proud man. People say that the chief characteristics of the Batak are their arrogance and their pride. My own pride was nurtured by the fact that I thought I was the only Christian in Palembang with a university degree — an

M. A. in law. I was not only a lecturer at Sriwidjaja University but also the chairman of the Association of Lawyers in Palembang. And, as if that were not enough, I was elected president of the town's Christian Intellectuals Club. With all my titles and offices therefore, and with the large salary I earned, it was no wonder that I began to look down on all the Christians I met.

In Christian activities my progress was much the same. In 1962 I was made the choir master of our youth group, and I soon despised everybody who could not sing. When the evangelistic team from the Bible School in East Java arrived at our town, their choir master asked me if we could unite the two choirs under his direction. I just scoffed, imagining that the combined choir would only be able to sing well under my own direction. I was so deluded that I thought our choir was the only one on the whole of Sumatra which could sing Handel's Hallelujah chorus.

But as if my musical presumptions were not enough, I borrowed a Bible commentary from a relative and began to study the Scriptures, not to find my way to Christ, but merely to discuss its contents with theologians. I was therefore spiritually arrogant as well.

Is there any hope for a man like this, that God will ever be able to bring him low?

The Turning Point

The evangelist during the mission in our town was Pak Elias. As he began to preach, his message started speaking to my conscience. However, when he came to the point of inviting us to go the front and to repent, I was still too hard and too proud to follow his advice. Instead of me then, a number of young people went out and confessed their sins. I was furious at the time and said to the young people later, "You didn't have to do that. You've already been born again through baptism and confirmation!"

This was the misconstrued Lutheran theology which had reached me through the German missionaries. In the end I was so angry that night, that I began to abuse the members of my own choir. Some of the girls were even driven to tears.

I tried to forget the whole evening but could find no peace. Instead of going to the pictures therefore or some other place of entertainment, I went along again to hear Pak Elias speak. The third evening he spoke about the way one should read the Bible. His message was a revelation to me, for up till then I had read my Bible just as if it had been a series of cowboy and Indian stories.

In the end I went to see Pak Elias after the close of one of the meetings. I was still feeling very proud and merely wanted to have an argument with him. "How," I asked, "should a person read his Bible? I've heard so many different theological views about the subject." Pak Elias replied, "How has Jesus taught you to read your Bible?" I just did not know what to say, for it had never occurred to me to ask Jesus about reading the Scriptures. Pak Elias then began to talk to me at some length, and for two hours he explained to me how I could become a real Christian. I felt a burden come upon my own soul. My past sins and my unimaginable pride loomed up before my eyes. For the first time in my life I asked the Lord that night to forgive my sins, and I was wonderfully saved.

From that moment on the Bible became an open book to me. Yet I was to make another wonderful discovery during that mission. There had been a number of difficult passages in the Bible which I had not been able to really understand. Later one day as I sat with Pak Elias again, without my even asking him, he began to explain the meaning of the very passages I had found so obscure. He was literally being guided by the Holy Spirit, and it showed me again just how much the Lord Jesus really cared for me.

A few months after the campaign had ended — and it had benefited every single church in our town — I found myself once more bogged down in a mass of problems relating to my work. I hardly had enough time to even pray. It was then that the Lord sent me a tutor in the form of my two-year-old nephew. I had told the boy that a Christian ought always to pray to the Lord Jesus before he goes to sleep at night. He was visiting us at the time and we had allowed him to sleep in the same room as myself. When we went to bed my little nephew asked, "Uncle, why aren't you saying your prayers? Have you quarrelled with Jesus?" This childlike question brought me to my senses. The Lord had chosen to use a two-year-old boy to be his witness and my counsellor. "By the mouths of babes and infants..." (Psalm 8).

Oppressions

It is time that we took a brief look at my family. I grew up in a so-called Christian home and my maternal grandmother had actually been an elder in a church. However, my paternal grandfather instead of being a Christian had been about the most notorious and most feared magician in Tapanuli, Sumatra. His name was Datu Parangongo. The thing that horrified me most as a Christian was the discovery that many people in our village are still in possession of the fetishes and charms they obtained from my grandfather. It was only when I heard Dr. Nahum speaking about these things that I realized my family was still threatened and oppressed by sorcery. It dismays me to think that while I am reading my Bible my own fellow countrymen continue to use the fetishes they received from my grandfather. Worst of all my own father still suffers as a result of these oppressions.

When I first made this discovery I sought all the more to testify to my parents and family about Christ. Yet I could get nowhere at all with my message. My father just rejected it coldly with the words, "You should have become a pastor. I don't need anything." My brothers and sisters too, although they are members of the church, want nothing to do with Jesus. I was driven to prayer and the Lord did not disappoint.

A little later Pak Elias paid a visit to our house. As he testified about the Lord Jesus, to my great joy both my parents surrendered their lives to Christ. Admittedly my brothers and sisters still resist the message, but I pray and believe that even their day will come. How I rejoiced to see my parents' zeal as they sought to show others the way to Christ after their own conversion. They began to study various Christian books avidly in order to learn how to help others become Christians. God grant that He will continue the work He has begun and finally convert my whole family.

Changes

When the Lord Jesus takes over a person's life nothing remains the same as it was before. I witnessed this in my own life.

Prior to my conversion I had been known at the university as the dreaded 'killer'. The students had chosen this nickname for me because of the way I would pick on those I did not like. Often when I felt an aversion for a particular student, I would defer his examinations for another year. As a Christian I realized the predicament I was putting these young people in, and I repented of my sin. Yet how much injustice still exists in the whole system of examinations in schools and universities today!

After my conversion my attitude in this respect changed radically. The students now became my friends. The situation so improved that they would wait by my car after lectures in the hope of getting a lift into town. Each day I became their taxi-driver.

Obviously, though, following Christ is not without its battles and trials. A problem which continually faces me is the actual amount of work I have to do. In 1968 I even thought of absenting myself from the East Java Bible School conference on account of overwork. However, so many people started praying for me that in the end I just dropped everything and went. But this too was the guidance of the Lord, for it was through the talks I heard at the conference that I first recognized the power the occult practices of my forefathers held over my life.

But I was not the only person in Palembang whose life experienced a sudden change in direction, for many other nominal Christians experienced the same. During the week of the mission literally hundreds of people came forward confessing their sins and accepting the Lord Jesus as their Saviour. I was amazed at the way that often a single phrase of the evangelist was enough to bring the self-confident Bataks to repentance. It was truly the work of the Holy Spirit himself.

None of the churches which participated in the campaign regretted their decision. The only church that had stood on the side-lines was my own, the Batak church, which had thought that the Bible School team had been a group of Pentecostals. But in this they were far from the truth. The message of both the evangelist and the team had been one of repentance and conversion, with no recourse to the ecstatic at all.

One of the consequences of the mission was the formation of some large prayer groups which have regularly met together ever since. We are very conscious that without constant prayer nothing will ever be achieved in Sumatra. I realize that this is also true regarding those of my own family who have yet to be saved. I have never had any difficulty in providing for their physical needs, but today their spiritual needs are far more important to me. I believe that the Lord will one day save them all. Perhaps you, the reader, will stand with me in your prayers. This is one of the reasons why I have written this short account, but there are two other reasons as well. Firstly, to show how my own life was once characterized by meaningless traditions of the church: that I was a churchgoer but not a disciple of Christ; and secondly, to illustrate my ignorance concerning the massive oppression which lay on our family due to my own grandfather, the chief magician. I thank God that he opened my eyes to this through his messenger Dr. Nahum, and that he has subsequently set me free. The praise is due to Christ alone."

XIII. AN ISLAND REPENTS

"God gives grace to the humble", says the Word of God. Pastor Gideon is an extremely simple and humble man. I have met no other man whose humility has impressed me so much.

In order to find out the details of his life I was forced to turn to those who know him well, since he does not like to talk about himself.

He is a pastor on the island of Rote which is situated just south of Timor and is nearer to Australia than any other part of the Indonesian archipelago. On account of the great shortage of pastors in the area over the last few years, Gideon himself has to care for a total of thirty different congregations. One pastor actually has to look after 48 groups of Christians.

In 1966 Pak Elias went with a team to Rote to hold a mission there. It was the first time that he and Pastor Gideon had met. Knowing that Gideon had warned his congregations to avoid the coming campaign, Pak Elias asked him, "Do you belong to Jesus?" "I've studied theology and passed my exams," came the reply.

After their conversation, Pastor Gideon's heart was in a turmoil. As the days went by he saw the numerous people who were being converted, the sick being healed, the possessed being freed, and confirmed drunkards being delivered of their alcoholism. On account of its sugar plantations, Rote is a source of a highly potent form of palm wine which the natives always used to carry with them in a flask slung at their waist.

The churches began to fill up in spite of the fact that their pastor still stood on one side. Gideon watched as the power of the Holy Spirit descended upon his fellow islanders, but he himself was not touched.

The two men met each other again. By now, however, the situation was completely changed. Pastor Gideon admitted, "I've been in the ministry for seven years and yet I've never seen a single person converted as a result of my work. Yet during one campaign under your ministry hundreds are converted. I think I know why. I've never really repented for myself and received the forgiveness of my sins, and I've certainly never been born again in the way that you describe. I'm going to resign. I can't go on like this!"

Pak Elias replied, "You don't have to give up your ministry, just start again, but this time with the Lord Jesus beside you. Come back to the Bible School with us and find out what we teach. I know it's not what people call modern theology, but at least it's the theology of the cross of Christ."

Gideon took the advice he had been given, feeling that he both could not and would not continue in a situation where his life and work were so fruitless. He therefore went to the Bible School in East Java for a year, and it was there that he experienced the power of the Lord Jesus in his own life.

When he returned to the island it was a changed man who stood in the pulpit to preach. His messages now began to have an effect, and the Holy Spirit used his subsequent ministry. In this way a man whose heart had been broken was given authority: the authority to prophesy and the authority to heal. Everything, though, took place quietly. There was neither noise nor sensationalism, unlike the ghastly background music which often accompanies the extremists. Gideon can fix his gaze on a man with unforgiven sin in his life, and tell him immediately what the problem is.

Before returning to Rote, Gideon accompanied one of the teams on a mission which took them close to the Portuguese border of Timor. He was motivated by a desire to reach his fellow pastors and to encourage and counsel them spiritually. In addition to this he hoped to be able to visit his own father who was also a pastor at the time. But he arrived too late. His father was drowned shortly before he came. Gideon used this shattering experience to appeal to the consciences of his colleagues. He knew very well the situation of the pastors on Timor. Many of them were living in gross sin. Many were involved in black magic and even fought each other with it. In one congregation for example, the pastor, the church elders, and a teacher, were engaged in a deadly feud, each using his magical powers in the fight. Gideon went to see the men one by one asking them, "Are you going to heaven when you die?" The old pastor replied, "I don't know, and the Bible doesn't know either." Speaking to another pastor, Gideon asked, "Are you ready for the Lord's second coming?" The man answered, "I'd rather Jesus didn't return yet, I'm not ready for him."

After touring the island of Timor, Gideon returned to his own small island of Rote. He realized that his first task was to evangelize the whole island, and for a year he continued to visit one congregation after another, preaching the gospel wherever he went. During this time the Lord confirmed his ministry in an unmistakable way. Over a thousand people were brought to Christ in this first year following Pastor Gideon's conversion. Large prayer groups began to spring up which became the backbone of his ministry. Each day he can rely on some 600

Christians to pray for the island, for the congregations, and for himself.

At the end of this year a wave of revival broke out on Rote. As Pastor Gideon walked to church he would find crowds of natives waiting outside unable to get into the building. They would listen to his sermon through the open windows. The only 'difficulty' he found was that sometimes the people would not allow him to stop, and he would have to continue preaching until 11 or even 12 o'clock at night. Whenever he felt like coming to an end the people would cry out, "Go on, go on." Such was the hunger for the Word of God which had gripped the natives.

There were occasions when Pastor Gideon was unable to stand the tropical heat in the overcrowded church any longer. "It's too hot," he said once, "I can't go on." However, the congregation soon found a solution." We must pray for rain so that the air will be cooler," they said. The sermon was halted. Many of the natives then began to pray for rain. As a result the Lord, who had so graciously poured his Spirit already upon them, sent rain too. It was just like Mount Carmel when Elijah prayed for rain: "Then he prayed again and the heavens gave rain" (James 5:18). In response therefore to his children's prayers, the Lord sent both the water of life and refreshing rain.

The only thing I can say to those who find these stories either strange or rather fanatical is, "Go to Rote and Timor yourselves and find out if these things are true. Yet don't approach Pastor Gideon too closely. He may tell you to your face what your unforgiven sins are, and this can be quite embarrassing."

What does Gideon's life look like from the outside? As a man he is completely devoted to his ministry. Like John Sung he consumes himself in the service of the Lord. Such men simply burn themselves out until no wick remains. Gideon himself cares little about his food or where he will spend the night. His time is spent in travelling from one of his 30 congregations to the next. It is no longer he that lives, but Christ who lives within him. At the present moment some 23,000 Christians stand behind him in his work.

An Indian proverb well describes the way he lives, "He who hunts lions, leaves mosquitoes in peace." In other words: "He who serves the Lord need not worry about anything else." Who of us is prepared to tread such a radical mountain pathway? How pitiful we often look beside such messengers of Christ! Something of the glory of God always rests on the life of a person in whom the image of Christ has already been formed.

There is much joy in heaven over every pastor who repents. How much more joy is there among the angels in heaven when an entire island repents?

XIV. THE REVIVAL ON TIMOR

Timor is one of the islands at the eastern extremity of the great Indonesian archipelago. It is actually nearer to Australia than to its own capital city. In 1964, out of a population exceeding one million, some 450,000 of the inhabitants belonged to the former Dutch Reformed Church. The number of pastors at that time, however, was only 103, far too few for the task. As we have already pointed out, one of the pastors had 48 different congregations within his care.

The spiritual state of the churches was almost catastrophic. This was due to a large extent to the way the Dutch had formerly administered the colony. Every minister in the church had at the same time been a colonial official. For this reason anyone who had wanted to obtain something from the government had been obliged to belong to the church as well. Timor, therefore, had never been evangelized, only Christianized. The former atheistic beliefs, the magic and sorcery, the promiscuity and alcoholism, all continued to prosper together.

This spiritual condition was a great burden to Pastor Joseph, the superintendent of the Presbytery in Soe. During the years preceding the revival, from 1960 until 1964, his work had almost driven him to despair.

Pastor Joseph is a man of great spiritual insight and understanding. The fact that his favourite books are those of Moody, Dr. Torrey, and Livingstone, speaks for itself. Next to Pak Elias he is better acquainted than anyone with the revival on the island.

From the point of view of the churches of the world it is important to know what reaction the church leaders on Timor had to the revival. The readers of the synod in fact met together on the 4th October 1967. They included Superintendent Joseph, Pastor Radjahaba, Pastor Meroekh, Pastor Baldey, and Pastor Micah. Besides these, Pak Elias and Pastor Gideon were also present on account of their direct involvement with the revival. After a good deal of discussion and a profitable time in prayer, they finally concluded that the movement which was taking place on Timor at that time was indeed the work of the Holy Spirit. Pastor Gideon, of whom we have already heard, was subsequently given the task of organizing the various teams.

God is sure to bless these church leaders for their decision. Unhappily in the Church's history it has frequently been the leaders who have most opposed the revivals when they have come, or who have at least stood to one side and refused to take part.

Although we have gone on ahead somewhat, it was necessary in order to have a clear picture of the framework in which the revival grew.

The Healing Movement

The revival on Timor was preceded by another movement of the Spirit of God. In October 1964 a teacher on the island of Rote received a vision. The Lord told him to travel to Timor and to hold a healing mission there. This may seem strange to Western minds, but one must try to understand the background against which such a command was given. There are practically no doctors at all on Timor and the neighbouring islands, at least not in the villages. Those who were sick would therefore seek the help of the sorcerers instead. The result was that almost every Christian in the area suffered some form of oppression from this healing magic. Little wonder therefore that the spiritual state of the Church literally cried to heaven. In view of this occult background it is understandable why the Lord should choose a man through whom to demonstrate his powers to the sick.

Jephthah, the teacher whom God had chosen, immediately went to see his own father who was a pastor on the island. Having told him about his experience, he asked his father to anoint him for his healing campaign. The father hesitated at first, wondering if the commission were genuine, but in the end, although he had never done anything like it before, he anointed his son for the task.

After his anointing, Jephthah prayed with the first group of sick people that he met. They were all healed. Encouraged by his initial success he decided to try and hold an actual 'Healing Campaign' in the first large town he came to on Timor. When it had been verified that a number of his cures were really genuine, the synod agreed to support the proposed campaign. The mission was a great success, and this led to the forming of a committee to deal with scriptural forms of healing.

Following the close of the campaign, a further week of healing was held in Soe. The wonderful miracles of healing which subsequently took place, aroused a great hunger for the Word of God within the Christians in the town. And so a movement was born which continued from October to December 1964. According to the various reports which were later confirmed by Superintendent Joseph himself, several thousand people were healed.

As time went on, however, the older Christians began to realize that there was a certain weakness in the healing movement. Somehow or other the preaching of the gospel was being neglected. Repentance and conversion were not the central theme. Nevertheless the healing movement can, as a result of prayer, be considered to be the forerunner of the later true revival.

The beginning of the Revival

In July 1965, David Simeon arrived on Timor with a team from the Bible School in East Java. He started to hold some evangelistic campaigns in both K. and Soe. As a result of this a definite biblical emphasis was brought to bear on the spiritual phenomena which had been taking place on the island. The team's message was one of repentance and rebirth, and of sanctification through the Holy Spirit. The work of that summer thereby became the spiritual birthday of the true revival which has broken out in Indonesia.

The campaigns were immediately followed by a huge outpouring of God's Spirit, which probably has no equal in all the history of revivals. The natives brought their fetishes out of their houses, piling them up in heaps and burning them. A wave of cleansing swept through the ranks of the Christians. But more important still, the Lord was able to call many of the islanders and use them to feed and spread the fire further.

Pastor Joseph later said concerning the work of David Simeon, "Just before the team from the Bible School left to return to East Java on September 1st 1965, Simeon preached his farewell message. As he spoke he seemed to be filled with the Holy Spirit in a special way, and what he said had an almost prophetic ring about it. 'I hope,' he said, 'that God will raise up teams to preach the word of the gospel, and that they will not only fill this half of the island with their message but the Portuguese half as well.' How and when this will take place I do not know. But the one thing I am certain of is that God is at hand and ready to fulfill these words."

The first actual witnesses of the revival on Timor were called through the ministry of the Bible School team.

Tamar had studied at the University of Salatiga on Java and was at the time headmistress of the Christian school in Soe. She was the first person to be called. Feeling that the Lord would have her attend the East Java Bible School, she told Pastor Joseph, Pastor Micah and David Simeon that she intended to go there. Pastor Joseph was anxious at first at the idea of losing an able teacher, for there was a genuine lack of Christian teachers in the area. And besides, a number of the teachers at the Christian school were Communists. Tamar too, had the trust and the affection of her pupils. But her mind was made up and nothing would make her alter her decision. When the Bible School team finally left, she asked Pastor Joseph if they could hold a valedictory service for her in the church.

The evening came. The church was packed with people. Starting at 8 o'clock in the evening, Tamar continued to speak until 1 o'clock the next morning. In spite of her five hour sermon, not a single person felt the slightest bit tired. God's Spirit had begun to work. As the meeting drew to a close, Tamar asked, "If anyone is ready to start serving the Lord tonight, raise your hand." The response was remarkable. When all the names had been written down, it was found that more than a hundred young people had raised their hands. Pastor Joseph decided afterwards to hold some classes on two nights of the week in order to instruct those who had registered their decision to serve the Lord.

We see here the difference between the tired churches of the West, and the revival area. In the West we continue to lament year after year the lack of candidates for the mission field or for full-time Christian service.

In Indonesia when one women speaks under the inspiration of the Holy Spirit, over a hundred people volunteer for missionary service in a single evening. And this was not just a flash in the pan as we shall quickly see. Since the revival began, many of the new converts have put their names down on the waiting list of the Bible School in East Java. So many people sought admittance that it was no longer possible to accommodate them all.

A Saul Became a Paul

The prophetic words of David Simeon were to be fulfilled much sooner than anyone would have thought possible. On the eve of her departure, Tamar started a chain reaction in the church. Stitting in the back row was a young man. As his friends raised their hands, he found himself following suit. But he became angry and the thought went through his mind, "Are you crazy? You can't do something like this."

Who was the young man? Because he had lost one of his parents, he had been living in the house of the local pastor since the age of seven. This, however, had not prevented him developing quite a godless attitude towards life. He was notorious for his fighting and brawling, as well as for his drunkenness. On innumerable occasions he had disturbed the church services, and had once gone so far as to break some of the windows while an actual meeting was in progress. The only reason he had been in the church at the valedictory service was because he had known Tamar personally, and had wanted to find out what all the 'fuss' was about. This then was the man whom the Lord had chosen to introduce his Church to a time of cleansing.

Some time after the meeting, Saul — as we shall call him — was sitting in his room swotting English. Suddenly everything around him went black. He could think of no reason at all for his sudden blindness. He put his face close to the lamp, but the only result was that he singed his eyebrows. There was nothing he could do but lie down on the bed and wait.

After about ten minutes had passed, a white figure appeared to him dressed in a long robe and with hair coming down to its shoulders. Saul knew at once that it was the Lord Jesus. As he fell to the floor in fear, he felt the blows of an invisible hand upon his body. He tried to get up again but found he could not move.

At this moment the Lord spoke to him, "What have you got there in your case?" Saul remembered that he had some fetishes in it. "Take them all out and hand them over to the pastor," he was told. Saul obeyed. When he returned to the room the Lord said to him, "You must be washed clean. I will then give you the task of cleansing the Church and preaching the gospel. You will pray with the sick and they shall be healed. Even death will be no problem to you. But remember this: the power is not your own but mine. Testify to the people in the church at the next service about what you have just experienced." As the Lord finished speaking, he vanished out of Saul's sight.

Saul was almost struck dumb. — When I spoke to him later, he told me in the presence of one of the missionaries, "My friend who shares the room with me came in while all this was still happening. Although he heard some footsteps and sensed that there was someone else in the room, he didn't see the vision at all." We can see here a similarity between this experience and the vision which Paul received outside Damascus when those who were with him heard the voice, but saw no one.

At the next service Saul asked to be given permission to speak. The pastor hesitated a little at first but finally agreed. When Saul finished his account, the power of the Holy Spirit seemed to fall upon everyone present. With one accord they began to confess their sins and to hurry home and fetch the articles of sorcery they possessed. That very night all the fetishes were burnt publicly before the church.

When Saul spoke later in the school he attended, the cleansing process was repeated all over again. As he testified of his experience to the pupils, they too fetched their amulets and fetishes, as well as their cheap novels and even their sheets of pop music, and making one heap of them all in the playground, at Saul's command they burnt the lot.

When the police heard about what had happened, they immediately went and arrested the 'ring leader', and taking him to the police station had him flogged for having caused such a 'serious incitement'. But now that the revival had begun, there was nothing to hold it back, although even at this stage the local pastor was still rather critical of everything that was taking place. This, however, was not surprising since for years Saul had been renowned for his hooliganism.

The First Team

The birthday of the first team was Sunday the 26th September 1965. Saul had spoken that day at both the morning and the evening services at the church in the presence of Pastor Joseph. A wave of repentance had fallen upon the whole congregation. As the young disciple had called upon the people to decide for Christ, many of the young people present had come forward. And so team number one was born. Saul chose 23 of the young natives to work with him.

When the team set out, they began to preach all over the island. Wherever the young disciples went, many people were converted and numerous others healed. The Holy Spirit had given the team three particular gifts: the authority to preach the gospel, the authority to heal, and the authority to prophesy.

Pastor Joseph later reported that in one town alone some 700 people were cured of their diseases through prayer and the laying on of hands. The following are some examples. Meeting a lame man on their travels, after they had showed him the way to Christ, they prayed with him and he was immediately healed. During one of the meetings, a child suddenly fell from its seat unconscious. Saul, who was the team's leader, was called. After he had prayed over the child it regained consciousness at once. The next example is even more remarkable.

The team once preached in a church from 8 o'clock in the morning till 3 o'clock in the afternoon. — One of the features of the revival is that the people lose all sense of time when they come under the influence of the Word of God and the operation of the Holy Spirit. — While the meeting was in progress a nine-year-old boy suddenly collapsed and died. His mother at once rushed to Saul and told him what happened. "We must finish the meeting first," the team leader replied. "We'll pray with the boy afterwards." All this happened only two hours after the meeting had started, and it was not until five hours later that Saul finally came to see the dead boy. As he stood beside him, he began to pray. It was then that the Lord said to him, "Blow into the boy's mouth and nose and put your hand on his forehead." Saul obeyed. After about a quarter of an hour the small boy began to move. Yet it was still some time before he became fully conscious again. Taking the boy with him to the front, Saul held him up before the congregation and gave praise to God. As a result of the miracle, many of the people present were converted.

I know the medical arguments that will arise in people's minds. The objection will be put forward that the boy was not really dead, only unconscious or paralysed. But even so, it would still have been a wonderful case of healing.

Before I actually witnessed these things with my own

eyes and ears, I too doubted the reports that were coming out of the revival area. Today, however, I can doubt them no more since I have actually spoken with the leaders of the revival themselves, as well as with Saul and several other leaders of the teams. It is the Lord Jesus and not people who is at work in Indonesia today.

The most important aspect of the ministry of Team 1 was told to me by Pastor Joseph. In the two weeks that the team was working in the town of N., some 9,000 people were converted. These are the type of figures one usually only associates with the Acts of the Apostles: 3,000 at Pentecost and 5,000 a few days later. It is greatly encouraging to know that the power of the Holy Spirit has not diminished since the first outpouring on the day of Pentecost nearly two thousand years ago, as a number of Christians have implied. We may perhaps be right in coming to the conclusion in the light of this revelation which the Holy Spirit has given us of his power, that we are living in the days just prior to the Lord's return. Everyone of the conversions we have just mentioned was accompanied by a mighty act of cleansing. Fetishes were burnt, stolen goods returned, old quarrels ended, and the sick were healed in their thousands.

Events like these should cause many evangelists and missionaries to examine their lives afresh. How does our own ministry compare with that of this team of 'laymen'?

The Lord first called me and took my life into his hands in 1930. Already on the day following my conversion I began my work of evangelism, and started to tell my school friends of my new found faith in Christ. As a result a number of them were converted. And so my ministry of intercession and counselling had begun. Today a total of 39 years have passed. Looking back through my records I find that I have preached now in more than 800 different churches in over a hundred countries of the world. At the same time I must have personally

counselled over 20,000 different people, but in spite
this I doubt whether in all these 39 years I have lea
9,000 people to the Lord. Yet this was the fruit which
was granted to Team 1 in just two weeks of its ministry.
Surely this is a fulfillment of the words, "And the last
shall be first." How insignificant our evangelistic labours
appear in the light of the work that God is doing through
these unknown disciples of Christ in Indonesia. The Lord
has no need of those who, out of conceit, imagine
themselves to be something. "God chose what is low
and despised in the world." The worldly halo of so many
famous men will pale into insignificance before the
spiritual greatness of many an unknown Christian saint.
Only those whose heads are held too high fail to realize
that all their proud boasting will one day be swept away
by the wind of the Holy Spirit.

XV. THE FIRE SPREADS

As yet we have talked very little about the methods used
by the teams in their evangelistic work. They usually
limit their missions to a few weeks at a time. After this
they return to their previous occupations. The only exception was Team 1, which held a campaign lasting several
months.

One of the problems which faced the young people
involved, was their schooling. They had in fact left school
and only returned at the end of their mission a few months
later. The teachers had set them some examinations to
see whether or not they could remain in the same classes
as when they had left. But the Lord was with them, and
not one of the 'truants' failed. This, too, revealed the
way in which the Lord blesses.

We must now accompany some of the teams on their
travels in order to see what the Lord does through them
and for them. The reports I have stem from several

sources, including personal conversations with actual team leaders and Mr. Klein, a missionary working in the area. Next in order of importance are the reports I received from the Church Synod on Timor, and also the accounts of David Simeon and Pak Elias who have both worked on the island. The facts facing us here have therefore been confirmed by many witnesses. This is an important point to make, for the events we are about to describe are so unusual that Western Christians will have difficulty in believing them, in spite of the fact that nothing is to be reported which is not already found in the Acts of the Apostles. Those who believe the Scriptures will have no difficulty in being able to accept the truth of these stories. But now let us join the various teams and hear what the Lord has done and is still doing in Indonesia today.

The Fire-Team

The uniqueness of this team exists in the fact that during their missions flames of fire have often been seen to descend upon the churches in which they preached. The team's testimony always resulted in a tremendous cleansing of the congregation. Drunkards would forsake their vice, thieves would return the goods they had stolen, and magical practices would be acknowledged openly.

The group initially worked among a Catholic tribe on the island, and many of the natives were subsequently converted. It was at this time that the question first arose whether or not the teams from Timor should cross the Portuguese border in order to evangelize on the other side. The eastern half of Timor is a Portuguese colony. The natives on either side of the border speak the same language. What were the Christians to do?

Prior to their conversion, the natives on the western side of the island had often crossed the frontier in order to steal cows. When the revival came, though, there were no more thefts involving cows. Instead, they began to cross the border to steal souls. A Christian who lives by the letter of the law would say, "That isn't scriptural. One must recognize and respect a country's borders." In reply, however, I would ask, "Who decided where the borders were to lie? Wasn't it just an arbitrary decision of the colonial powers, whose only thought was to claim as much land as they could for themselves? What kind of crime is it when a team of natives crosses the border in order to win the people on the other side for Christ?"

Another objection will be, "But why don't the teams go through the proper legal procedure and apply for entry visas?" The answer is, "If they did so, they would never be able to hold their missions, since the authorities on the other side of the frontier are Catholic. In fact they are such staunch Catholics that there are reports of Protestant missionaries already having been killed in the area." One Protestant missionary who actually obtained a visa was, one might say, generously supplied with an aeroplane by the Catholic Church in which to leave the country immediately. It would be too much to expect ecumenicalism to have reached the eastern part of Timor yet.

I cannot believe that God will hold anything against these native Christians for allowing their missionary zeal to drive them to cross forbidden frontiers in order to show others the way to Christ. It must not be forgotten that the Catholics in the eastern half of the island are no better than what the Protestants in the west were like before the revival came. The heart of man is the same, irrespective of whether it beats under a Catholic or a Protestant flag.

The Teams' Provisions

No one who traces the birth and development of the teams will cease to be amazed at what he finds. They practise quite literally the words of Jesus in Luke 10 : 4,

"Carry no purse and no bag on the journey." The teams either set out with no provisions at all, or at most with only enough to tide them over the first few hours. Who then provides for them? Have we forgotten the experience and the higher mathematics of brother Dan already?

Once when the Lord chose two married couples to work for him, the husband of the first couple asked, "Lord, who will provide for us?" In reply the Lord said, "Your wife must fast for 14 days in the way I show her." His wife obeyed and began to fast. After the first seven days she was told, "Take a coconut and a banana. Drink half the milk of the coconut and eat half the banana. Put the second half of the banana and the rest of the coconut milk aside for later." Again she obeyed. When the 14 days were up, the Lord told them, "Go and see if the banana and the milk are still fresh." To their astonishment they found that they were both as fresh as they had been 7 days previously. Usually in the tropics when fruit has been opened it goes bad in a day.

Although the woman had fasted for 14 days, she felt no exhaustion at all. The Lord made it clear to the couple that He could keep them both alive on the same amount of food if he wanted to. The two couples joined each other after this and formed the third team, after which they set out on their mission of evangelization.

The experiences of Team 31 also illustrate the way God answered the question of daily provisions. Once when the team was working in a village, just as they were about to leave, they were given nine bananas to eat on their journey. The team, though, consisted of 15 members. When they stopped later to rest and the bananas were distributed, everyone received a whole banana. I realize that a rationalist will find a story like this absolutely impossible to believe. But we need only think of the five loaves and the two fishes mentioned in Matthew 14:19 which were sufficient to satisfy the needs of over 5,000 people. The God who supplied their needs still exists today.

The team experienced a similar miracle on one of their other missions. They stayed once with a couple whose child was on the point of death. When the father, however, repented of his sins, the child was healed. Before the team left, the family begged them to stay for a meal of rice and meat. Quite naturally it was very difficult for them to find enough food to satisfy their 20 guests. The team had grown in size through being joined by some of the elders of the churches they had visited. The Lord, however, in his mercy remembered this family. He told the team members to take only two spoonfuls of rice and two pieces of meat each. As the rice was served, everyone present suddenly saw a hand appear over the food and bless it. They were all completely satisfied.

Another native by the name of Barnabas had a very similar experience. He is the 32-year-old leader of Team 4 and has five other helpers on his team with him. On the 10th February 1968 the Lord commanded him to go to a village about 50 miles away from Soe. He was to preach the gospel there. The Lord told him, "Take no food or water for the journey, and do not rest until you have reached the village." This was without doubt quite a test, particularly when one remembers that Timor is in the tropics; and 50 miles is more than a day's march. Barnabas obeyed and set out on his journey. Later, when he began to be overcome with hunger and thirst, he asked the Lord if he would give him something to refresh him. At that moment a gust of wind blew a tamarind fruit towards him. Holding his hands out, he caught it. However, instead of eating it at once, he first of all asked, "Lord, is this for me or for someone in the village?" The Lord replied, "It's for you." After giving thanks therefore, Barnabas ate the fruit. It was both sweet and very juicy, and afterwards his hunger and thirst did not return until he had reached his destination.

This story, too, shows us that the God of the manna

in the wilderness and the ravens of Elijah is still alive today.

These wonderful experiences should not, however, make us crave for miracles. The most important thing is not miracles, but rather the saving of people from death to life in Christ. Our desire should not be for the sensational, but rather for a personal knowledge of the Lord Jesus himself. These miracles of the Lord's provision are merely a demonstration of the fact that the Lord accepts responsibility for those whom he has commissioned to go out and preach the gospel. Indeed, the number of people who are bearing the good news is already very large. In the first year of the revival alone, 72 different teams came into existence. Since each team consists of anything from 4 to 28 members, this means that about 1,000 messengers of the gospel are already under way. And everyone of them travels without a purse, without security, and with no sleeping arrangements or previous plans, basing his mission entirely on the promises of God. Is this not a tremendous testimony and challenge to the sluggish and tired Church in the West, which has so little, compared with its brothers in Indonesia?

The Blind Receive their Sight

In Matthew chapter 11 we have the story of how John the Baptist sent some of his disciples to Jesus to ask him, "Are you he who is to come?" Jesus answered them, "The blind receive their sight and the lame walk, lepers are cleansed and the deaf hear, and the dead are raised up, and the poor have good news preached to them."

During Jesus' lifetime the world experienced the greatest time of revival it has ever known. However, each time the Church has experienced revival down through the ages, its history has again reflected the events of the gospels and the Acts of the Apostles. And so it is with the revival in Indonesia.

Yet in addition to this, anyone who has the opportunity of comparing one revival with another, will be astonished to find that the Indonesian revival is more closely connected with the revival of the New Testament than any other in the history of the Church.

Let us hear a little about the work of the teams in this respect. The experiences of Team 48 are particularly impressive. The young leader is a 25-year-old illiterate girl by the name of Anna. Both her parents are dead, yet like herself, her four brothers and sisters are today all involved in the Lord's work.

The Lord called Anna with the words of Matthew chapter 10. As she was unable to read, she had someone read the words aloud to her later. Anna is spiritually one of the most authoritative messengers of the revival. The first gifts she received from the Lord were four songs which she was able to learn off by heart. When she sang these gospel messages, those who listened were converted.

She is an excellent 'home' missionary, and as she goes from house to house, she asks the people to bring their idols out and to destroy them. She has the gift of prophecy, too, and is able to tell people to their faces what sins they have committed.

One day she entered a house and met a woman who was blind. After she had shown the woman the way to Christ, the Lord commanded her to pour some water into the woman's eyes that she might be healed. In this way the woman received her sight. Encouraged by her initial success, Anna began to ask the Lord every time she met someone who was blind, to give her the power to heal the person. As a result she was able to heal a total of ten blind people in the name of Jesus. This only happened, however, after the blind people had confessed and repented of their sins. It is events like these that distinguished the revival from the healing movement which, as we have said, originally preceded it. In every case of healing the person's own salvation takes pride of place.

The condition of the soul is always more important than that of the body. In this way the Lord Jesus is magnified in the eyes of those who are sick. This is the reason why the revival has continued on its present healthy course.

Once when Anna met a person who was deaf, the Lord said to her, "Put your finger into his ear and pray with him." She obeyed and the man was immediately healed.

On other occasions she has even prayed for those who have died, although only if the Lord directly commanded her to do so. She never took the responsibility of the decision upon herself. Once she was led to a two-year-old child who had died. After she had prayed for him, he was raised up just like Jairus' daughter of so long ago.

Anna's life and ministry are an example of how a Christian can be led and directed by the Lord. She only goes to the places where the Lord sends her. Bearing in mind her illiteracy, His commands are not always easy to obey. She has had to visit schools and government offices, and also speak to pastors about their sins. However, wherever she travels, the Lord always prepares a place for her to stoy. She refuses to use a mattress or a pillow, and prefers to sleep rather on the floor. Each night the Lord tells her what her tasks are for the following day. In 1967 the Lord even told her the name of a missionary who was soon to visit the island. When he arrived, he was astonished to find that Anna was able to greet him by his name.

One of the most difficult tasks the Lord gave her, fell on the 10th February 1968. She was told, "Go to the government offices and testify about me there." She obeyed. The officials listened to the message of their illiterate visitor, and in the end 20 men were converted.

At about this time Anna was ordered to visit the house of a minister whose three children were continually falling ill. In a vision prior to her visit, she was shown a two-edged sword. On arriving at the house she discovered that such a sword had in fact been in the house since the time of the Dutch, and that it had an occult history behind it. She told the minister that the sword would have to be destroyed. Afterwards the children were completely healed.

Anna is by no means the only person whom the Lord has used to restore the sight of the blind. Many of the teams have had similar experiences in their work of evangelization. We can illustrate this with two further examples, both of which are well attested, since a number of pastors were present on each occasion. The first instance was described to me by a pastor who has become actively involved in the work of the revival.

At one of the church meetings on Timor which was attended by three pastors, one of whom was a woman, and by the president of the Synod, a 58-year-old blind man was healed through prayer and the laying on of hands. The blind man was quite startled when he found that he could see. One of the church elders said to him, "Throw your stick away and walk down the aisle to show everyone that you can now see." As the man obeyed, the woman pastor, who was watching it all take place, started to doubt and said, "The man is lying. He wasn't blind at all." At that moment the hand of God came upon her and she was struck blind herself. There is a story very similar to this in Acts 13:11, in which Elymas the sorcerer became blind when he tried to oppose the apostle Paul.

In the revival in Indonesia one finds that almost every event has its counterpart in the New or Old Testaments. When the moderator of the Synod heard about the blinding of the pastor, he asked, "Who was responsible for making her blind?" No one was able to answer him. The Lord had taken it upon himself to act. For three days, as a result of her critical attitude, the woman remained blind. During this time the believers continued to pray for her. Then, when the three days had passed, she confessed her sin and repented, and the Lord gave her back her sight.

We will finish by mentioning just one more case in which a person was healed of blindness. The man concerned was 46 years old, and had been blind since birth, or at least from very early childhood. Illnesses like this also occur in China and other parts of the Far East. After a member of the team had showed the man the way to Christ, he prayed with him under the laying on of hands. With this the man's eyelids opened and some blood came out. The man could now see, but he was somewhat confused, for he had never seen anything before in his life. Here again, I was told the story by a pastor who was present at the time, and who could guarantee the truth of the account.

Because we can so easily forget, let us remind ourselves: if Jesus opens the eyes of a spiritually blind person, the miracle is far greater than if he were to heal a person suffering from physical blindness. We must never try to shift the emphasis of the Scriptures on account of these wonderful events in Indonesia. Jesus is much greater than all the miraculous deeds that can be done in his name. Nevertheless let us still rejoice that the Lord can glorify himself so marvellously.

The Dead are Raised

We have already heard of one case where a person was raised from the dead during the ministry of Team 1. There is one team in particular, however, which stands out with regard to experiences of this nature. The leader of this team is mother Sharon.

Like Anna, she too is illiterate. One day the Lord appeared to her in a long white robe, and he said to her, "I have called you to preach the gospel." I can imagine the objection that many theologians may raise at this point. "Why must we have all these visions?" they will ask, "our faith should rest on the Word of God alone." I agree with this comment. However, I would ask in reply, "How can the Lord reveal himself to an illiterate person who is unable to read the Bible?" In situations like this, the Lord must use unusual means. And besides, must the Lord always ask the theologians first, how he should reveal himself to people? If this were the case, present day Christianity would be even worse off than it is already.

When the Lord Jesus revealed himself to this illiterate woman and called her into his service, she replied, almost in the words of Jeremiah, "But I can't preach; I'm not educated; I don't understand anything about the Bible." The Lord, however, overruled her objections. After forming a team with three other people, she set out to testify to the Word of God and to pray for the sick. As a result, a number of people were raised from the dead through her ministry.

The first case of this was later checked by Pak Elias who was able to talk to the mother whose child had been brought back to life. The child had been dead already for six hours when mother Sharon arrived. After someone had read the Scriptures, mother Sharon prayed with the dead child and when she had finished, its life had returned.

Another instance was confirmed by the missionary Mr. Klein. A child had been dead for two days. Ants were already crawling about over its eyes and body. The parents, however, instead of burying the child on the first day, as is the usual custom in the tropics, called for mother Sharon. Two days later she arrived. After a time of prayer the child was restored to life.

We have before us therefore testimonies from the ministry of three separate teams. The first team experienced the miracle of the dead being raised at the town of N. The other two teams experienced the miracle under the leadership of the two illiterate women, Anna and mother Sharon.

As a fourth witness to the raising of the dead we can

turn to another Christian pastor who is also a native of Timor. He told me about two people on a neighbouring island who, after they had died, had been carried out of the hospital in which they had been patients. After prayer, however, they had both come back to life again.

It must again be pointed out that the raising of a spiritually dead person is a far greater miracle than a physical return to life. In Luke 15:24 we read, "This my son was dead, and is alive again." The spiritual conversion and rebirth of a person is a greater miracle than a bodily resurrection. We should always remember this, lest, as a result of the deeds which God is presently accomplishing in the revival area, our spiritual lives be side-tracked along a false trail.

XVI. MIRACLES

Miracles are not an end in themselves. They are merely signposts designed to point us to the Lord. Miracles are not the most important thing, but only of a secondary nature. They are but a confirmation of the Word of God. At the end of Mark's Gospel we read, "The Lord worked with them and confirmed the message by the signs that attended it." The preaching of the gospel is of first importance. The accompanying signs are merely a form of confirmation. Anyone who tries to build his Christian life on miracles will soon fall prey to extremism and a hopeless wilderness of inner impoverishment. The Word of God is our foundation and our daily bread. Miracles are really the exception; signs which the Lord occasionally erects. In times of revival the question of miracles is nevertheless very acute. In the case of Indonesia for example, some amazing events have come to pass. And yet every miracle that has happened there has its parallel in the pages of the Bible.

Esther is the leader of Team 17. There are 15 members

in the team including herself. One day the Lord spoke to her and said, "Go to Rote." At once the team hired a boat belonging to a Moslem and set out for Rote. On their way there they ran into a severe gale. The Moslem said to them, "If your God will answer your prayers and calm this storm then I will believe in him." The team prayed, and within a few minutes the sea was completely calm. The Moslem was converted, and afterwards he renamed his boat 'New Life'. With God all things are possible. The Lord Jesus who stilled the storm on the sea of Galilee (Matt. 14) is still alive today.

Team 49 was working once among a tribe of sun-worshippers. As they were holding a meeting in one of the buildings, the rain began to pour down in torrents. Suddenly, however, the rain stopped, and the sun began to shine brightly. At that moment the team saw Jesus in the skies standing above the sun. As they went outside to look, about half the congregation followed them. Taking their opportunity from the vision which was witnessed in full daylight by everyone present, they began to preach. "The Lord Jesus," they said, "stands before the sun which he has made. You must worship him and not the object that he created." As a result of their testimony, 20 of the natives were converted. When an account of what had happened was told in a nearby village, some of the sick people there were at once healed. Are we not reminded here of the vision in Revelation chapter 1, where it is written of Jesus, "his face was like the sun shining in full strength"?

The Lord Jesus did not only give his messengers their provisions, but he gave them travelling companions too. Team 31, which worked under the leadership of Pastor Gideon, often travelled during the night. At the time of the new moon, the tropical nights can be fearfully dark. On account of this the Lord on occasions has gone before them in the form of a shining light, in the same way as he once accompanied the children of Israel in the wilderness. Also when it rained, the team did not get wet. The rain would fall on either side of the path along which they were walking, but not on the path itself. I have heard of experiences like this from other mission fields. In my book 'Name über alle Namen Jesus', there is an account of a similar event involving the Eskimo Christian, Esther Egak.

Team 47 has also on several occasions experienced a miraculous light. They were told one day to go to the town of N. At first they tried to hire a car, but the owner, a Moslem, was unwilling to allow them to use his vehicle. So they set out on foot. On the way the Lord suddenly told them to stand still and to pray. They obeyed. The car then drove up behind them and they got in and were driven to the next village. That night the head teacher gave them a room to sleep in, but there was no light in it. In spite of this the room was lit the whole night by a supernatural light from the Lord. The next day they travelled on. In the next village there was no light in the church. This time the Lord illuminated the church for them.

We have a miracle here similar to the one recorded in Acts 12, when the prison cell of Peter was suddenly brightly lit by the appearance of an angel. Then in Revelation 22 we find another biblical illustration of an event like this: "And night shall be no more; they need no light of lamp or sun, for the Lord God will be their light."

These signs involving light are simple illustrations of the fact that the Lord wants to be our light, and one day will be our light for evermore. Those who are familiar with the kingdom of God will find nothing unnatural about these miraculous signs. We are simply faced here with the fact that the Creator is able to use his creation for his own purposes. The universe contains many more possibilities than we can ever imagine. It is true that nuclear research is for ever making fresh discoveries, yet scientists are only able to discover what has already been embedded in creation by God.

Some of the miracles of the revival in Indonesia appear at first to be rather strange. Yet even so, I find that they are not completely unfamiliar to me. I have sometimes asked myself concerning certain occult phenomena, what the biblical counterpart of a demonic miracle really is. In Japan for example I have heard of Shinto priests who practise levitation. They are able to disappear from one mountain peak, and ten minutes later reappear on another peak which is anything up to 12 miles away. I was told about some almost unbelievable achievements by the aborigines in Australia. They said for example that members of their tribes are able to run from the east coast to the west coast of Australia in a matter of only four days. Humanly speaking this is impossible, since it means that the runner would have to travel an average of nearly 600 miles a day. Among the Tibetans and the people of Haiti I heard of the so-called phenomena of 'riding on the wind'. By this means magicians are capable of travelling enormous distances in only a very short time. But all these feats can be traced back to the workings of the same demonic powers.

These phenomena must also exist on a scriptural level, and we do in fact find similar events recorded in the Bible, although they occur on an entirely different plane. For example, Enoch was translated, and Elijah went up by a whirlwind into heaven. Philip too was once caught up by the Spirit of the Lord, and Jesus himself ascended into heaven from the Mount of Olives. In every case here we have an example of the overcoming of both gravity and distance by the power of God.

Let us now turn after this somewhat lengthy introduction to a miracle of this nature which was experienced by Team 47. The team was commanded by God to go and preach the gospel in a village which was about 48 travelling hours away. Setting out on foot, they arrived at the village within a space of four hours. On their arrival they discovered that the villagers were already assembled together in the church. They described how they had heard the sound of a trumpet coming from the mountain calling them to the meeting, and they said that they had thought it had been the team which was calling them. However, the team did not have a trumpet with them. There were altogether 50 people in the church who were ill. Everyone of them was healed, including three people who had been dumb from birth. Afterwards their tongues were loosed, and they began to speak.

In order to add the last straw to the troubles and doubts a person may be experiencing while reading these reports, we will quote just one final example. Our story-teller is Nathan, a local district officer who has already been the leader of a team. Nathan described to me how another team under the leadership of a Christian named Ruth was threatened by a group of soldiers. Some non-Christians had stirred the soldiers up against the team, and one evening a corporal sat down with his men and began to work out a plan to stop the Christians' work. While they were actually discussing their plans, the team met together for a time of prayer. As they were praying Ruth had a remarkable experience. She suddenly saw herself among the soldiers, and was able to hear them discussing their plans against the team. She was convinced that she had actually been with them. The soldiers, however, had not been able to see her. When Ruth had returned, the Christians began to pray that the Lord would make their enemies so tired that they would give up the plans they were making. And so it happened. The soldiers were so overwhelmed by the desire to go sleep, that they put aside all thought of harming the team and went home to their beds.

The question facing us is how to understand such experiences in the light of the Scriptures. First of all we have the stories of how the angels of the Lord opened the doors of prisons on two occasions: Acts 5 : 19, and 12 : 7 f. Then we have Paul's own account of how he was caught up into the heavens: 2 Corinthians 12 : 1—4. Has God forgotten how to do these miracles today? Are we only his stepchildren? Is it not still true that Jesus Christ is the same yesterday, today and forever?

We have no need of miracles like this in order to be saved. However, if God chooses to act in this way during an extraordinary revival, we have no right to doubt the things he does. And anyway, the only reason for our doubt is that we put more trust in our own understanding than in the living God. We have forgotten to live in the world of the Bible. Therefore everything has become so strange to us. One day these illiterate natives of Timor will sit in judgement over those of us who pride ourselves on our own intelligence.

Our reason, however, has still more challenges facing it. The communion services being held in the revival area are naturally large. As we have already mentioned, in some places anything up to 9,000 natives have been converted in a matter of two weeks. Understandably these new-born Christians desire to partake of the Lord's supper. For them, though, it is not so much a feast of remembrance as a time of real fellowship with the risen Lord. With the advent of these large communion services therefore, one is confronted with the question: where does all the wine come from? The islanders who have experienced so much of the Lord's help already in the problems they have faced, made this into a subject for prayer also. A little later the Lord gave them the command, "Fill some large vessels with spring water." Fetching the water from a spring, they prayed over it for several hours. When the time came for the celebration of the Lord's supper, the whole church testified that the water had become wine. This has happened now on three separate occasions.

We have here a repetition of the miracle of John

147

chapter 2. The question again arises whether we are going to erect a theology which depends upon our own intellects, as is the case in most parts of the world, or whether we are going to put more trust in God than in our own small minds. For myself, on account of his sufferings on the cross and his resurrection, Jesus is great enough already without having to refer to the miracles about which we have been hearing. However, we must realize that the natives in Indonesia, in their desire to celebrate the Lord's supper, would be robbed of something if they had either no bread or no wine with which to remember their Lord's body and blood. Is the Lord Jesus given the title Wonderful Counsellor in vain? We have a God who works miracles! O sing to the Lord a new song, for he has done marvellous things (Psalm 98 : 1). I would prefer to take my stand beside these simple and illiterate Christians on Timor, sharing their childlike faith, than with the present day rationalists who attempt, albeit unsuccessfully, to tear the world of the Bible apart with their reason. It would be a very small God who permitted his plans to be upset by the so-called philosophers of today.

XVII. SIN AND DISEASE

There exists a general connection between sin and death, and sin and disease. Paul writes in Romans 6 : 23, "The wages of sin is death." Through the original fall of mankind, disease and death entered into the world. And we are all involved in this calamity. "Therefore as sin came into the world through one man and death through sin, so death spread to all men because all men sinned" (Rom. 5 : 12).

We must not, however, short-circuit this general relationship between sin and disease. The thought should never even enter our head, let alone be voiced in the presence of a sick person, that, "He must have done something wrong, else he would never have fallen ill."

Jesus himself had to fend off this false conclusion on more than one occasion. In Luke 13 : 4 he asks his disciples, "Or those 18 upon whom the tower in Siloam fell and killed them, do you think that they were worse offenders than all the others who dwelt in Jerusalem?" In John 9, referring to the man who had been born blind, the disciples asked Jesus, "Rabbi, who sinned, this man or his parents, that he was born blind?" Jesus parried their shortsightedness with the reply, "It was not that this man sinned, or his parents, but that the works of God might be made manifest in him."

The Bible therefore confirms the fact that there is a general connection between sin and disease, but it rejects the idea of a special causality, that every single case of illness is directly caused by some particular sin.

The Scriptures, however, do not exclude the idea of special rules applying during a time of revival. Revivals are always exceptional circumstances and, although it need not necessarily be so, ever since the time of Christ they have been characterized by the extraordinary. At such times God himself intervenes personally.

The truth of this can be seen in every revival, and it is being illustrated afresh in the current movement of God's Spirit in Indonesia. We find there that the Lord is speaking to the simple native people by means of dreams, visions, angelic appearances, and direct speech. At any other time we would treat these supernatural events with the greatest of caution, and even at the centre of the revival itself one must be on one's guard, for the devil ever seeks to inject his own demonic visions and psychical experiences into the genuine work of God. Indeed, Satan is the great deceiver, and he loves to cause disorder wherever he goes.

The events in Indonesia show us how God is moving

among these simple Christians in a way he has seldom moved before. The result is that every daily event is affected by his presence, and every experience has an entirely new significance about it, for Jesus stands in their very midst.

In the case of the healing of the sick this means that when the Lord commissions one of his messengers to tell a person, "Destroy your fetishes, then you'll be healed," the promise comes true. This does not mean that the members of the teams can heal people whenever they want to, but rather that they ask the Lord concerning each individual case. If through the gift of prophecy they are shown the cause of the illness, in a special instance like this the very root of the evil is revealed.

The healing of the sick in the Indonesian revival — and also in other genuine revival movements — is not opposed to the teaching of the Scriptures. The only thing that did not correspond completely with the biblical pattern was the earlier healing movement. Yet the Christians on Timor recognized this for themselves. The healing movement was really only a forerunner of the genuine revival in much the same way as John the Baptist was a herald of the coming of Christ.

With these few thoughts from the Scriptures in mind, let us turn now to one or two brief examples which, although they fit into the framework of the revival, cannot be used as a pattern for the Church in general. If this happened, misconceptions would soon arise and lead to error.

As we have already mentioned, Team 31 has been greatly blessed in its work among the sick. The young evangelists counsel the natives very thoroughly before they attempt to lay hands on them and pray for their recovery. When a special meeting is held for those who want healing, the Word of God is expounded first. Next those who are ill are asked to write their diseases down on some cards. If a person cannot write, a Christian does this for him. The cards are then collected and a team member again explains that healing depends entirely upon the Lord. They are also told that no one need expect to be healed if he is unprepared to hand his life over to Christ completely. Only after this very basic preparation — which can sometimes take several hours — do the individual team members pray with the sick people under the laying on of hands. But now the natives feel the power streaming through them. The meeting is closed with a time of testimony and people are encouraged to go to the front and to give praise to God. Frequently every person present is healed, although there are times when only about 90 % of those who seek healing are cured. When this is the case, those who are still ill are counselled and prayed for afresh. As a result the work develops in a sound and sober fashion.

Team 32 was once sent by the Lord to a certain village in which 36 people were ill. After preaching the gospel to them and showing them the way to Christ, the team told them that they would first have to surrender their lives to the Lord before they could expect to be healed. But even if they were not healed, they added, the Lord still expected them to hand their lives over to him.

When the team subsequently prayed for the 36 natives, 32 of them were immediately healed. We can mention one special case which illustrates the connection again between sin and disease. A small child had been on the point of death. The Lord showed the leader of the team the cause of the illness. The child's father had been called into full-time service by the Lord but had refused to go. As the leader told the father of his sin, he repented and the child was immediately cured. Having quoted this example, however, it should be pointed out, to avoid misunderstanding or misconstruing what has been said, that not one of the other 35 natives was confronted in this way and told, "You have sinned! Therefore you are ill." This would have been the same shortsighted conclusion which is often made all over the world. Only in one case did the Lord reveal to the leader that a particular sin lay behind the illness of the person concerned.

Team 47 has also experienced a number of healings during its ministry. For example, they were called once to a woman who was unable to give birth to her child. She had already been in labour for eight days when the team's leader, a woman of 35, went in and prayed for her. As she was doing so she was suddenly shown that the husband was guilty of disobedience. When the Lord had called him to follow Him, he had resisted the call. Finally he repented, and as a result his wife was able to give birth to their child.

In February 1968 this same team had a similar experience. Their leader was again called to visit a woman who was unable to give birth. As she began to pray, the Lord said to her, "Both the parents are addicted to alcohol. I will not help the woman until they have given it up." However, the couple were not prepared to repent of their habit, and as a result, when the child was finally born, it seemed as if it were dead, and did not breathe for a total of eight hours. The parents were terribly worried and in the end confessed that they had sinned. When they had done so, the Lord said to the team leader, "Touch the child's tongue near the back of its throat." When she did so, the child immediately began to breathe normally. Over ten people were present at the time who witnessed the miracle.

The leader of Team 2, named Abel, was given the following task. He was called to see a family whose child had been quite ill for a number of weeks. It was unable to eat, and cried continually. When Abel arrived, he asked the father if he had any fetishes in the house. The man hesitated and tried to avoid the question. The Lord then showed Abel that there were indeed articles of sorcery in the house. When the father finally confessed to the fact and brought them out of his house — there were many of them — the child began gradually to quieten down. As the last fetish was brought out, the child stopped crying completely. Abel prayed again and at once the child sat up and asked for something to eat. When two bowls of rice were brought, it ate them hungrily.

These examples illustrate how the sins of a father and a mother often affect the children. As parents we have a great responsibility regarding our children. "The iniquity of the fathers is visited upon the children to the third and the fourth generation." Christian parents should not only pray for their children, but for their grand-children and great-grandchildren as well. I feel a great responsibility myself in this respect, particularly when I see how easily the grandchildren and great-grandchildren of well-known Christians fall into gross sin.

XVIII. SIN AND JUDGEMENT

The relationship between sin and judgement is very similar to the one we have just described between sin and disease. However, even if one were able to find a number of examples of God's judgement on people, it would be incorrect to generalize from particular cases. If God were to punish everyone immediately they sinned, the world would soon become just one big concentration camp. Similarly, if God were to require the death of each sinner, no one would be left living upon this earth.

We must therefore be careful not to put all the events of the revival over a common denominator. The Lord is sovereign, and is free to act as he will. God cannot be pressed into a predetermined mould. The Holy Spirit is independent of everyone and refuses to be told how and when he ought to act. It is almost blasphemy when we as ordinary human beings try to order him around. He acts, he works, he determines, he decides, he judges, he blesses; so let us once and for all decide to leave our pious thoughts and selves out of the picture.

a) Let us quote first of all a few examples illustrating quite clearly how God punishes people.

Team 31 worked for a while in one of the larger towns on Timor. As a Catholic policeman listened to their message, he began to laugh and said, "What you're saying is stupid." When the team had left the town, the policeman set out one day with his cart to fetch some wood from the forest. Arriving in the jungle, he stood his rifle up in the cart with its bayonet uppermost. As he was heaping the wood on to the cart, the rifle suddenly fell over, driving the bayonet into him and killing him immediately.

Nathan, who was the district president, became the leader of Team 11. Together with his team he went to do some evangelizing in a town in the north of the island. However, the so-called Christians living in the area incited the police to stop them preaching there. As a result, the police president who was a nominal Christian as well as a drunkard, forbade them to work in the area. The team was at first discouraged, but then Nathan went to the police president and asked him, "Who ordered you to stop the team from working here? Was it the government, or have you done it on your own authority?" The president was a little embarrassed and finally admitted, "It was the Christians here. They started worrying me so much that in the end I issued the order about the team." Following their conversation the order was withdrawn. When Nathan returned to his team he found them meeting together in prayer. Without telling them his news, he joined in praying with them. Suddenly the whole house was shaken as if by an earthquake. It was just like the account in Acts 4:31, "And when they had prayed, the place in which they were gathered together was shaken." Following this experience a number of team members stood up to prophesy that God would punish those responsible for the order forbidding them to preach. Three months later, while the police president was away from home, his house was burnt to the ground. There was nothing to be saved from the flames.

God's judgement therefore does not fall upon unbelievers only, but on nominal Christians as well. This is illustrated even more vividly in the next example.

Pastor Joseph was once accompanying Team 3 on one of its missions. This again illustrates how even pastors can change their minds and begin to work with the teams. Pastor Joseph is in fact the superintendent of the Presbytery on Timor. When the revival had originally broken out he had at first stood to one side, wondering if it were truly the work of the Spirit of God. However, as he witnessed the wonderful things the Lord was doing in their midst, he was convinced. Today he is one of the leading figures in the revival. But it is also significant to find that in spite of everything he is only a member of a team and not its leader. This is a good example of how God does not look on a person's title or education — no, every leader is chosen solely by the Lord himself.

The team was on its way to visit a certain town on the island, whose church was torn by jealousy and a struggle for power between two sections of its congregation. The chief culprits were a couple of Christian teachers. When they heard that Pastor Joseph was coming with a team to their town, they decided to give him an official welcome. On hearing of this, however, Pastor Joseph said to them, "I haven't come here on an official visit. I'm just a member of the team." And so for about two weeks Team 3 lived and worked in this almost ruined church. It was then that the Lord showed them that the two teachers would have to be relieved of their offices in the church and replaced by two other men. The whole congregation was agreed. Hardly had the team left the town, however, than the quarrelling broke out afresh. The friends and supporters of the teachers tried to invalidate the decision of the team. By now Joseph and his fellow team members had arrived back in Soe, and it was only then that they heard of the latest news. They sent a message at once warning the quarrelling Christians that the judgement of the Lord would fall upon them if they started to destroy the church all over again with their continual strife. The men to replace the teachers had been chosen by the Lord himself! But the quarrelling did not cease. As a result a terrible act of judgement fell upon the church. Twenty-nine of the people involved in the strife suddenly died of a mysterious illness. The story was reported to Mr. Klein on the 11th February 1968. The chief witness to the whole affair was Pastor Joseph himself.

b) Another form of judgement is that which serves to correct. A few examples.

Team 31, a team I have already mentioned on several occasions and whose work I particularly value, was working in a certain village when its leader, Pastor Gideon, entered into a house where a child was ill with whooping-cough. As Gideon began speaking with the father, who was in fact an elder in the local church, he discovered that the man was really opposed to the revival in the area. Gideon then said to him, "You are spiritually proud. That's why your child is ill." When the father heard this, he confessed his sins and repented. They now prayed for the child and it was immediately healed.

A certain family, on hearing about the work that the teams were doing, began to mock and to laugh. The result was that their child suddenly fell ill and had to go to hospital. The Lord then spoke to Judith, the wife of the leader of Team 2, and told her to go and visit the family in question. When she met the parents, she said to them in the name of Jesus, "You have insulted the Lord by criticizing the teams. Repent, and keep your child at home. The Lord is able to help him." Heeding her words, the parents repented and their child was immediately healed.

Once when Team 17 travelled to Rote to hold a mission there, the local church leaders refused to show them any hospitality. "They're only coming here to sponge on us," they claimed. On the evening following this remark, one of the leaders started trying to light his paraffin lamp. In all he attempted to light the lamp eleven times without success. It was then that the Lord spoke to him and said, "You have spoken evil of the team. Make up for this and help them." The man repented and was ready to obey. At once the lamp started to burn. And what a wonderful time that evening was. When the team had finished testifying to the church, 20 people were converted, and a little girl who had been lame was healed. In the next village a total of 400 out of 500 sick people were cured of their diseases.

c) Thirdly, some forms of judgement lead to the sanctification of the Christians involved. The following are two examples of this.

The leader of Team 43 was a Christian woman by the name of Abigail, who was illiterate. Although the Lord had called her, her lack of education had made her hesitate to obey. Then one after another of her children began to fall ill. She called one of the team leaders and asked him to pray for them. The Lord, however, said to the man, "Abigail's children are ill because she has not obeyed my word." When Abigail herself heard this, she repented at once and started to obey. As she went from house to house carrying the Christian message, the Lord gave her the authority to heal. She met an old man with a wound that refused to close up. After showing him the way to Christ, she prayed with him and at once the wound began to dry out. Her own children too, never fell ill again. — On another occasion the Lord told her to go to the local prison and to talk to the prisoners about Jesus. However, when she left home, she went instead to a hospital to witness to the patients there; but the Lord had mentioned nothing about this. Later, as evening approached, realizing that there was no time to visit the prison any more, she started for home. On the way she became lame. She could not take another step. It was then that she recognized her disobedience, and she asked the Lord to forgive her: her foot was healed immediately. — This illustrates how we can often look for tasks which the Lord has not assigned us. God does not want activity, but obedience.

Team 45 was led by a 43-year-old teacher. He had originally been called by the Lord through a dream. The teacher had found his own dirty clothes being taken off and a new robe being put on instead. At the same time he had heard a voice saying to him, "This is the mantle of Elijah." When he had woken up, he doubted whether the dream was genuine. That day, however, one of his children burnt his arm. The teacher called one of the leaders of the teams and begged him to pray for his child. It was then that the Lord showed him that he was guilty. Repenting at once, the teacher was ready to obey his call. He was subsequently given the authority to heal and the authority to cast out demons.

XIX. THE PRESENCE OF JESUS IN THE INDONESIAN REVIVAL

The revival in Indonesia is still very young, and it is therefore not possible to pass a final judgement on it at the moment. God grant that we will never have to before the coming of Christ, and that this wonderful outpouring of the Spirit will not cease until the Lord himself returns to take the torch of the gospel from the hands of his messengers.

The Presbytery on Timor waited a long time before it pronounced its judgement on the nature of the revival movement. An administrative body not only has the right but also the duty to act with care. How often have religious movements been labelled as revivals which have been little more than psychical epidemics far removed from the work of the Holy Spirit.

What did the leading church people have to say after observing the revival for a year? First of all they produced some very sober statistics. Within the revival's first year, 80,000 people were converted to Christ; 40,000 of these had previously been Communists, and the other half heathen. During the same interval of time some 15,000 people had permanently been healed. Church attendance had likewise grown phenomenally. Some churches which had previously had only about 30 people attending their Sunday services, after the first year of the outpouring of God's Spirit had congregations numbering anything up to 500. Many of the churches were just not large enough to cater for the increase in numbers. But in addition to these facts it had been observed that a wave of repentance and sanctification had swept through the formerly decaying church. Over a hundred thousand fetishes had been brought out and destroyed by the island's inhabitants.

This first year had also seen the birth of 72 evangelistic teams which had travelled throughout the area with no financial aid at all, preaching the gospel message.

These statistics only apply to the state of affairs at the end of the first year. One of the pastors on the island told me that today, at the end of the revival's third year, the figures have grown considerably. The number of those who have been converted has risen to over 200,000. It is almost impossible today to see the picture as a whole. The story on one island, for example, is almost unbelievable. Before the revival began, there were hardly any believers there at all; the number did not even reach treble figures. And today there are some 20,000 converted Christians among the island's inhabitants.

The number of teams has also grown steadily and has

passed the 200 mark already. The total number of those who have been healed probably exceeds 30,000.

These figures clearly represent a great victory for the Lord Jesus in Indonesia today; but the figures alone fail to reveal the special characteristics of the revival.

The growth in the number of Christians has utterly changed the numerical structure of the churches. It would be interesting to compare the church registers showing the actual numbers attending communion in the year 1963 and the year 1966 or 1968 for example. If one were not to know that a revival had taken place, the question would immediately arise, "What happened to increase the church attendance some twentyfold in these years?" The growth in the weekly offerings tells a similar story. Whenever the pockets of Christians are touched, something is sure to have taken place. Pockets are the last places to be surrendered to Christ. The door of one's bank account is always the last door which is opened to Jesus, if it is ever opened to him at all. But the temporal structure of the churches has also changed. In 1963 the congregations would soon have complained if the minister had gone on preaching for more than a couple of hours. Today, however, the Christians will not allow Pastor Gideon to leave the pulpit until he has preached sometimes for seven or eight hours at a stretch. The believers in the revival area have lost all sense of time, all sense of hunger and thirst, and all sense of the value of money. On top of this, the very social structure of the churches has changed too. Class divisions have simply faded away. The pastor or the superintendent become members of a team led by a simple layman chosen and appointed by the Lord, and Pak Elias' sister, a woman of noble birth, sits and talks with a simple illiterate woman about their common Lord.

The values and the standards of the Christians have been completely changed. The only thing that remains which is of any worth is that which speaks of, or points to, or originates from Christ. "He is the head, that in every-thing he might be pre-eminent" (Col. 1:18).

This brings us now to the most wonderful characteristic of the revival: the reality of the actual presence of the Lord Jesus Christ. How difficult it is for us as Christians to discover the will of the Lord. Yet these simple natives experience almost every day direct encouragement and contact with their ever present Lord.

Naturally, as a theologian I am well aware of the fact that every sect appeals to its own revelation from the Lord. The false prophets of the Old Testament did the same. The 'lumen internum', the inner light of divine vision, often stemmed from a demonic source or the human heart. It is a well-known fact that where the Holy Spirit is at work, the devil is not very far away. This is the danger threatening every revival, that the demonic and the divine stand so close together.

But such a danger should never lead us to insult the Holy Spirit and to reject his own work. To use a simple example: it would be foolish to say that because children are prone to disease, women should stop giving birth in order to ban these diseases from the earth.

We should never be forced out of a fear of the demonic to attempt to deny or to explain away the wonderful fact that Jesus is speaking directly to his children in Indonesia today. In no other revival since the first century has the presence of Jesus and his direct guidance and leadership been so much in evidence.

The reality and the ever present experience of the Lord's presence within the revival area has an eschatological significance which perhaps even the simple Christians on Timor have not fully recognized.

A Sign of the Lord's Second Coming

The more I consider the terrific events which are happening today on Timor, the more I am convinced that God has something to say through them to the whole world. The Indonesian revival is not just a small nationalistic affair, but is rather something which concerns the whole of the Body of Christ.

A dream of Pastor Joseph will help illustrate what I mean. But before I describe his dream, let me first point out for the sake of my critics: I realize that the Word of God is a thousand times more important than any dream that a man may have. However, I have already mentioned the spiritual reality which exists in Indonesia today, and this dream lies on the same level. Besides, Pastor Joseph is one of the maturest and most sober leaders of the revival as well as being the superintendent of the Presbytery in Soe. In his dream Joseph saw a host of people drawn from every nation under the sun standing in front of a church. They were singing a hymn together, and although the tune was the same, each was singing in his own mother tongue. When he woke up, Pastor Joseph asked the Lord to explain to him the meaning of the dream. The reply was, "The dream means that the revival on Timor has a world-wide significance."

We are living in a time when 'Satan's throne' has already been erected in the Western world. Theologians have explained away the divine sonship of Christ, and have set up the primacy of their own reason instead, as the French did during their revolution in 1789. Throughout the world it is no longer God but man who is being worshipped. God's Spirit will not suffer this folly to continue for ever. This blasphemy of the theologians will soon be swept aside like the tower of Babel.

In the face of this world-wide rebellion against God, the Lord Jesus has begun a new work in one of the most insignificant corners of the world today — the islands of Indonesia. Yet it is not with the wise or with the theologians that he has begun, but with the simple and illiterate islanders. He is again choosing the despised and the ignoble of the world, that in the coming kingdom of heaven they may sit in judgement over the noble and the élite. Whoever has eyes to see, let him see! So many, however, are blind, and compromise their lives away. The Church is filled with blasphemers who love to occupy the 'chief seats', not to mention our places of learning whose professors are often inspired by the very devil himself. But there are still exceptions: those who as yet have refused to bow the knee to Baal, preferring rather to endure mockery and trials in their discipleship of Christ.

Perhaps we can mention here just one brother who has chosen to walk this steep and narrow pathway. Once when Prof. Dr. Michel of Tübingen entered the lecture theatre, he found a scrap of paper lying on his desk. It was a note from one of the theological students, which read, "Michel is your name and a Michel (colloq.: fool) you are; and what you teach is rubbish!" This well illustrates the spirit of rebellion in the world against God and the followers of Christ.

God has therefore seen fit to begin anew and to light his lamp afresh in one of the most contemptible corners of the earth today. This light, however, is not only meant to act as a counterbalance to the current demonization of the human spirit — no, it is more than that. It concerns the last things; or better, the Last One. But who is this person? Who ultimately stands above the present chaos of all human values? Who is seated at the controls of this world? Who is going to have the final word? To whom has God given a name which is above every name? The answer is, to the One who collapsed under the weight of his cross on the way to Golgotha's hill; to the Man who bore the curse of sin as he hung upon the tree; to the Man who descended into Hades to preach to those imprisoned long ago; to the One whom death could not hold; to the Lamb of God with whose praises the heavens are filled!

He is the Coming One, and his are the footprints that can be seen more clearly on Timor than anywhere else in the world today. The revival on Timor is an eschatological event. Many of the natives have indeed prophesied that the hosts of heaven are already preparing themselves for the great and glorious day.

XX. THE REASON FOR THIS REPORT

The revival in Indonesia can teach us many lessons. We should be first of all filled with joy that the Lord has so graciously granted his earthly children this wonderful time of blessing. We often become so tired when we see that nothing has happened after years of praying for revival. Yet God is not bound by our desires, but acts where he chooses and wills.

The spiritual outpouring in Indonesia should also spur us on to live more holy lives. The natives on Timor felt compelled to surrender their fetishes and idols and have them burned. Is it not the time for us, too, to surrender all our secret and sinful idols to Christ? Every idol we possess brings a hidden ban into our lives which robs us of our fruitfulness in service. The revival's message to us is therefore, "Children of God throughout this world, purify yourselves from sin, for without holiness there can be no fresh outpouring of blessing."

The events occurring in Indonesia should also stimulate our faith. The extent of our unbelief is revealed by the fact that we query in our hearts the miracles which have recently taken place there. For years we have read of these phenomena in our Bibles, yet when they occur in our own lifetime, we find we cannot believe.

Then again, the revival should open our eyes to the greatness and the glory of the Lord. As a young Christian years ago I often used to read the words of Jesus in John 14:12, "He who believes in me will also do the works that I do; and greater works than these will he do, because I go to the Father." The words 'and greater works' have often filled my mind. I could never really grasp what they meant. Then after following Jesus for 39 years, I saw these words being literally fulfilled on Timor.

Last but not least this 'Acts of the Apostles' on Timor demands that we as Christians must be prepared. We must prepare and arm ourselves for the coming day of the Lord. As my book 'Der Kommende' shows, God is already preparing Israel for that great day; but he is preparing his Church on earth too. The revival on Timor should surely wake us up to this fact.

Our Responsibility

The reports from Timor, however, as well as encouraging us, should also drive us to prayer. Although the Indonesian revival is probably the greatest the world has known, it is faced with more dangers than any other in the history of the Church.

The enemy has summoned the armies of hell in an attempt to destroy this movement of the Spirit of God. Today we are facing the greatest 'world war' the enemy has ever fought since the time of Christ. A fearful battle is taking place in the spiritual world which only those with prophetic insight can see. Indonesia is Satan's number one enemy today. Every child of God in this world is therefore duty bound to join in the fray and to intercede for the revival.

A number of the Christians there have already fallen victim to pride; the many miracles of healing and the raising of the dead can easily go to a person's head. Whenever this has happened, they have lost their authority at once.

A number, too, have fallen into the sin of immorality. The communal life of the teams not only represents a challenge, but also a danger. These too, have lost the authority the Lord gave them.

Others have fallen prey to money. Those who have been healed were naturally grateful, but those who had healed them should have remembered the words of the Lord Jesus when he said, "You received without pay, give without pay" (Matth. 10:8).

Some have also fallen into disorder. To be led of the Spirit does not mean that one will override every rule and regulation and live completely without restraint.

Thanks be to the Lord: those who have fallen have repented and returned, allowing themselves to be corrected by their brothers in the faith. Their humility showed that the Lord had not given them up.

Because we have been able to share a little in these wonderful events, we have an obligation to pray for this revival in Indonesia. Revivals are not the place for pious dilettantes. When Satan begins to mobilize his armies, believers too, must mobilize and strive together in their prayers. One need characterizes Christianity today: the need to pray. The ministry of intercession is practised far too seldom among Christians. All too readily we allow our threatened brothers and sisters throughout this world to fight and battle alone: believers in Communist countries are often forgotten; Christians in Red China are neglected; and while Indonesian Christians are withstanding the murderous attacks of the arch-enemy, we stand back and watch. Without realizing it, we have become guilty of the blood of many of our brothers in the faith. This is the main reason behind the writing of this book: that Christians will be stirred up to consider and to help their brethren in the farthest corners of this world. Who can hear this call? Although we cannot all be missionaries, we can nevertheless visit the mission-fields daily in our prayers. As a young man, Hudson Taylor bought a map of China and knelt on it each day while he prayed for the lost people of that land. To be a 'map missionary', far from being the worst, is rather the best type of missionary to be.

What a wonderful surprise it would be in eternity if every believer in the West were to be met by some brown, yellow or black Christians who said to him, "Did you know that the Lord saved us as a result of your prayers?" It is true that many Christians already will be greeted by these words, but the question is, will we be included among them?

But our story has not come to an end. We began our description of the Indonesian revival with an account of the lives of two of its forerunners. We now come to the story of another man whom God has been particularly pleased to use as his instrument in Indonesia.

XXI. PAK ELIAS

The following paragraphs describe only briefly the biography of a man whom God has blessed in a particular way in the revival in Indonesia. I have intentionally left this story to the end, for I felt that the Lord's 'biography' should really come first. It can never be stressed enough that this is not a matter of giving glory to a man. Any form of hero worship which develops around a well-known evangelist or preacher robs the Lord of the honour due to his name. Yet everyone of us is prone to push himself into the foreground. If this happens, the work of the Holy Spirit is quenched. I am therefore well aware of the dangers involved in describing the life of a man who has been much used by the Lord.

It is a part of God's method in dealing with mankind to select people to fulfill specific tasks. There are three aspects to this phenomenon: the task itself, the time of its accomplishment, and the chosen man. Thus, at the time of the Exodus for example, the task was the deliverance of the children of Israel from Egypt, the time was the climax of their afflictions, and the chosen man was Moses. In almost all of God's dealings with the Israelites we find this same divine triangle. When we think of the building of the temple, we find that the task was to house the ark of God, the time was the inauguration of the Kingdom, and the man whom God had chosen was Solomon. Or if we consider the ministry of John the Baptist: the task was to prepare the way for the Messiah, the time was shortly before His appearing, and the man was the solitary voice crying in the wilderness. The same applies to the history of the Church. Taking the Reformation for an example, we see that the task involved was to renew the Christian Church, the time was the threshold of our modern age — linked as it was with the discovery of America and other countries of the world — and the man for the task was Luther.

The Indonesian revival reveals the same pattern. David Simeon and his brother stood at the revival's threshold with Pak Elias as one of the students at their Bible School. Today the Lord has raised the former student above his teachers, for Pak Elias is a native of Indonesia, and the Lord has seen fit to choose the Indonesians themselves for the work of this revival.

The task at hand was the renewal of the almost petrified church on Timor, and the conversion of the Moslems. The God-appointed time was after the conclusion of the conflict with the Japanese, the Dutch, and the Communists. There was to be no fighting with one's back against the wall. The instrument whom God had chosen was Pak Elias.

Biographies tend to be rather tedious. For this reason I will keep my comments to a minimum. Pak Elias was born in 1928, the youngest child in a family of seven. His father died only three months after his son was born, which meant that his childhood and youth were characterized by hardship and need.

Pak Elias' early years were marked by numerous political upheavals, but one of the benefits he gained from this was a knowledge of the dialects of Timor and Ambon, as well as Indonesian, Japanese, Dutch, and English. These languages are in many ways a reflection of the actual education he received: a junior school on the island of Rote; high school on Timor; a teachers training college on Ambon; a teacher in Java, and finally a post in the academy of Bandung — an education not only marked by political change but also by the distances involved. The actual perimeter of this great archipelago measures some seven or eight thousand miles. Therefore both linguistically and geographically, Pak Elias' education was very broad. One can see God's 'style' already behind the course of his life. Was not Moses prepared for forty years in Midian before God called him for his task? Were they wasted years which David spent with the Philistines before he received his crown? — God's purposes are often not recognized till later. Was it therefore due just to a whim of God that Pak Elias was tossed to and fro among the islands of Indonesia as a young man?

In spite of a lack of money to help him in his studies, Pak Elias' career was quite exceptional. He was periodically forced to work for some of the time in order to save enough to study further. But even so, his above average intelligence enabled him to complete his academic work before his fellow students. By the time he was 23, he was already headmaster of an intermediate school in M. Further studies led to his appointment as the principal of a teachers training college in the same town. By the age of 29, as well as being the director of an academy and a university lecturer, he was also the headmaster of a high school with 2,000 pupils. An exceptional career indeed!

Pak Elias was a much respected person in church circles too. By the time he was 24, he was the leader of the Christian youth work in Bandung, and at 26 he was already an elder in the local church. In addition to this, each Sunday he would preach to the 2,000 pupils of his school and the 200 students of the training college. A great work indeed!

In both his public and his church life, Pak Elias was recognized as a born leader. Then something extraordinary happened. In November 1957 Dr. Roland Brown of the Moody Bible Institute in America held a mission in East Java. When Pak Elias attended the meeting on the 18th November, he was gripped by what he heard, and when the invitation was given to come to the front, he felt constrained to obey the command; but the courage failed him.

That night a terrific battle raged within his heart. A voice began to say to him, "You haven't been born again." But in reply the devil said, "But you've been preaching for seven years now, and you are the elder of a church." The inner voice persisted, "You are proud. You are building on your successful church and private life." Again the devil answered, "You've lived a good life. You're on the right road. There's nothing wrong with the way you live."

The battle continued. Finally the tempter urged him, "Stay away from the meetings. There's nothing in them for you."

But in spite of everything, Pak Elias returned the next day to listen to Dr. Brown speak. Again the message gripped his heart. As the missionary urged the people to confess their sins publicly, forgetting everything, Pak Elias got to his feet and walked to the front. Accepting Jesus into his life, he surrendered himself completely to the Lord.

Pak Elias' conversion came like a bombshell to the local Christian church. The ministers, church elders, and teachers, and even the ordinary church members became angered by his move. With one accord they began to say, "He was either all right before, or else he's been an utter hypocrite." The real reason, however, for all the anger and offence that arose as a result of Pak Elias' conversion, was the people's subconscious fear that their own sense of security was being threatened.

This is an old problem for many official churchgoers are simply quite unable to grasp what it means to be converted and born again; and the same is true with many of the ministers and elders of our churches.

The conversion of Pak Elias and his new contact with the Bible School in East Java resulted very soon in him being deprived of his office of elder in the church. How symptomatic this is of Christendom today: the Church endures the blasphemy of its ministers, it endures drunkards, gossips and liars, but a man who by God's grace has been converted, it finds very hard to endure. For many years Pak Elias was forbidden to preach in the churches again. Yet he was affected very little by this ban for the fire of God burnt so fervently within him that he began to preach on the streets instead.

Poisoned by Ashes and Sulphur

In 1960 Pak Elias took up his studies again. Attending the Bible School in East Java he sought to be equipped afresh. The spiritual atmosphere of the school answered the cry of his own heart. By 1961 he was already engaged in evangelistic tours covering the islands of Celebes, Java, and Timor. When the organization 'World Vision', which helps orphans and needy children, recognized the worth of this zealous man of God, they invited him to become one of their vice-presidents. 1963 found Pak Elias doing further evangelistic work in Borneo and on Rote. It was during this work that he first met Pastor Gideon, who was subsequently converted through his ministry.

But 1963 was also a year of crisis. On the 17th April the Agung volcano on the island of Bali erupted and buried a number of villages. Pak Elias, who was holding a mission there at the time, helped carry many of the children to safety on his moped. The roads, however, were sometimes covered to a depth of several inches with hot ash and, as a result, Pak Elias' lungs became seriously inflamed. At hospital the doctors started fighting for his life, but in the end they told his relatives, "It's no use; both lungs are almost completely burned. It's only a matter of days before he dies." The time of crisis arrived, and his wife was called to the hospital and told in her sorrow, "He won't last the night." Pak Elias' temperature had risen to 106 degrees. The inflamation had spread to his liver as well. At midnight, between the 30th April and the 1st May, however, the apparently fatally ill patient began to sing. Turning to his wife he said, "This isn't my last night on earth. I have to glorify the Lord Jesus. God has given me two verses confirming his will, 'We went through fire and through water; yet you have brought us forth to a spacious place' (Psalm 66:12), and, 'When you walk through fire you shall not be burned, and the flame shall not consume you' (Is. 43:2). I have gone through fire, but the Lord will deliver me." His prediction came true. That night Pak Elias' condition began to improve. By the following day he was already well along the road to recovery.

While he was still at the hospital, it became clear to him that he would have to leave the organization 'World Vision' and devote his life to the preaching of the Word.

The Doors Open

In 1964 Pak Elias set out again on a preaching tour of Java, but the churches were still closed to his ministry. He received an invitation to visit Sumatra, and travelling there he witnessed the great revival among the Moslems of which we have already heard.

One night Pak Elias was suddenly awoken by the Lord and shown that he was to preach before thousands of people. At the time he had no idea what the prophecy could mean, but the following day, after the churches had remained closed to him for a total of seven years, he received an invitation to hold a mission in Bandung. The letter mentioned that every church in the area would be taking part in the coming campaign. Pak Elias could hardly believe his eyes. All the churches — for him, the outlaw? He sent no reply at first, but then after a few days had passed, he received a telephone call conveying to him the same message. But still no word from the Lord. Pak Elias did not know what to do. Finally, a week later, two people arrived from Bandung with another written invitation to preach at the coming campaign. Three invitations! This must be the will of the lord; Pak Elias decided to go.

The mission in Bandung was a great occasion. 52 different churches and pastors took part in the work, and a team of 75 Bible school students from East Java turned up with their teachers to assist in the preparation of the campaign. The churches were amalgamated into four groups according to districts, while the teachers and students laboured together in preaching. During this time of preparation many were brought into a vital relationship with their Lord, and these were subsequently trained in counselling classes to help in the real campaign which was soon to follow. Pak Elias was the instrument God had chosen for the task. Every evening between 8,000 and 15,000 people came to hear the gospel preached, and altogether some 3,000 accepted the Lord Jesus as their Saviour. The new converts, however, were not allowed to drift away and meetings were arranged in which to build them up through the Word of God. This follow-up work lasted for three months, and the whole campaign for 18 weeks.

Business men and university lecturers and students were also gripped by the Word of God, and as a result of the mission Pak Elias regained the support and the trust of the churches which had previously rejected his work, or which had at least stood coldly to one side.

In Luke 9 : 1, 2 we read, "And Jesus called the twelve together and gave them authority over all demons and to cure diseases, and he sent them out to preach the kingdom of God and to heal." Where, we ask, is this authority in evidence today? Although the Church is often filled with orators, there are hardly any witnesses of Christ; and the number of Christians with the authority to heal or to cast out demons is even smaller.

Pak Elias has already said on several occasions, "I have no authority to heal, and neither have I the authority to raise people from the dead." On the other hand he speaks little about his authority to preach and his authority to cast out demons. But this is a good sign, for in my own experience, those who really possess spiritual gifts hardly mention them at all, whereas those who speak freely about their gifts usually have none at all.

Now let us listen to an unnerving story from the Bible School itself. A man with magical powers applied for a job as a driver at the Bible School and was accepted. He had learned his magical arts in Mecca and Medina. Once while he had been in India, he had allowed himself to be buried alive for four weeks. And now this man with the devil's own powers was a driver at the Bible School! The students and teachers, however, gradually became aware of his presence, and as time went by they witnessed his ability to kill dogs and cats and other animals through his powers of concentration.

The Bible School leaders were forced to intervene. Summoning the man to see them, they questioned him about what he had done. "Is it true," they asked, "that you can kill animals by means of your magical powers?" "Yes," replied the man, and he then added, "I can not only kill animals, but I can kill people too." Looking at Pak Elias he went on to say, "Don't look into my eyes.

174

If you do, you will die within five seconds." Realizing the challenge to his faith, but at the same time experiencing the peace of God within his heart, Pak Elias returned the gaze of the magician. "Look into my eyes," he said. "In the name of Jesus I bind the evil powers within you." The five seconds passed, but nothing happened. The two men continued to stare at one another. Suddenly, about a quarter of an hour later, the magician fell to the ground unconscious. His flesh had become as hard as wood. Not wanting the man to die, Pak Elias addressed him again. "In the name of Jesus Christ I command you to get up," he said. The magician regained consciousness once more. His magical powers had been defeated. As the Christians talked with him further, he confessed to having four gold needles embedded in his arms. These were a source of much of his magical power. When he challenged some students to try and cut them out, the knife could make no impression at all on his skin. Again Pak Elias began to command in the name of Jesus, telling the needles to come out of the man's arm. At once they started to move and they slowly came out one by one. The magician finally succumbed and promised to surrender his life to Christ. However, he failed to keep his word, and so later when it was discovered that he still had some of his old fetishes, he was finally relieved of his job. In spite of being one of the worst magicians in East Java, this man had been able to stay in the Bible School for four months. We can see here the subtlety of Satan whereby he smuggles his emissaries into the Church of Christ in order to cause chaos in its ranks.

It is seldom recognized by Christians that this is one of the methods Satan uses to disrupt the kingdom of God. One of the rather more sober members of the Pentecostal movement told me once, "We've sometimes found that even spiritistic mediums have slipped into our meetings and begun to speak in tongues, with the result that the disorder that followed was laid at our feet." His observation was an encouraging sign of his own spiritual and biblical outlook.

At one meeting when Pak Elias and Pastor Gideon were working together on Timor, Gideon had been preaching for about half an hour, when a woman in the audience suddenly stood up and tried to disturb the meeting. The woman was in fact a sorceress, and she started contradicting everything that Pastor Gideon said. If he cried out that there was power in the blood of Christ, the woman would shout out that this was not true. Finally Pak Elias turned to Pastor Gideon and said, "We must silence this woman, otherwise we'll get nowhere. This is Satan's work." Then addressing the woman, Pak Elias called out, "In the name of Jesus Christ I command you to be quiet and to come to the front and listen to our message." At once the woman stopped her cries and came to the front. At the close of the meeting she asked to be counselled, but was unable to believe. In spite of this, everyone present, including the local pastor and church elders, had witnessed the power of Jesus in their midst.

In his ministry Pak Elias has experienced many similar disturbances. During a large meeting at which another sorceress was present, the woman, in an attempt to disrupt the proceedings, suddenly rushed to the front and fell to the ground as if dead. When two people went to see what was wrong with her, they turned to Pak Elias and said, "She's not just unconscious, she's dead." Pak Elias, however, would not have the meeting interrupted and carried on with his message. Then as the meeting drew to a close, he called out to the woman, "In the name of Jesus, stand up!" At once the woman arose, and confessing her sins, she was wonderfully saved.

Pak Elias flew once to the island of S. in order to hold a mission there. Before he arrived, a Moslem sorcerer living on the island had a vision in which it was revealed to him that a dangerous man would be arriving soon from Java and that this man must be killed. The sorcerer, having been told by the devil to go to the airport, discovered that he was unable to carry out his planned assassination on account of the large number of policemen who happened to be there. Pak Elias then went to a house in which a meeting was to be held. The sorcerer followed him, but because of the large number of people present, he was again unable to get near enough to kill him. At the end of the meeting Pak Elias went outside to speak to the additional people who had gathered there. The sorcerer looked for a place from which to put his plan into effect. He was a skilled stone-thrower, an art which is frequently practised on the Indonesian islands still today. To increase his chances of success, the man had stuck a number of needles into his cheeks to enhance his magical powers. Finding a suitable spot, he drew back his arm to throw his stone. Suddenly it became quite stiff; he could not move it at all. At the time Pak Elias knew nothing of the events that were taking place. As the meeting closed and he gave the invitation for people to come forward and repent, the sorcerer came out to the front and confessed his plot to murder the evangelist. He said later, that as he was going to throw the stone, the ground had suddenly moved beneath his feet. The sorcerer made an open confession of all his terrible sins and thefts, and next day he began to go from one family to another returning the goods he had stolen. He even returned the very shirt from off his back, for that was stolen too. It was a wonderful victory for the Lord over a man who had wanted to kill one of his messengers.

The Moslems on the island once demonstrated against

Pak Elias and the other Christians there. As his brothers in the faith sought to protect him from the attack, Pak Elias said to them, "Let them come; those who are with us are more than those who are with them." And so the Moslems advanced. Suddenly a man stood up from among the audience which had come to hear the Christians preach. He was a high-ranking army officer. Turning to the approaching crowd he called out to them, "If you don't stop your demonstration and quieten down at once, I'll order my soldiers to shoot. I've come here to hear what the speaker has to say." With that the demonstrators stopped, and after a few moments they all sat down. Following the meeting, in spite of the position he held, the officer came to Pak Elias and said, "I need Jesus; show me how I can find him." His request was granted. — He must surely have been the brother of the centurion we read about in the Acts of the Apostles chapter 10.

On another occasion, as Pak Elias was about to use a flannelgraph to illustrate the state of the human heart, a crowd of Moslems, which had been stirred up by two sorcerers, approached. The Christians wondered how to defend themselves. Stopping in the middle of his message, Pak Elias told them not to worry and began to read Psalm 2 out loud, "Why do the heathen rage . . ." When he had finished, he said, "The gospel must be shouted out in the darkness." While this had all been going on, both the sorcerers were involved in accidents, the one on his moped and the other in his car, and before the meeting had drawn to a close, they had both been admitted into hospital.

The last attack we shall describe had an even worse ending for the opponents of the cross. Again the Moslems had sought to hold a demonstration during one of the large meetings of the Christians. Two men in particular were the chief instigators of the plot. What was the result? A week later one of the men drove over a precipice and was killed, while the other, setting out to sea in his boat, was caught in a sudden squall and drowned when his boat overturned. On account of these incidents the demonstrators, who had regarded these two men as their leaders, became alarmed. Although they had just written some letters to the government complaining of the work that the Christians were doing, the letters were never sent. Instead the Moslems had torn them up saying, "It's too dangerous to get in the Christians' bad books." In this way every attempt of Satan to hinder the work of God resulted in a blessing for the Christians.

> Be Thou our great Deliverer still,
> Thou Lord of life and death;
> Give us the grace to praise Thy name,
> With this our latest breath.

XXII. WISDOM LIES AT HIS FEET

Pak Elias, by the grace of God, has been allowed to reach both the intelligent and the illiterate, the high and the low, with his message. For the Holy Spirit, however, these distinctions simply do not exist. Whoever imagines himself to be something, is nothing in the sight of God. On the other hand, whoever recognizes his own poverty and nothingness, receives the grace of God.

We have already heard how a local university lecturer at Palembang, acknowledging his own poverty of spirit, found Christ at a mission which Pak Elias was holding in the town. The story was repeated in Bandung where a woman lecturer also found the key to eternal wisdom. The apostle Paul described this wisdom by saying that it was "to know Him and the power of his resurrection" (Phil. 3 : 10).

There is no pathway higher than this. Even if one were to plumb the depths of the creed, one would find no greater thought. It is Jesus alone who must ever be central in our thoughts; no man, no matter what spiritual gifts he may possess, may challenge this central place.

Now let us hear the testimony of a quite exceptional woman. She is not only a lawyer, but also a lecturer at Bandung university. When I met Mrs. Mapaliey in Indonesia I became very interested in her work for, like myself, she had written her doctor's thesis on the subject of occultism, entitling it, 'A Brief Survey of the Various Forms of Occultism in Indonesia Today'. Furthermore, she has agreed to translate my book 'Between Christ and Satan' into Indonesian. But now we will let her speak for herself.

"Two years ago Pak Elias held a mission in our town. During the week a well-known pop-singer and musician was converted. He was so filled with a love for the Lord that he at once phoned me up and asked me if I would be prepared to sing at some of the meetings. I agreed, and each night sang a song on the theme of the prodigal son, little realizing that it was a song about myself. As the week progressed, a great change started to take place in my heart. Each message I heard made me increasingly aware of my own inner poverty, so much so that I finally surrendered my life to Christ.

As a result I asked Pak Elias to visit our home, hoping that some of my relatives would find their way to Christ too. I was made very conscious again that evening of what I had received from our Father in heaven: the forgiveness of my sins, a future hope, and a joy that no one could take away.

Prior to this wonderful experience, my life had mainly been governed by a traditional church outlook. Although my own father had been a pastor, and had taught us from childhood to say our prayers, we had never been led to the point of surrendering our lives to the Lord.

Apart from my studies therefore, my years at school and college had been governed mainly by sport. I was a passionate tennis player, and my hobby had been to collect as many trophies as I possibly could.

Mediumistic Abilities

It is strange how many Christians know nothing of occult bondage, even though they may be suffering from it themselves. It was terrifying to me to discover one day that I was one of the very people to whom the words of Exodus 20:5 applied. My own grandfather in fact had been a sorcerer. In spite of my father being a Christian, a line of mediumistic powers ran through our whole family and found expression particularly in my own life. Already when I was a child I had noticed these mediumistic phenomena. I would sometimes hear voices whispering or singing to me, while on other occasions I would sense the presence of invisible spirits around me. If I met a stranger, I would immediately know what type of person he was and what his thoughts were. On top of everything, I used to have dreams that came true, which made me afraid to dream at all.

One example comes to my mind. After my marriage I dreamt one day that two doctors were leaning over me; one of them was an Indonesian and the other a Westerner. I even remembered seeing the operating lamp. Next morning I told my elder sister about the dream and she is therefore my witness. A week later I suddenly started suffering from some severe pains in my stomach. The doctor suspected that it was my appendix and thought an operation was necessary. It was then that my dream was fulfilled to the letter.

My two daughters have likewise inherited these mediumistic abilities. Our elder daughter has a marked telepathic disposition and is also hypersensitive. This means that she is able to sense things around her more than other people. She is almost like a radio receiver which can pick up the invisible signals around it. Moreover, she has contact with the world of spirits, and many is the time she has woken up at night after experiencing battles in the spirit world. Our other daughter also experiences supernatural things like seeing ghosts.

People in our house notice these things also. For example, the cook twice said that she saw me in the dressing room when I was not even in the house. On another occasion the chamber maid said that she saw a Balinese idol dancing about in the porch, tapping the window pane rythmically as it did so. My daughter had run into the room at the time and demanded, "Who's knocking on the window? It's getting on my nerves."

The ghosts seemed to plague everyone in the house; we just did not know what to do. Several months after the mission, David Simeon arrived in the district with a team of students from the Bible School. When I told him what was happening, I was surprised to discover that he was not only acquainted with such phenomena, but that he also knew how to drive the spirits out of the house. After the team had gone into each room and prayed, and had commanded the powers to leave in the name of Jesus, the house was completely freed.

The Lord taught me a number of lessons through these very trying experiences. I had first of all failed to realize that my own life could still be burdened from my grandfather's side, in spite of the fact of my father being a Christian. Occult oppressions are therefore able to bypass believing generations and appear again in unbelieving generations which follow.

The second lesson I learnt was that in spite of my own repentance and conversion I had still not been freed from the occult burdens in my life. Specialized counselling is essential in this area.

Thirdly, and this was the thing that distressed me most, I learnt that my own daughters had inherited these same mediumistic abilities.

Yet this was not all. Our own house had been affected by the strong mediumistic powers which we possessed. Oppressed people can therefore produce a form of bondage on the actual material things around them.

These were four very explicit lessons concerning the effects of sins of sorcery which can sometimes be passed on to the third or fourth generation. However, I would never have had the courage to have spoken openly about these phenomena unless I had not learnt one further lesson. This was that although we are faced with genuine powers stemming from the arch-enemy of our souls, the power that is ours in the victory of Christ is far greater. He has defeated the powers of darkness. Therefore through him, and through him alone, we can overcome the might of our foe.

This was the greatest lesson I could have learnt: that Jesus is still, and always will be victorious over all the powers of Satan and hell.

Looking back, I can now understand why God allowed me to go through all these experiences. Although many people are gripped by the powers of darkness in Indonesia, apart from the Christians from the Bible School in East Java there is hardly anyone in our country capable of dealing with this difficult counselling problem. At least, I have never met anyone who would have been prepared to face the enemy in the name of Jesus. Since my own deliverance the Lord has led many people to me whom I have been able to advise and help. This difficult school has therefore taught and prepared me to aid those who are occultly oppressed.

The wonderful and victorious power of the Lord Jesus is the only answer this world knows to all the powers of sorcery."

With this, the testimony of Mrs. Mapaliey ends. I was

personally greatly encouraged to find that completely independently of my own work in this field, a university lecturer in East Asia has been led to the same conclusions as I myself concerning occultism. We only met for the first time in 1968, but after reading through one of my books she said, "This is exactly what I have discovered for myself. Can I translate this book into Indonesian?" I believe that this was the leading of the Lord.

XXIII. A PLANTATION OWNER FINDS CHRIST

At the Bible conference in East Java I had the pleasure of meeting Mr. Taneng-Djin. He spoke to me in German. He is an extremely gifted man speaking several languages, and has travelled extensively throughout the world. We will let him describe his story in his own words.

"I was born in 1905. Both my parents were devout Confucians. For my education I attended a Dutch school. On account of our strong religious convictions, my wife and I were married according to the rites and customs of the Confucian faith.

Our marriage was blessed with three sons: Boon, Hooi and Leong. They studied in Rotterdam, London and Amsterdam. Leong became well-known as an outstanding chess player, and in 1963 he became an international master.

My wife and I were very religious, although we knew nothing at the time about the Lord Jesus. We began to pray to God in 1932, but rather like the Athenians in Acts 17, he was still unknown to us.

The Second World War and the time of the Japanese occupation was a very difficult time. We were persecuted in all sorts of ways and the taxes were very high. The war was followed by the trouble between the Dutch and the Indonesians. This also affected us a great deal.

But then came the real tragedy: our gifted son, Leong, became mentally ill. On receiving a telegram from some friends in Europe informing us that Leong had been admitted to hospital, I left at once to fly to Amsterdam. The doctor told me that Leong was suffering from an incurable form of schizophrenia. This was a great shock to me. As I spoke to other doctors about my son's condition, I was told, "Take him back to Indonesia. He has a better chance of improving at home and in the sun."

So it was that we flew back together to Bandung. On our arrival Leong received further treatment. The doctors prescribed exactly the same drugs as he had received in Holland: Largactil, Librium and Serpasil.

Hardly had it become known that our son had arrived back home again than his old friends began to call at our house. They urged him to play chess for their club again. Leong had in fact been in the international team which had travelled to Leipzig for the Chess Olympics held there in 1960, and he had obtained 16½ points out of a total of 20. His friends therefore wanted him to go with them to Europe again for another tournament in 1965. All this, however, only served to make Leong's condition worse, and the result was that he was admitted to a military hospital for further treatment; but the conditions there were hopeless.

We did all we could to obtain his release from the barred rooms of this hospital. When we did succeed, the patient again quietened down. In our ignorance, though, we then made a disastrous mistake. We allowed our son to be treated by an astrologer. Parents concerned for their children will try almost anything, and yet so much of what they do is wrong. The very last thing we should have done was to expose Leong to the powers of darkness.

As a result of the talks we had had with a Christian missionary who had tried to show us the way to Christ, by the end of 1965 we had recognized that our Confucian faith was leading us in the wrong direction. However, we were still unprepared to take the right path. Nevertheless we started that year to pray to the Christians' God.

In March 1966 Pastor Simeon from the Bible School in East Java arrived with his wife in the town to hold a series of meetings there. Mrs. Simeon in particular spent much time with us trying to lead us to the Lord. Our hearts, however, were as hard as diamonds, and we still found it impossible to decide for Christ.

In May of the same year, Pak Elias arrived in Bandung with his team. As he encouraged the people at the meeting to come to the front and to repent of their sins, we at last decided to take this step. For the first time in our lives every burden was lifted from our shoulders. We were greatly concerned at the time, however, about what our aging parents who were still Confucians would think about our decision. Hurrying back home, I told them what we had done. They were very shocked and started saying, "Now we're all alone. Who's going to sacrifice to us when we are dead? No one will come to our place after they've died." I tried to comfort them, but it was no use. At that moment Leong and my wife arrived at the house. One could sense at once the new-found joy they had through having accepted the Lord Jesus as their Saviour. My parents too, could actually see the change, and as a result they reconciled themselves to the step which we had taken.

With this a great joy entered our home. Jesus had changed everything. Later we experienced the added joy of receiving a visit from Pak Elias. While he was with us I confessed my sins before him, thus confirming the fact that I had truly accepted the Lord. My son's illness also cleared up completely. The doctor in Amsterdam had therefore been proved wrong. When there is humanly speaking no more hope, there are still a thousand and one opportunities open to the Lord. His arm is never as short as the shortsightedness of man sometimes imagines.

On the 21st July 1966, my wife, Leong and myself were all baptised. The old had passed away; behold, everything had become new through the Lord Jesus Christ. Looking back today, I simply fail to understand why I never accepted the Lord Jesus earlier in my life. Why are we so foolish as to pass the Lord Jesus by for years, when he is the only source of the most precious things in the world: the forgiveness of our sins, and a peace with God which the world cannot ever take away?"

The revival in Indonesia has touched the very depths of my heart. Ever since I left those distant islands, the words of the wonderful Christian choir from the island of Ambon, which they sang to us in German to welcome us to their land, have been echoing through my mind:

Jesus my joy, Thou pasture of my heart;
Jesus my crown, how I long for where Thou art!
Jesus, Thou art mine, and I belong to Thee;
Dearer on earth is nothing else to me.

ASIA'S GREAT OPPORTUNITY

Since the original publication of this book in Germany, I have been able to make a further visit to South East Asia, the essence of which is described in the following pages. Within them you will find an account of a series of experiences that have moved me most deeply. An interval of 16 months separates the events of the previous chapters from those recorded here. We are thereby presented with a fresh survey of what is currently taking place in the Far East, a survey that will cause us to hold our breath in suspense.

In the European Olympic Games a custom still persists today of a relay of runners who set out from the ancient Greek town of Olympia, where the original games were held, by whom the Olympic flame is transferred from torch to torch until it reaches its final destination. The runners in this relay carry the flame from country to country and from continent to continent, to the city in which the Games are to be held.

Here, in this procession of torches, we find an illustration of the spreading of the gospel message. Some 1,900 years ago the good news began to be relayed around the world. The first station consisted of the lands of the Mediterranean area during the time of the Roman Empire. Rome stood at that time at the central point of the then known world. For this reason, as we have already hinted at in the previous chapters, it was destined to become one of the first centres from which the gospel message was spread abroad.

The inner decay of the Christian Church was not long in following the collapse of the Roman Empire. The so-called vicar of Christ by now had little in common with his Lord. The spiritual centre of Christianity was therefore to be gradually transferred to central Europe. And so the flame journeyed on. The missionary work of people like Columba, Pirmin, Boniface, Ansverus and numerous others of the Teutonic race, prepared the ground for the new area of civilization under whose protection the gospel was to be propagated further. The Reformation therefore, with its two main branches of Calvin and Luther, introduces us to the second station in the relay of torches which began at Pentecost.

The theological renewal at the time of the Reformation was closely followed by a spiritual revival in the form of the Pietist movement. In this way, men like Spener, Francke and Zinzendorf became midwives to a spiritual deepening and supplementing of the Reformation faith. The Pietist movement was destined to become the scriptural seedbed of the many missionary ventures of the 18th and 19th centuries. For 350 years Germany, together with Switzerland and the Scandinavian countries whose religious history is closely connected with hers, remained the spiritual centre for the propagation of the Christian message.

But God's will was that the flame of the gospel be carried further still. Every race and every continent was to be given its opportunity. The 18th and 19th centuries also saw the rise of the British Empire. The fruit of this development is evidenced today by the fact that one can travel almost anywhere in the world using English as the lingua franca. This has been of an enormous help to both the missionaries and the gospel. It is easy to see why the torch was to be transferred to the English-speaking world, for in this way the whole globe lay open to the message of Christ. This third major centre of the good news embraced lands on either side of the Atlantic. In

Britain the names of men like Wesley, Booth, Spurgeon, George Müller and Hudson Taylor shone in the darkness as God raised each of these men up to be the founder of some great Christian movement. In America those chosen and used by God to serve as his tools included C. H. Finney, Moody, Dr. Torrey and many others. As we think of Billy Graham today, it almost seems as if he is the last great light to shine from this Anglo-American missionary centre. The torch must continue its onward march.

Today, as we move further into the second half of the 20th century, the world is facing a massive upheaval. The neo-rationalistic philosophical and theological outlook has almost extinguished the light of the gospel in the Western world. The centre of gravity is therefore shifting eastward to Asia. But those familiar with the history of Africa and Asia will wonder why Africa is seemingly overlooked in our story. There is a reason. Africa has already experienced a mighty awakening in the form of the Uganda revival. This, too, gave birth to a number of evangelists and missionaries, perhaps the most well-known being William Nagenda. However, the Uganda revival was neither privileged nor destined to send a host of missionaries into other parts of the world. It possessed but a limited power to radiate the gospel to other continents. Why was this? Although it is not easy to talk about the negative side, it must be admitted that the Christians in Uganda suffer from a rather unhappy characteristic. They are simply too sure of themselves. A Japanese Christian, Professor Shimizu, once said to me, "I found that the attitude of the Christians out there was a little repugnant. They didn't seem to be ready to accept anything from another brother, although they expected other Christians to listen to them." This has been my own impression on a number of occasions too. When the leading Christians lose their humility, a revival rapidly goes downhill. This seems to be the reason why Uganda has been unable to reach out successfully and evangelize the other continents.

In Indonesia, however, the circumstances are better. The revival there, although only four years old, is already sending out many missionaries into other parts of the world. And so a fourth great centre for spreading the gospel message is developing. The relay of torches has probably, with this fourth station in the Asiatic world, arrived at its most crucial yet. Over one thousand million people are living today in Asia, and every one of them needs to grasp hold of the gospel in order to avoid being ruined and destroyed by the massive bulwarks of darkness found in their midst. It is possible that Asia is to be the last great missionary centre before the second coming of Christ. A gradual shifting is therefore taking place from West to East. The spiritual strength of the West is rapidly declining. Many missionary societies have already lost what spiritual authority they once possessed, and yet too often they remain unhappily oblivious of this fact. Others are merely a 'smoking flax', and are near to being extinguished. Indeed, one of the most well-known spiritual leaders of Asia has been heard to say, "In the last century the West sent many renowned missionary workers to us. This era, however, has almost passed. For every sound Western missionary who arrives here today, we receive another two with an unscriptural theology and no commission from the Lord." This is one of the results of having so many modern theologians teaching and lecturing in the missionary colleges of the West. What good can come of this? While I was actually writing this account in the Far East, the president of a missionary college here said to me, "When we send our enthusiastic young missionary recruits to the West in order to receive further theological training, they return having lost almost all the inner spiritual power that they ever had. Western theology simply destroys a Christian's faith, and, instead of building him up, robs him of his power." As a result of this, the Asian Christians are being forced to begin training their young people themselves. They have had to sever themselves from the West and found their own colleges in which, if they hope to retain the young Christian's faith, they have to forbid the teaching of Western theology.

Asia's time is approaching. No other continent has drunk so deeply of the blood of Christians martyrs. Asia's soil is saturated with blood. In every Communist country of the world the cries of the saints reach up to heaven. Is God unable to hear? Surely not, the revival in Indonesia is already His answer. This new centre of missionary activity is already sending out teams of evangelists to Japan, Thailand, Pakistan, Germany and other countries. There is obviously no lack of opposition, yet this is all part and parcel of the growth of the Kingdom of God.

I. THE BULWARKS OF DARKNESS

In South East Asia one finds many strongholds acting as blockades to the gospel message. The chief fortress of darkness, however, is Communism, no matter whether it appears in a Chinese, Russian or neutral garb. The present population explosion, and the threatening world food shortage, only serve to promote its growth. The very spirits of hell have become incarnate within this political system. This can be supported by examples from many reliable sources. For example, in one Communist prison, the guards arranged a horrifying and blasphemous ceremony. A Christian minister was forced during a communion service to distribute excrement and urine to the communicants. This is simultaneously a case of both blasphemy and torture. What a revelation of Satan! And this is not just an isolated case. One can read of further examples in the books written by Pastor Richard Wurmbrand, a man who has personally witnessed similar atrocities in Communist prisons. There can be no doubt at all about the Satanic origin of these tortures.

The second bulwark resisting the Christian missionary work in Asia is the religions of the East, particularly Islam. The Moslem faith has experienced a renaissance of a more aggressive outlook. In the past, in many areas, Moslems had developed a certain tolerance. Today, however, although many of the younger Moslems are losing interest in their mother religion, there is nevertheless a growing hostility towards other faiths among the more convinced disciples of Mohammed. Having mentioned this already, we will content ourselves by simply quoting a few more recent examples which illustrate this fact.

On the 1st October 1967, 29 churches and church buildings were destroyed on the island of Celebes by a large crowd of Moslems in a single night. In spite of the fact that a church organ was burnt in front of his house, a president of the police living in the neighbourhood of one of the churches, took not the slightest bit of notice of what was happening.

In northern Sumatra a number of acts of persecution took place against the Christians in 1968. On the island of Banjak 300 Christians were threatened with death if they did not leave the island immediately or accept the Moslem faith. Although some 25 Christians capitulated, the remainder fled to the nearby island of Nais leaving behind all their worldly goods.

In the same year the Moslems destroyed the Christian church in the village of Asahan. The Batak, a Christian tribe who outnumber the Moslems on the island, were so furious that they destroyed two of the island's mosques in revenge. One can understand why they reacted like this, but at the same time it was not scriptural, and such a reaction would never have occurred in the revival area itself. As Christians, we must never retaliate. In fact this retaliation merely supplied the Moslems with fresh material for their anti-Christian propaganda. For the Batak it was a disastrous reaction, for it simply illustrated how far away they are from the real teachings of Christ.

In the months of September and October 1968 in southern Sumatra, four Christians were killed by some Moslems in Marta Pura. They had only recently been converted to Christianity from the Islamic faith, but they had had to pay for their conversion with their lives. However, their sacrifice was not in vain. Shortly after the death of these four Christian witnesses, 60 other Moslems were converted. The last specific act of persecution in 1968 was a Moslem attack on a church in Kedini in East Java, when the building was simply burnt to the ground.

The year 1969 immediately ushered in a new series of Moslem attacks on the churches in the area. On January 17th the Dutch Reformed Church in Djatibarung (West Java) was destroyed. The next blow fell in Slipi, a suburb of Djakarta, on the 28th April. Within the space of two hours a newly constructed church was destroyed by a mob of some 500 Moslems. Although, as before, a general of the army was living only 50 yards away, he was, to quote, "completely unaware of the disturbance." I have visited the site of the ruined church. The building had only been completed two months prior to the attack. Without any form of outside help the Christians had managed to raise over £3,000 to have the church erected, and for the poor Indonesian Christians this had been an enormous sacrifice. But on top of this, since the attack the authorities have refused all permission for them to begin rebuilding.

The minister who founded this church in Slipi is at the same time pastor of another three congregations. These, too, have become the targets of Moslem attacks. He is prevented from preaching at one of the meeting places because the Moslems in the neighbourhood have threatened to use force to stop any services being held there. At another of his churches the Moslems have erected their own mosque on a site immediately adjacent to the church building. Woe to the Christians if they had attempted to do the same!

My host, who is the minister of the largest church in the town, has his own church lit by bright flood lights day and night. "We just don't know when we'll be next on the list", he told me.

The third bulwark of darkness erected in Asia against the Christian faith is occultism. The Eastern religions, together with animism, are so entwined with magic and spiritism that the demonic forces often reach deep within the Christian churches themselves. Many nominal Christians, although paying lip service to the Bible, still retain their old fetishes, protective spells, and healing magic, to which they always return when danger threatens or when they are in need.

The revival on Timor began with the islanders bringing their fetishes out of their houses and burning them. Very briefly we can tell the story of how just one of the nominal Christians was delivered from his bondage to fetishes. Mark, a young man of 26, had witnessed some tremendous events during the revival but he had been left completely untouched by them at first. For a number of years he had been an active charmer, and many people had been in the habit of turning to him when they had needed help. Finally, however, the Lord met him in the spring of 1969 and gave him a direct revelation. One evening at about 6 o'clock Mark saw a shining figure approaching him. He fell to the ground and lost consciousness, and lay there as if dead for 14 hours. Ants crawled into his mouth and eyes and ears, and his relatives were convinced that he had died. The next morning, though, at about 8 o'clock he regained consciousness. He told the people of the dreadful things he had experienced. He had been taken to the very gates of hell. A horse which had been covered with blood, and on which numerous people had been sitting, had galloped past him. Then a voice had called out, "This horse carries to hell people who have not forsaken their sorceries." He had had other visions which had likewise terrified him. After this dreadful experience he burnt all his charms and fetishes. The Lord then called him to the special task of being a team leader. I was able to meet this brother myself when I visited the area in which he lives.

In addition to these bulwarks of darkness, a new threat is appearing in South East Asia, which I have referred to already on several occasions. By this I mean the deadly modern disease of Western intellectualism and destructive biblical criticism. Some Christian students recounted to me how they were forced to leave the theological college in D. for fear of being robbed of their faith. In K. they face the same problem, where both a Dutch and a German theologian teach the present day brand of modern theology. On the very island on which the Lord has revealed himself so mightily, Satan has established his own seminary! Because of this the Christian students in the revival area were forced to arrange a conference at which to decide what their attitude should be to this new but very real threat.

Another difficulty facing the genuine work of Christ in Asia today is the missionary practices of the Catholic Church. In this so-called age of ecumenicalism some almost unbelievable things are taking place. As this report was being written, the moderator of the Reformed Church told our international team of some terrible events which had occurred quite recently. He gave us some examples of the Catholic intolerance in the area, and described instances of the unspiritual attitudes of the Catholic missionaries working here. In the northern part of the island, the Catholics put the following scheme into practice: they renamed some 60,000 animists in the area, baptised them, and then registered them as members of the Catholic Church. Yet not one of the 60,000 animists accepted Christ as a result of his registration. I repeat, this was reported to me by the actual church authorities on the island, and can therefore not be looked upon as just a piece of malicious anti-Catholic propaganda. — We shall be hearing more about the actions of these newly baptised Catholics a little later.

We can see that Asia bleeds from many wounds. Yet the glorified Lord has ignited a fire in Indonesia which will continue to burn till He returns to this earth again. In the past the messengers of the cross used to travel from Europe and America to the East. Today we find our Asian brothers and evangelists journeying west to a civilization which has been drained of all its power by rationalism.

II. THE BIRTH OF A BOOK

Let us turn for a few moments away from these meaty matters, to a story of a lighter nature. Much of this book was born in a region close to the equator under a burning tropical sun. A shirt and a pair of trousers is already almost too much clothing for the type of climate one finds out here. Mosquitos and other insects buzz around my arms and feet. A glass of lukewarm water stands on the primitive table beside me. Since leaving Germany not a single cold drink has wetted my lips. Wherever I have travelled the only refreshment available has been a glass of either hot or lukewarm water. Brown-skinned native children stand around the little table at which I am working, staring in amazement at the portable typrewriter set before me. They have never seen anything like it before. The noise of their chatter and laughter blends with the sound of the older natives sitting nearby conversing loudly with one another. A short distance away a group of some 25 people are singing revival hymns and clapping their hands in tune to the music. A weak paraffin lamp, which keeps going out, stands on the table beside me. I take some cream and rub it into my skin to repel the insects, and try to keep the noise out of my head by putting ear plugs into my ears. But on top of all this, I feel almost overcome by exhaustion through having attended so many meetings. And some of these have lasted for as many as 12 hours at a time. What an effort it is to try and concentrate! I find it almost impossible to put my thoughts down in an orderly fashion on the paper in front of me.

III. THE BIBLE AND THE IRON CURTAIN

The Communist beast which has risen from the very abyss itself has lain for many years over Asia, and it smothers almost every move which is made in the area in the name of freedom. Its claws continue to grope towards those few lands which as yet have withstood the pressure it puts upon them. Communism's lustful aim includes not only the subjugation of all the peace-loving peoples of the world, but also the extinction of the Church of Christ.

With God's help I have been enabled in my travels to visit almost every one of the countries in the Far East. Wherever one goes, one is faced with a different set of needs. In one area the problem consists of a lack of rice, in another a lack of employment, but in every single country with the exception of Ceylon one finds a common need for the Bible, the printed Word of God.

This famine of God's Word has been particularly laid on my heart with regard to one of the countries of South East Asia. I cannot mention any names for fear of endangering the Christians working in the area. Countries under Communist rule the world over allow neither Bibles nor Christian literature to cross their borders. However, in order to dupe the West, a few Bible colleges are allowed to remain open here and there. But even in these the same shortage of Scriptures exists. In the country I am particularly thinking of, there is only about one Bible for every six students, and so when their training is ended, they are forced to leave with nothing to aid them in their ministry save those portions of Scripture they have managed to copy out while at college. "Isn't it possible to get Bibles to these people?" I asked. "Yes," a missionary replied, "the British and Foreign Bible Society has already printed Bibles in their language. The unhappy thing is that they are still lying around in London, since it's illegal to import them into the country." "Hasn't anyone thought of a way of getting the Bibles to the people who need them?" "Oh yes," he replied again, "500 have already been sent." He then went on to tell me excitedly how the Bibles had finally found their way into the country — unfortunately the method used cannot be described at the present time. Suffice it to say that the missionary has learnt from the Vietcong how to cross frontiers which seem almost impassible. Hatred is not the only emotion that can cause one to be inventive, for a love for Christ and his Church is even better at opening doors where no doors seem to exist. Desiring to know more I questioned the missionary further, "How many more Bibles do you need, and do you know what they would cost?" "Well, we could use a further 500 Bibles immediately, and maybe up to 10,000 New Testaments," he replied. "We could get these through the so-called iron curtain. Concerning the price, though, the Bibles from London cost about £1 each, but the New Testaments are a lot cheaper."

The idea of taking Bibles through the iron, or red curtain as it really is, gave me no rest. A few mornings later I went and found the missionary again and said to him, "I'll make you a promise. I and my fellow helpers from Germany and Switzerland will supply you with these Bibles and New Testaments without cost." And so we agreed: the Bibles should be ordered from London while the New Testaments should be printed in either India or Hongkong in order to allay the cost.

Will you pray for the success of this campaign? Our one desire as Christians should be that the message of our Lord and Master be spread throughout the world, and this includes those places where man has apparently forbidden its entry.

IV. A VICTIM OF THE RELIGIOUS BEAST

In the book of Revelation we read in chapter 13 of the beast and the false prophet which will one day appear on this earth. These are destined to terrorize mankind in the last days. This Satanic alliance represents in effect the union between on the one hand a political, and on the other hand a religious power. It is to be an 'arranged marriage' between Church and State, between the beast of Communism and the beast of false religion.

It would be an over-simplification to equate the religious beast with the Catholic Church. Religious fanaticism exists as much among Protestants as among Catholics. But basically every religion which excludes the Lord Jesus and the Holy Spirit is, in the last analysis, Satanic. By their fruits you shall know them.

Some years ago I made a number of visits to the Latin-American countries where the majority of people subscribe to the Catholic faith. In Colombia, which could almost be called the Spain of South America, I met a missionary who told me the following story. A Protestant evangelist was pulled out of his bed one night and kidnapped in full view of his wife. A few weeks later the evangelical Christians received some small packets containing dried flesh. The duplicated letters which accompanied the packets claimed that the flesh was in fact the flesh of the kidnapped man. This claim was followed by the threat that anyone not prepared to forsake his Protestant faith and return to the Catholic Church — outside of which there was no salvation — could expect a similar fate. Of course, it could not be proved that what was in the packets was the kidnapped man's flesh but, whatever the case, he was never seen again. The missionary affirmed, "I can guarantee as a Christian the truth of the story I have just told you."

Since this particular episode, terrorist acts in Colombia against Protestant Christians have on the whole ceased, but this is mainly due to the adverse publicity they received, and the disapproval expressed by certain governments concerning such persecution. However, the religious beast is still very much alive, and it continues to raise its head whenever the time is right.

In South East Asia a fresh blow was struck on the 28th March 1969. The facts were confirmed in the court case which followed. There can be no doubt at all about the actual validity of this report.

To avoid the possibility of any form of revenge being taken on those involved, the names of the people and the places will be omitted. However, let it be said, I not only wrote the story in the country in which the crime took place, but I have also preached on more than one occasion at the actual home town of the victim himself.

After much prayer and preparation a group of Bible students felt compelled by the Lord to go and preach the gospel in a Catholic area near the country's border. Many people may immediately retort: "Well, that was wrong to start with. You don't need to send Protestant missionaries into an area where a Catholic church already exists!" Yet in answer to this, no one would be so foolish as to suggest that all the people living near a Catholic church, or even a Protestant church for that matter, will automatically be Christians. Christ's disciples are always in the minority. "The way is narrow which leads to life, and few there be who find it," said Jesus. Nominal Christians always need to be evangelized in the hope that some may be converted.

And so the young soldiers of the cross set out, travelling from one Catholic village to another. They went from house to house inviting the people to their meetings, and the Lord blessed their work. In each village there were those who found the Lord Jesus Christ as their Saviour. But this stirred up the anger of the leading men in the villages, and a form of denominational hatred broke out — a hatred which never comes from above, but from below.

After a campaign lasting for several weeks the group decided to return home. One of them, however, we can call him Stephen, said to his friends, "Last night the Lord told me that I must continue working here on my own. I must stay and evangelize the area more." The other Christians respected his decision, and so, after a long period of prayer together, they finally parted. Nevertheless, although they left their brother behind, they continued to remember him in their prayers.

In his subsequent ministry, Stephen received confirmation that his decision had been in line with the will of God, and the Lord used him mightily in his service.

According to the local by-laws, Stephen had to inform the mayor of each village of his presence before he could start his work. In one of the border villages the elders called the local council together. After a lengthy discussion in a dialect which Stephen could not understand, they called for six men who, they told him, were to accompany him to the next village. After leaving the village and walking for a distance of about three miles, Stephen sensed an evil force about him. Stopping, he raised his hands into the air and started to pray. There was a flash as one of the six men struck at him with a bush knife, cutting off the fingers of his praying hands. A second blow followed which severed a hand from one of his arms. Stephen sank momentarily to the ground. Then with renewed strength he raised his bloody stump into the sky and started praying again. At this moment a third blow struck the back of his neck killing him instantly. His body was then dragged into the bush and hastily covered with earth.

But the murder could not be hidden. Before the day was out the whole village knew. Summoning the villagers therefore, the mayor explained to them that the reason Stephen had been killed was because he had been a Communist. He went on to warn them, saying, "If anyone talks about this outside the village, he'll be killed. No one else is to know what has happened."

However, in spite of the warning, within a few days an account of the crime reached the police station in the nearest town. The note included not only a sketch of the place where the body was hidden, but also the names of all those who had taken part in the assassination. The message had been left unsigned; it would have been too dangerous to have done otherwise.

From the information they had received, the police soon found the body of the murdered missionary. Since the crime had been instigated by the Catholics, the Protestant police president ordered six Protestant policemen to take part in the arrests and so prevent the people involved escaping. At sunrise the next day the police surrounded the mayor's house. They told him to summon all who had either planned or taken part in the crime. In this way everyone involved was arrested and, together with the mayor, imprisoned in the district jail. At the time of writing they were still awaiting trial.

In their confessions, the murderers described their crime minutely and claimed that they had been urged to commit the murder on religious grounds by the village elders.

The most significant thing for the Christians, however, was not so much the confessions of those involved, as the actual circumstances surrounding Stephen's death. As he had been cut down by the knives of those accompanying him, not one cry of pain had crossed his lips. With no thought of revenge in his mind he had departed to be with his Lord in a spirit of prayer and utter peace, content to know that his Saviour had counted him worthy of suffering for His sake.

And so another martyr has been added to the list in South East Asia. But the seed will surely bear fruit, as it did with that other Stephen who was stoned to death outside the walls of Jerusalem so long ago. "Lord, do not hold this sin against them", must surely have been the cry of both.

When Stephen's body was finally recovered, a small sensation ensued. Although the feet had remained exposed in the hastily dug grave, the process of decomposition was not so far advanced as is usually the case in the hot tropical climate of the country. This news soon spread around the Catholic village and many of the people began to beat their breasts, saying, "We have killed a saint, we have killed a saint."

V. IN THE INDONESIAN REVIVAL AREA A SECOND TIME

Supernatural Food

I was first able to visit this area in which the fire of God has been lit in 1968. Ever since that time my heart has longed after the work which God is currently doing in Indonesia.

In the spring of 1969 I had the great joy of being together with Pak Elias and David Simeon when they visited Germany and spoke at the meetings I had arranged for them in Stuttgart and Bretten. Although on both occasions there was insufficient room in the actual meeting places for all those who had come to listen to the messages, it was a source of even greater joy when Pak Elias told me that he would be willing to accompany me to the centre of the revival area on Timor later in the year. I find it almost impossible to put into words the events I have subsequently been able to witness and experience, and apart from my own conversion in 1930, I look upon this second visit to the Indonesian revival area as the greatest spiritual event of my life.

As a prelude to our trip I was able to participate in yet another Christian conference in East Java. Daily the people present were brought face to face with the Lord Jesus. The climax was reached at the valedictory service at the end of the conference which lasted for nine and a quarter hours.

In Europe three hours would have been quite enough for me at any meeting. Yet the strange thing was, even after nine hours I was neither tired nor exhausted. In fact I was rather quickened. David Simeon and his brother talked with me after the meeting, and I commented to them about this fact. "It's the spiritual atmosphere," I said. "There's a complete difference between an atmosphere which drains your strength away and one which renews it. In the West, many missionary conferences, instead of quickening a person, have an atmosphere about them which leaves one exhausted afterwards."

In the revival area, the believers attending these conference meetings, which can last anything up to ten or even twelve hours a day, are supplied with a spiritual manna by God's angels themselves. It is true that we know from the Bible that things of this nature have happened in the past, but today their occurrence is rare. Timor, however, is an exception.

Natural Food

One of the people I was privileged to meet on Timor was Philip, who was also a native of this island. A spiritual atmosphere seemed to radiate from this humble and simple servant of Christ. I was unable to obtain his story from himself, since, like many of the islanders, he spoke little about his own experiences but rather of the Lord. His friends and fellow workers, however, had some tremendous stories to tell. Philip is the leader of Team 36. On one occasion when he arrived at a village with ten of his team members, intending to hold a mission there, he was met by the minister of the local Reformed church and told, "It's no use staying here, the village is very poor, and there is simply not enough food for you and your friends."

The team was driven to prayer, and they asked their Lord, "Lord, are we to stay here, or to move on?" "I have brought you," replied the Lord, "and so I will supply your needs while you stay."

Next morning, very early, they commenced their first meeting which lasted until 3 o'clock in the afternoon. By then the young missionaries were feeling hungry, for they had had nothing to eat since the previous day. Turning to the Lord again in prayer they asked Him to take care of their needs. "Fetch the minister and the local elders and leading Christians together," the Lord commanded them. They obeyed, and subsequently 39 of the local Christians gathered with them to pray. Suddenly they had a vision, and they saw before them a table spread with a white cloth and covered with foods of every sort. Everyone of the fifty people present saw the same vision. Next some hands appeared which distributed the food richly among them. It was then that the real miracle took place. They found that as they put the food into their mouths they really had something to chew. It was now real. That evening the experience was repeated, and during the three days in which the team stayed at the village, the miracle was repeated on altogether eight different occasions. The local minister, the church elders, and other leading Christians in the area, as well as the eleven members of the team, were all witnesses of this event.

We have in the Bible a record of the feeding of the four

and the five thousand. Now from Timor comes the feeding of the fifty. But there are other examples of how the Lord has supplied the daily bread of his messengers.

Neither the rationalists nor the modernists of today will be able to accept what is to follow. However, in this instance it is not their opinion that really matters, for their attitude leads them to reject every miraculous event recorded in the Bible and elsewhere. The only advice I can give such people is, "Come and see for yourselves." The reason for my own visit to Timor was in order that I too might be able to share in the Lord's revelation of himself there, and if God so will, this will not have been my last visit to the area. It is true that one is able to feel the Lord's presence in every corner of this world if one has surrendered one's life to him, but Timor has become a present day 'mount of transfiguration'.

The Wine of God

We now come to a series of miracles which are astounding Christians throughout the world. At the time of writing, the miracle which occurred first at Cana in Galilee has been repeated on Timor already on eight occasions.

We will turn first of all to a first-hand account from the leader of the church in the central region of the island. Pastor Joseph is a member of the Reformed church and received his theological training in the West. During the conference in July 1969 he gave a complete account of the events as they had happened, before a group of some 120 missionaries and students drawn from all four continents. The day was in fact July 12th. I was personally present at the time and afterwards received a translation of his report in English. Such details as these are necessary since the events we are about to describe are truly stupendous. I have actually preached now on several occasions in the church in Soe where the miracle occurred, and have ascertained that the facts stand up to investigation. But now let us listen to the report of Superintendent Joseph himself.

No vines grow on the island of Timor, and so wine made from grapes just does not exist there. The importing of wine is also impossible on account of the extreme poverty of the island's inhabitants. However, there exists a form of palm-wine to which many of the natives are addicted on account of its high alcoholic content. Before the revival there was indeed much alcoholism on the island, but as the Spirit of God took hold of the people many of them broke their wine and spirit flasks and gave up their evil habit. In addition to this many of the stalls at which alcohol was sold were also smashed to pieces. Everyone of the converts on Timor renounced his habit of drinking palm-wine.

This, however, raised some serious problems in the life of the church. The Reformed Church had always used palm-wine during its communion services. Since therefore the churches were regularly pervaded with the smell of alcohol when they celebrated communion, the custom was a great source of temptation to those who had been freed from their alcoholism. Moreover, drunkards outside the church used this as an excuse for continuing with their habit. "If the church agrees with drinking palm-wine," they said, "it can't be a sin to drink alcohol, and so we don't have to confine our own drinking to the church."

The believers prayed for a solution, and the Lord was soon to reply. On the 9th September 1967 one of the Christian women heard the Lord's voice say to her, "I will change water into wine at the communion service in October." This prophecy was repeated again on the 13th and the 17th of September. The woman, who was a member of one of the evangelistic teams, conveyed the message to the leading Christians in the area. And so, as the day of the communion service approached, some vessels were filled with water and prayed over by the Christians. Then the miracle happened, and the church in Soe experienced its first miracle of water being changed into wine on the 5th October 1967. Superintendent Joseph was actually present at the time.

In December 1967 the miracle was repeated at the next communion service. The Lord again announced the forthcoming miracle some weeks before it was to take place. On each occasion he chose a different team to pray for the water before the change occurred.

Superintendent Joseph went on to say that up till the time of his giving his report, the miracle had occurred at every single communion service they had held since the first miraculous service in October 1967. As I have said, this amounted in all to eight occasions.

On the 7th December 1968 Pak Elias and his wife were also both present at one of these communion services when the miracle took place. He told me that at the time he felt so wretched inside that he had to confess his sins all over again although he knew the Lord had already forgiven him once.

Following one of these communion services, two bottles of wine were left over. As the time for the next service approached it was announced that teams number 4 and 11 were to participate in the fresh miracle, and seven bottles of water would be required. However, since only five bottles were available at the time, Joseph agreed that one of the Christians should empty both the full bottles and use them. When the brother had done this, he returned home only to find his own wife lying on the floor suffering from a severe haemorrhage. She had vomited about the same amount of blood as he had emptied wine from the bottles. Kneeling beside his wife he prayed for her healing. He then hurried to see Superintendent Joseph and told him what had happened. Calling the elders of the church together, they returned quickly to the man's house and prayed over his sick wife. She then recovered.

After this experience the men asked the Lord, "If you don't want us to empty out your wine, what do you want us to do with it?" They were told in reply that the wine should be used for the healing of any who were sick, and in particular for those who were suffering from anaemia. The Christians obeyed.

As a result of this distribution of the wine to the sick, it was discovered that when the wine was left to stand it gradually went sour. It remained dry for about the first week, but by the fourth week it would be completely sour. This fact is reminiscent of the story of the manna the children of Israel received in the wilderness which began to stink when it was kept longer than was necessary.

Many of the missionaries who heard the report of Superintendent Joseph naturally asked, "Was it really wine or was it just the juice of crushed grapes as certain Christian teetotalers believe?" The answer is quite illuminating. It was neither — nor! The wine tastes and smells like genuine wine, and yet it contains no alcohol. Perhaps this will end the quarrel between those whose opinions differ on the matter. Both sides are wrong, and both sides are right. One wonders how many of the theological problems that trouble us will be answered in the same way.

Western theologians will find this recurrence of the miracle of Cana in Galilee almost scandalous. Many of them have already rejected the miracles of the Bible, and will therefore be quite unable to understand the present events taking place on Timor. The accounts written here will simply be explained away as mere fanaticism. But this is understandable. Five years ago, if I had suddenly been faced with reports of this nature, I too would have refused to believe them. I can therefore sympathize with the person who has genuine doubts. However, the problem of doubts can soon be solved. One can visit the centre of the revival in Soe whenever one wants to. The reported events can therefore be checked, and perhaps, if the Lord will, even experienced for oneself.

Yet the revival church in Soe is by no means a mere tourist attraction. No one can approach the table of the Lord if he is unwilling to follow the Lord. And besides, the curiosity and sometimes deceit of those who visit the area can be dealt with quite embarrassingly. Anyone arriving here with some unforgiven sin on his conscience, or with deceit or an impenitent attitude in his heart, can, under certain circumstances, find that his secret sins are exposed and brought into the light. The Lord quite often gives a member of one of the teams a message for some unrepentant person present, which can strike right home to the person's heart.

VI. I AM A WITNESS

How unworthy I am! I have often robbed the Lord of the glory due to his own name and have been disobedient at times, and have often gone my own way. O, how my service for the kingdom of heaven accuses me! And yet I, too, have been a witness. God's mercy is beyond our understanding. I have witnessed the changing of water into wine.

Following the believers conference in East Java, an international team set out under the leadership of Pak Elias to visit the actual revival area in Indonesia. In addition to our leader, our team included three professors from Japan and Pakistan, as well as a young American missionary. We represented altogether five different nations, and were in fact the very first international team to have the privilege of becoming acquainted with the centre of the revival area. It was a moving experience to be permitted to take part in this tour. Pak Elias said to me, "You are the first visitor from Germany to have experienced the things you are now seeing taking place."

I can only repeat: this is a privilege I have neither earned nor deserved.

We finally reached Soe on the 16th July 1969. The journey had utterly exhausted us. The road conditions out here are simply inconceivable to people living in either Britain or Germany. Although we arrived several hours late, we discovered that the members of the church had waited for four hours to welcome us into their midst.

During the next few days we went from one meeting to another. Some meetings lasted for as much as twelve hours a day and thereby illustrated the type of spiritual appetite the local people must have to be able to absorb and digest so much spiritual food.

During our stay on the island, in company with the whole church, we were privileged to witness the changing of water into wine on two separate occasions. These were the ninth and tenth occasions on which the miracle had taken place. Can anyone imagine what it is like to be considered worthy to stand in the very presence of God?

Superintendent Joseph told us that the Lord had informed him six weeks previously that the coming international team would be celebrating the communion service with the church in Soe. But six weeks ago the team had not even been thought of. It had only been formed two days before our actual visit at the believers conference I have already mentioned, and then only after much prayer.

On July 5th a group of twelve men and women were commanded by the Lord to pray for the changing of the water into wine. Six women were given the task of fetching the water from the well the Lord had indicated. The water was then poured into a large vessel in the presence of 18 Christians, and covered with a piece of cloth. On Friday the 18th July at 12 o'clock the Lord told them that the transformation had taken place. Taking the cloth off the vessel they found it was true — the water was now wine. When I saw the amount of wine that there was, I said to one of the leading brothers, "That won't be enough for the 700 or 800 people coming to the communion service." He agreed, but went on to say, "We will just have to wait for further instructions from the Lord." On Saturday at 10 o'clock in the morning the Lord gave the required instructions: "Meet together tomorrow morning at 4 o'clock, draw some water out of the well I show you, and pray for the water until 7 o'clock." They obeyed. Next morning at seven the extra water had again been changed into wine in the presence of eighteen witnesses.

Whenever the miracle occurs the Lord directs a different person or group of persons to fetch the water and to pray for its change. In this way the wonderful privilege is shared. Moreover, on each occasion of the miracle the Lord has directed that the communion service be held at a different location. The miracles are thereby experienced by the whole church, and no one knows beforehand who is to be chosen next to participate.

A number of problems are raised, however, by this miracle. It is not difficult to imagine, for example, the kind of objection that one will meet from the rationalists. But the phenomenon is not one of mass hypnosis. Neither is it a question of trickery or fraud. Those involved have included the local pastors, the local doctor and magistrate, and even the governor of the district who has in fact only recently become a Christian himself. We will be hearing his own story very soon.

I can understand the genuine queries that will arise in the minds of even Christians. Humanly speaking I know miracles are incomprehensible, and even the simple inhabitants of the island have doubted at times. When, however, one Christian woman actually expressed her disbelief, on the occasion of the next miracle the Lord commanded her to be present when the water was drawn from the well, and that she should stay by the water until the miracle had taken place. Thus, with her own eyes, she saw the water change into wine. Falling to the ground, she begged the Lord to forgive her unbelief. One of the brothers told me his own story: After the occasion of the first miracle he had expressed his doubt and said, "If the miracle really happened, I'll give away my own cow." Imagine his surprise when on the next occasion the Lord directed that he should be the one to draw the water. Going to the designated well, hardly had he poured the water into the vessel he had with him, than he smelt the odour of wine. Looking down he saw that the water had already become wine. Placing the vessel on the ground, he knelt down and begged for the Lord's forgiveness.

It is quite remarkable to see how detailed the Lord's instructions are with regard to the execution of this miracle. The obedience of those involved is absolutely essential. Once the Lord sent six Christians out to fetch water without telling them which well to go to. Outside the village they were suddenly commanded to stand still. "Lift up that stone," they were told. They obeyed, and there they found a spring of water with which to fill their vessels. By the following day, however, the spring had dried up again.

Another time the 18 people who were praying were ordered to take the wine to Pastor Micah. Arriving at his house and being met by his wife they quite naturally gave the wine to her, asking her to pass it on to her husband. Although their disobedience had been only slight, the wine changed back into water once more. They consequently had to fast and to pray for another three days before the Lord wrought the miracle a second time.

On the ninth occasion of the changing of water into wine at which I was also present, the Lord directed a group of 12 people to begin fasting two weeks before the actual communion service was to be held. During this time the Lord allowed them to eat only half a banana a day, together with just a table-spoon full of rice and half a glass of water to drink. Relying on this meagre ration the Lord commanded them to pray for several hours each morning before setting out to work. This frugal diet, however, resulted in much blessing.

On Sunday, July 20th, we celebrated the much longed for communion service. Some 600 Christians from the surrounding district took part. I have never in my life experienced such a feast of the Lord. Who can comprehend the joy we had of being able to sit at the table of the Lord which had been decked with his very own wine? The taste remained in my mouth a full ten minutes after I had partaken of the cup.

What is the actual significance of this miracle? One thing it definitely is not, and that is a mere sensation. Basically it is a means by which the Lord is aiding these poor Christian folk who have never even tasted fruit juice, let alone wine. It must never be forgotten, however, that the changing of a man's heart is a far greater miracle than the changing of water into wine. There are greater gifts than the gift of miracles, Jesus himself being the greatest of God's gifts to this world. Indeed, his incarnation, atonement, resurrection, ascension and coming again, are all greater gifts than the gift of water being changed to wine. The salvation of a soul is greater than the quenching of the body's thirst. And besides, our faith is not founded upon miracles such as these, but rather upon the Lord Jesus Christ and the promises of God. If we can but grasp this fact, then the way will be open for us to rejoice aright in the fact that the Lord is presencing himself with us in the 20th century and is exhibiting the same power and the same glory as he revealed during his actual earthly life nearly 2,000 years ago. It is indeed marvellous to find that God is still working miracles in a day in which the theologians of the Western world are erasing the selfsame miracles from the pages of the Bible, attributing them instead to the myths of Greece and Rome. However, the present events in Indonesia are not a myth, but rather a direct revelation of the power of the Lord himself.

This miracle of changing water into wine has yet another meaning though. When Jesus came to Cana in Galilee he stood at the threshold of his miraculous ministry. The miracle described in John chapter 2 was the first of the signs that Jesus did in Galilee, and it was not by chance that it took place at a wedding feast. The coming of the Messiah is a time of great festivity and joy. In the same way Christ's second coming for his Church, and the future hope of the marriage feast of the Lamb, is the greatest and most joyful event we have to look forward to. This present day miracle is therefore of an eschatological nature. The 'marriage feast' is at hand. The Lord is at the doors. Both the Lord's first and second coming are to be introduced with a time of great joy, and it is this joy that Christians are experiencing already in the revival area in Indonesia. In fact many of the prophecies uttered there point to the nearness of the Lord's return. It is entirely possible that this miracle of water being changed into wine will continue to occur in the revival area until He appears. But now a further story that will shed even more light on this 20th century miracle.

VII. MOTHER LI

Mother Li was first called by the Lord on the 17th November 1965. She was told, "You must go to New Guinea and preach the gospel there." Mother Li replied, "But Lord, I'm uneducated. Can't you send two of my sons instead?" She had in the back of her mind the request which the mother of the two sons of Zebedee had made to the Lord in Matthew 20:20. Accepting her prayer in part, the Lord postponed her call till later.

Mother Li is the mother of eleven children. To have obeyed the Lord's command immediately would have been fraught with many difficulties. But perhaps this had not been the Lord's intention. Indeed, when he had first spoken to her he had fixed no date as to when she should go. I can illustrate this from my own experience. About 40 years ago the Lord called me and said to me, "Go into all the world and preach the gospel to every creature" (Mark 16:15). However, I had to wait 25 years until this commission was fulfilled. But then, suddenly, every door seemed to open at once and since that time I have been able to visit, in a missionary capacity, over 100 different countries and to preach the gospel on every continent of the world.

And so, this simple Christian woman had to wait. In 1967 her husband died. But even this may have been part of God's plan, for the man may have been unwilling to allow his wife to leave their eleven children and travel to a distant land as a missionary. In the meantime the Lord answered her prayer concerning her sons, and it will not be long now before the two sons will have completed their missionary training and become missionaries in their own right. However, the Lord did not go back on his original command. In spite of the fact that she is now 47 years old, He called her again and said to her, "Next year you must preach my Word in Java. After that I will send you to New Guinea as I promised." If one were to meet this utterly simple native woman it would almost be impossible to believe that she could fulfill such a missionary task. However, one has to learn an important lesson when in the revival area, for the Lord often seeks to use the humblest of people to fulfill the greatest of his tasks. Spiritual authority comes not as the result of possessing outstanding spiritual gifts, but rather through obedience.

The period of waiting did not pass in vain. The Lord gave Mother Li two specific charges to fulfill. First of all he called her to be the leader of the prayer group which was to pray for the changing of the water into wine at the communion services. She was told that she would lead this group from April 1968 until December 1970. After that time the Lord promised to call someone else to take on this job, although she was told that she would still remain a member of the group. In addition the Lord promised that He would work this miracle at every communion service during her time of office, which amounted to a total of four communion services each year — two for each church. This was a tremendous promise, particularly in view of the fact that many Christians from the Western world are making great efforts to visit the centre of the revival area. Yet tourists who come out of curiosity will have little chance of experiencing these great events, for the Lord seeks out his own for himself.

The second commission she received referred to the settling of disputes among the pastors of the churches and the churches themselves. Mother Li thereby became the leader of the Peace Team.

Her first job was to reconcile two of the pastors who had been at enmity with one another for over nine years. A reconciliation had already been attempted by the president of the National Council of Churches, but this had failed. In spite of making a long and difficult journey in an attempt to bring the two antagonists together, he had had no success in his mission. When Mother Li arrived to see them, however, the Lord gave her the authority to act as peacemaker between them, and the two men were reconciled. Travelling continually by foot, Mother Li has journeyed from one end of the island to the other, reconciling pastors and elders and other Christians to each other, as the Lord has directed her.

At the conference we attended I failed to notice this simple woman among the many other people present. However, a few hours before my departure she came up to me and handed me a woven mat to remember her by. This expression of love from such a simple handmaid of the Lord impressed me greatly, and I later discovered just how much time it took a person to make one of these mats. They first of all have to obtain the threads from certain roots and bark. These they then spin, colouring them with natural dyes made from berries and other plants. Next the weaving begins, but they possess no complicated weaver's loom to help them with their work. Pak Elias, having grown up in this part of the world, told me, "It takes anything up to six months for a person to make a table cloth out here." One can see therefore the actual worth of one of these seemingly insignificant pieces of cloth. And yet I was presented with altogether three such cloths by the Christians out there. I felt quite ashamed. Yet the love of Christ has truly entered into the hearts of these people, and of this we will now hear further.

VIII. THE LOVE OF CHRIST

The revival expresses itself in two ways in the lives of the people it touches. It stirs up a deep love for Christ on the one hand, and a sincere love of one's neighbour on the other. The 150 evangelistic teams have fulfilled the commission of Luke 9:3 to the letter, and have gone out without bag, without purse, without money, and without food. They have as a result had to put up with many hardships, but nothing has daunted them in their resolve. At Soe during a conference there, I was able to witness at first hand the frugality of the 43 teams present at the time. The 250 or so people who attended the conference expressed not the slightest anxiety concerning what they should eat or where they should sleep. In fact, because of the insufficient room in the houses many of them slept under the trees at night, and this included not only team members but also many other Christians from all over the island. Their love for Christ made them oblivious to every hardship, and they lived together willingly in a state of true poverty. Each morning they would meet before sunrise to pray for their daily bread, little knowing just how their Lord would supply their needs. It was extremely moving to listen to one of the Christians, Pak O., as he wept at a church meeting and begged the Lord to take care of these faithful messengers of the cross.

As we have said, the second fruit of this outpouring of the Holy Spirit is a love of the brethren. This love rests upon every single relationship on the island. Instead of the strife which once existed, neighbouring families now meet together between five and six in the morning to pray and to read the Word of God. Walking through the village at sunrise one can hear the sound of these family devotions coming from every quarter as the people sing praises and pray in loud voices to their Lord. Even the police have felt the effect of this change. For years the government endeavoured to put an end to the heavy drinking and fighting which existed on the island, but without success. However, since the revival broke out all this has ended. Where the people sing to the Lord, the spirits of darkness flee.

This selflessness and love has taken on forms which I have never seen in the Western world, and its strength and purity is almost unique. As the hundreds of visitors poured in from the outlying districts, hospitality was offered to them as freely as it was possible. In one particular home for example, with only a thatched roof over our heads, some 40 guests were catered for in a single day. On other occasions I twice counted some 30 to 35 people in the house, and the very minimum number present was always nine or ten. The words of Acts 4:32 apply literally to these people: "Now the company of those who believed were of one heart and one soul, and no one said that any of the things which he possessed was his own, but they had everything in common."

I was able to talk once to the father of a family with whom our international team stayed for a whole week.

In addition to ourselves, they had welcomed other visitors into their home each day we had been there, in spite of having six children of their own to feed. Since the father had only a very minor office job from which to obtain his income, we asked them what the secret of their scriptural mathematics was, which could make so little stretch so far. In their answer they told us of the way in which the Lord had led them to himself, and how they had both been wonderfully saved when the revival had first broken out. The wife had been the daughter of a minister. Her father, however, had died when she had been only three years old. Although she had grown up in the traditions of the church, she had never come to know the Lord Jesus personally. When the spirit of the revival had swept across the island, she had been caught up in its power and had finally confessed her sins and accepted the Lord as her own Saviour. Following this, she now started to pray for the conversion of her husband who was an officer in the airforce at the time. Under President Sukarno he had flown in many missions during the time of the uprising in Celebes, and had been responsible for the deaths of many people. But then the revival arrived and many of the natives began to turn to the Lord for salvation. Prevented by pride, he sought to avoid his own conversion. However, the Lord struck the officer down with a severe illness. He developed a dangerous boil which can sometimes have fatal consequences in the tropics. The doctor informed him, "If the boil bursts internally it will kill you. If it bursts on the outside you will live." His wife, who had prayed a great deal for his spiritual welfare, begged a believing pastor to come and see him. The Christian brother prayed with the patient in accordance with James 5 : 14. The very next day the boil burst externally, and soon the officer was completely healed. As a result of this experience the officer was finally converted. Not wishing to remain in the airforce for fear of having to kill more people, he took his opportunity and left, taking up a poorly paid position in an office instead. And so today, receiving just a minimal wage each week, he acts as host to the many messengers of Christ who arrive in the town. His house is in fact a focal point of missionaries and evangelists. But what of the secret of their daily provisions? His wife told us, "The more we give to the Lord and to his servants, the more blessings we receive in return. We find that the giving of hospitality leaves us not with less, but with more than we started with." The Lord will accept nothing from us without repaying a hundred-fold.

IX. KUSA NOPE

Kusa Nope is the fourteenth member of a line of kings which has ruled in Timor for many generations. Up till the year 1948 he had continued to hold the title of King of Amanuban. Then, after the departure of the Dutch colonial powers, he had been elected governor of the district of Soe. However, the people had continued to address him as king just as before, and his appearance and behaviour made this title well-deserved. Before we go on to say anything more about him, let us first listen to his own testimony of his conversion. Although I have had the opportunity of meeting three different kings from Africa and Asia during my life, it was Kusa Nope who made the greatest impression on me through our almost daily contact with him during our stay in the district under his administration.

"I was born in 1910 and spent my early school years in Soe. My mother often used to send me to the Sunday school of the local church, but I understood little of what they taught me there. Later I attended the high school in K., and then continued my studies in Makassar on the island of Celebes. The only reason I carried on going to church there was to keep up appearances with my friends. I didn't want them to think I was a heathen. However, when my friends themselves began to stay away from church, I soon followed suit. At the outbreak of the Second World War I returned again to Soe. I was even baptised at the time, yet I was still not a real Christian. The only aim I had was to earn a lot of money, and to attain a high position in life. I just didn't think about Jesus at the time. At first it seemed that everything was working against me, and I had a lot of trouble with the government, with my friends, and even with my own family. Yet I had to overcome all these problems alone and without the help of Jesus.

In 1967, however, a mission was held in Soe. It was then that I first surrendered my life to Christ. A short while later a simple native Christian woman came to me with a message from the Lord saying, "You have got 18 fetishes in your palace at N. as well as many others at your sacrificial site on the mountain of Tonbis. You must destroy them all." At the time I was so busy that I soon forgot all about her message. Inwardly, I suppose, I just did not want to obey. Later, when I did in fact have a little space in which to breathe, I was invited to attend a congress of the government which delayed my obedience further. On returning to Soe I became very ill and had to go to the hospital in K. for treatment. After keeping me under observation for some three weeks the doctor advised me to travel across to Java to receive further treatment at one of the university clinics found there. At the time I had a blood pressure of 230, as well as many other complaints. That same night the Lord spoke to me and said, "Do not go to Java. Return home to Soe instead." When I saw the doctor the next morning and told him of my decision he merely shook his head. However, in the meantime I had become convinced that the illness was from the Lord, and that it had resulted from my not having obeyed his commands concerning the fetishes. Back at Soe the Lord finally brought me to the place where I was prepared to destroy all my objects of sorcery. Together with a team of 70 believers we decided to climb up to the sacrificial site on the mountain of Tonbis. I was so weak that in the end I had to be carried. When we did finally reach the site we proceeded to destroy all the fetishes.

Following this we next renamed the mountain, Horeb, calling the neighbouring mountain, Mount Zion, as the Lord had directed us to do. I felt convinced that when the fetishes had been destroyed I would at once get better, but this was not to be. I asked the Lord therefore if I was still to go to Java for treatment. "No," was his reply, "go back to your office and work." This seemed very strange at the time for I was still very weak, but in those days I had to learn the important lesson that one has to believe without seeing, and to obey without questioning. After much hesitation, however, I went along to my office again. The people there were quite astonished to see me arrive for I had lost some 30 pounds in weight since last I had been there. Yet now I was back at work my strength quickly returned and I was completely healed. The most difficult aspect of all these trials was the learning of obedience. It is only through Jesus, and through obedience to him that one can find any form of fulfillment in this life."

Having heard the testimony of the king himself I would like to go on now and fill in some of the details behind his story.

When our international team originally arrived at the airport in K., Kusa Nope was already there waiting to meet us. Pak Elias turned to me and asked, "Have you ever heard of a king meeting an evangelist at an airport before?" The king, who we discovered was an extremely humble brother in Christ, sacrificed two whole days in order to be able to accompany us on our six hour journey from K. to Soe. Only those who have travelled along these roads can understand what a sacrifice this really was. On our way we suddenly came upon a bus bearing the name 'Horeb'. Stopping, we learned that not only had Kusa Nope renamed the two mountains with the names the Lord had told him, but he had given two of his buses these names as well.

After our arrival in Soe we were twice invited to be the guests of the royal family. In addition to this the king himself attended the conference meetings almost every day. When it was finally time for us to leave, he again ordered some cars to drive us back to K. The next day we found yet another car, complete with a chauffeur, waiting to drive us wherever we wanted to go. The impression received by all the members of our team was that here was a king who was also a brother in the Lord.

While I was in the area I was able to hear the report of the 70 believers who had accompanied Kusa Nope to the top of the mountain of Tonbis. The actual destruction of the sacrificial site had been a veritable battle against the powers of darkness. The following paragraphs contain a short account of the events as they actually took place.

The kings of Amanuban have been in possession of a sacrificial site on the mountain for hundreds of years. Some 300 years ago one of the princesses was sacrificed at this very spot. The idols rewarded the people greatly for their worship, and the forefathers of Kusa Nope had been able to fulfill almost every desire they had had at this altar of sacrifice. Yet events of this nature are almost inconceivable to Westerners, who usually banish them to the realms of myths and fairy stories.

When the team arrived at the site, the Lord showed them that there were over a hundred different fetishes hidden there. Even Kusa Nope himself had not known just how many occult objects they would find. At first the Lord had told the eight team leaders to stand in pairs at the four points of the compass. He had indicated next that the members of the king's family should stand in the middle of this square, with the 62 other team members standing around them in a circle. The fetishes themselves were brought from their hiding places and put in a heap. They all now began to pray together and to sing hymns of victory to the Lord. At that moment the eight team leaders suddenly found themselves being physically attacked by some ghost-like figures. They were seized by the arms and at the same time heard voices asking them, "Why are you trying to drive us away from this place? We have a right to be here." To this the leaders replied, "We are doing this on the authority of the Lord Jesus. We don't come in our own name." On hearing this the figures suddenly rushed away through the trees, knocking some down as they went. As they watched them leave, the team leaders saw them change into what looked like bulls and rams.

The team was now told by the Lord to stand in the form of a cross. Twelve of the elders of the former heathen tribe and twelve elders of the Christian church were made to form the central beam, while the eight team leaders had to form the cross-piece. They then started to pray and to command the powers in the name of Jesus to leave the sacrificial site and not return again. At the same time a great fire was lit and the fetishes were thrown into it and burnt. Those which could not be burnt were broken into pieces and thrown away. To me it was very significant, however, to find that the Lord had said to them at the time, "Do not simply destroy the fetishes and charms, but pray a prayer of renunciation over each of the articles beforehand."

Everyone of the 70 team members was a witness to these events. Later, however, three other fetishes were destroyed, but this time only in the presence of one other Christian worker.

And so the ban over the life of the king was broken, a ban which had affected the whole of the royal family. The result of this was a feeling of complete liberation. As governor of the district the king today holds a monthly prayer meeting with his 80 fellow officials, during which time he reads the Bible aloud and joins with them in prayer. They also meet together in a similar way each Saturday at midday after the week's work has ended.

Governors in Indonesia are elected to office every four years. At the last election there were naturally many people who opposed the re-election of Kusa Nope. Neither the non-Christians nor the Moslems were happy with his being governor. However, the Lord spoke to him one day and said, "Do not fear, for you shall be re-elected. I have placed you in this office to fulfill what I have purposed." And so the promise was fulfilled. The Lord has in fact often conveyed his wishes to the king, sometimes using one of the team leaders to pass his message on. For example, I was sitting in his home one day when a very simple Christian woman arrived with a message from the Lord referring to his actual administration.

This is true also of the pastors of the local church. Occasionally one of the church members has been given the text on which his pastor should speak. In fact on some occasions the actual church services have been interrupted for the purpose of passing on a message. Once when Pak Elias himself was preaching in Soe, a woman who was filled with the Holy Spirit stood up and interrupted him while he was actually speaking. Yet in all these circumstances the Lord's discipline continues to reign supreme. Up till now there has been no sign of the lack of restraint which is so often found among members of the extreme sects. And yet this is almost sure to come. Every revival seems to boil over in the end. It is basically a question of whether or not the people involved will continue to accept the discipline and correction of their fellow believers and the Word of God.

It is the duty of Christians throughout the world to pray and to intercede for this revival, that it may continue along a pathway ordained by God. We should also pray for the leaders of the churches and for the king himself,

that God will keep their spirits humble and will use
them in the service of their fellow countrymen.

X. A GOVERNMENT OFFICIAL BY THE GRACE
OF GOD

Nathan is the secretary of the government in Soe. I was
able to meet him on two occasions, once in East Java and
the second time on Timor itself. The impression Nathan
makes on one is unforgettable. His life is a testimony
in itself, and a person can be blessed by meeting him
without a word being spoken at all. Indeed I have experienced this myself. He is one of those few people in
whom the image of Christ has already been formed.
One of the missionaries, who like myself attended the
conference in Java, said of him, "Of all the tremendous
testimonies we have heard, Nathan's impressed me most."

Nathan based his brief report on the words of Isaiah
57 : 15 which read, "For thus says the high and lofty One
who inhabits eternity, whose name is Holy; I dwell in
the high and holy place, and also with him who is of a
contrite and humble spirit, to revive the spirit of the
humble, and to revive the heart of the contrite."

One of the secrets of the revival is the humility of
the believers involved. In the other revival areas of the
world, in Korea, Uganda, and Taiwan, although the same
is true to a certain extent, it appeared more noticeable
to me on Timor. The Christians there possess truly broken
and contrite and humble hearts. In one's fellowship with
them one feels as if one is covered with filth from head
to foot. This feeling of unworthiness is so great that one
is overwhelmed with a desire to run away and hide.
It seemed so out of place when they asked me one day
to step up into the pulpit and preach the gospel to them.
On several occasions I have felt compelled to say to them,
"No, it's you who must preach to me, not I to you."

However, this feeling of unworthiness is not engendered by the natives themselves, but rather by the Lord who reveals himself so mightily in their lives. While I was staying with them I continually felt as if the eyes of the Lord were looking straight through me. For days it seemed as if Jesus was standing above me and reproaching me for my sins. This was not a vision in the true sense of the word, but rather something that could be recognized with the eye of faith. The only prayer I could think of uttering was, "Dear Lord, if you don't free me from this feeling of despair I will be lost." I resolved in my mind that if it were the Lord's will, this would not be the last visit I made to Soe. And I feel indeed that God would one day have me return.

But now to Nathan's own testimony of the Lord's dealings with him. In 1965 one of the teams on Timor was told by God to make Nathan one of its members. Coming to this senior government official they said to him, "The Lord has told us that you are to join our team." Nathan was a little perplexed; he was old enough to be the team leader's father, and educationally was far superior to him. Was he to subordinate himself to this simple young man? And if he did, what would the authorities say? He told the team of young people he would have to think over what they had said and ask the permission of his superiors as well.

Quite surprisingly the head office gave him its official consent on the 5th October 1965. The government even supplied a car to take the team on the first part of its evangelistic mission. When they were finally dropped by the car in the evening they went on walking until about 11 o'clock that night.

It was during this march that they first experienced the help and the presence of the Lord. For the whole of the time a light shone around them and illuminated their way. Nathan looked up into the sky to see if it was the moon that was causing the shadows, but as yet it was not to be seen. Other evangelistic teams have also experienced this miraculous light on their travels.

As they approached the village they were making for, they found the villagers already coming out to meet them. They were crying and frightened, for they had heard a loud voice speaking to them and telling them to accept the message of the gospel. Meeting together in one of the houses they immediately held their first mission service.

When the team did finally get to bed, it was already well after midnight. Nathan was restless. He kept asking himself, "What's going to happen in the morning? Where are we going to get some food to eat?" It was the dry season at the time, and besides, there was already a shortage of food in the area. Next day, however, when the team met together for prayer, the Lord said to them, "Walk one kilometer out of the village and there I will give you some food." Although Nathan still doubted in his heart, he obeyed the Lord's command with the rest of the team. As they reached a spot exactly one kilometer from the village, they suddenly saw a man coming towards them. They discovered when they began to talk to him that he was an elder of the local church. He was carrying a bottle of palm-juice at the time, and he offered it to the team for them to drink. And so their breakfast had been supplied. In the East when there is a famine, the people are content with far less than their brethren in the West. The young missionaries were inwardly moved by the way in which the Lord had supplied their needs, and they were unable to hold back their tears as they drank the juice that the man had offered them.

On their arrival at the next village the team found shelter in the house of an old man who lived there. Their new host was somewhat worried by the number of his guests. How could he feed nine people when there was a famine in the area? In spite of the fact that the team tried to console him, their words were of no avail.

And so they turned to prayer. However, although the Lord comforted them with the words of Matthew 4 : 4, "Man shall not live by bread alone, but by every word that proceeds from the mouth of God," the old man continued to doubt. Suddenly the second miracle of their daily sustenance occurred: a poor man arrived at the door with some rice and a chicken for the team to eat. With this the spell was broken and the old man began to cry and to repent of his unbelief. The team could only praise their Lord for the richness of his provision for them.

Each day they were confronted with fresh problems concerning their daily bread. Next morning for example, having left the house early in search of something to eat, their host returned later with a sad expression on his face. There was nothing to be found. However, while he was still speaking, two other people arrived with some rice and meat for the guests. With one accord they fell to their knees and thanked their Father in heaven for his daily love towards them. By now Nathan had already repented of his doubts, and yet, as each new miracle occurred, he never ceased to wonder. He noticed that the team made no plans of its own but waited in faith upon the Lord for all its directions. This is true obedience — something which has almost been forgotten in the West. Yet if we would only obey him, no matter what the cost, the Lord would always provide.

The provision of their daily bread was not the only miracle that Nathan witnessed on their evangelistic tour. Indeed this was but a side issue, for the most important aspect was the converting of souls to Christ. In this realm too, the team had many marvellous experiences. As was inevitable, they met with a lot of opposition to their work. In their times of united prayer, however, the Lord would actually show them the faces and the sins of those who sought to oppose them. In this way these young disciples of Christ had already prayed a great deal for their enemies before they had ever met them in the flesh. They were usually told by means of prophecy what problems and difficulties faced them at each village, before they had even arrived there. On entering a new village therefore, the team was often forewarned of the battle that awaited them. The following is an example of this.

In one of the villages the team was called to the bedside of a man who was very ill. One of their basic rules was to pray together for each family before they entered the house. As they were therefore praying for this particular man and his household, the Lord spoke to them and said, "There is a curse upon this family, for the father has stabbed another man through the tongue several times." When the team finally entered the house they confronted the man with the sin that the Lord had told them he had committed. "Will you repent of your sin?" they asked him. "Yes," he replied, "I will." He then went on to confess to them that as a soldier he had once shot a man down and thrust his bayonet through his tongue several times as an act of revenge. By faith the ex-soldier took hold of the forgiveness that exists in Christ, and he surrendered his life to the Lord. It was then that another very interesting fact came to light. After he had committed the crime he had just confessed, his wife had borne him another child. By now the child had reached an age when he should have been able to talk, but when the team saw him they found that he was not even able to utter a single word. Following the repentance and conversion of the father, however, the team prayed for the child under the laying on of hands. Next day the child could speak; the curse had at last been lifted.

As had been happening throughout the revival area, wherever the team went, the villagers would bring their fetishes and charms out of their houses and burn them. It was just like at Ephesus in Acts 19. When the occult ban had been broken many of the villagers accepted the

Lord Jesus as their Saviour, so much so that the glory of God rested on their whole campaign. As Nathan ended his report, he begged for just one thing. "Please, pray for me and for the other Christians on Timor, that we will never become the victims of spiritual pride."

XI. GOD CALLS THROUGH VISIONS

The prophets of the Old Testament were often called by God through a vision at the beginning of their prophetic ministry. Isaiah for example saw the Lord high and lifted up in the temple, while Jeremiah was shown a rod of almond and a boiling pot on the day that the Lord called him into his service. Ezekiel, too, was the recipient of many visions from the Lord. And so we find that in the Old Testament the seeing of visions was closely connected with a person's prophetic ability. The same is true today on the islands of Indonesia. We find that the prophecy of Joel 3 : 1 and Acts 2 : 17 is being fulfilled in our midst: "Your sons and your daughters shall prophesy, and your young men shall see visions, and your old men shall dream dreams." The revival on Timor therefore, has both a prophetic and an eschatological nature, and this is confirmed on almost every occasion a person there is called into the Lord's service. Let us listen for example to the story and testimony of Philip, the leader of team number 36, and a man with whom I was able to enjoy wonderful fellowship when I stayed at his house and listened to the story of his own life.

Philip was called by God on the 12th September 1965. As he went out into his garden at about 5 o'clock in the morning, he suddenly saw a shining figure with long white hair standing some five yards away in front of him. The chickens were so frightened by this visitor that they started flying down from the trees in which they commonly roost on Timor. The dog, too, started barking in alarm. Philip was quite scared and asked himself if what he was seeing was either a nun or the devil. It was well that he asked this question for the strange phenomena of incubi and succubae, about which I have already written in other of my books, occur on Timor also. Quite often for example, the devil will appear to a person in the form of a being of the opposite sex in order to lead him astray. Full of horror Philip ran back to the door of his house only to be met by his cousin who cried, "I've just seen a star fall into the garden." "Where?" Philip asked him urgently. His cousin pointed to the spot where the shining figure had been standing only a moment previously. Philip was now sure that he had not been suffering from a hallucination.

When he had at last calmed down, Philip went out into the garden for a second time and began to water his apple trees. Suddenly he heard a voice say to him, "Water people." Although he thought it was a rather strange thing to hear, he went on with his work and started to do some digging in one corner of the garden. The voice spoke to him again: "Dig the hearts of men." Well, this was even stranger, he thought. How could one dig a man's heart with the crow-bar he held in his hand? It would kill the person! Like many of the islanders he could only understand the meaning of words in their literal sense.

But now the voice went on to explain the meaning of the words he had just heard. "To water people," it explained, "means to give them the water of life, and the water of life is the Word of God. To dig the hearts of men means to renew them with the Holy Spirit. The weeds in the garden are a picture of a person's sins which must be pulled out by the roots, otherwise they will grow again. Pull out the weeds therefore, dry them in the sun and then burn them. When the land has been cleansed, begin to plant, and you will reap much fruit. Remember, the thing that counts is not how nice the stalks look, but rather the type of fruit each stalk bears."

Following his 'spiritual lesson' Philip saw a vision in which he himself was preaching to a crowd of many hundreds of people who were standing in the garden. His message was based on the thirteenth chapter of Luke, and he was talking about the unfruitful fig tree. He noticed that the audience consisted of people from Africa, China, and Europe, as well as soldiers and policemen, and they were all standing listening as if rooted to the spot. He spoke out louder in order to make himself heard by all the people present, but even this was not enough and so he moved nearer to the gate of the garden that others might be able to hear what he was saying. After he had watched himself preach for a total of five hours, the vision disappeared. Instead of the crowd he suddenly found his mother and his brothers standing around him looking at him as if he had gone mad. It was only then that he had noticed how much time had passed. He was covered in sweat.

"Come into the house and have something to eat," his mother begged him. "Man shall not live by bread alone," replied Philip, "but by every word that proceeds from the mouth of God." Up till then Philip had had little contact with either the church or the Bible. He began to tell his family, however, about the vision, and afterwards went into another room and started to pray. It was the first time he had done so for years. Suddenly he saw some white writing in front of him which read, "Read John 14 : 12." Fetching his Bible — he knew no texts off by heart — he read the passage concerned. "What do you mean, Lord?" he asked. "I can't become an evangelist. People like that have to leave their home and lead a very poor type of life."

That night at about 10 while Philip was again praying, he was given his second vision. Two shining figures came up to him and dressed him in a shirt and a pair of trousers, at the same time putting a hat on his head and a sword in his hand. They then told him to read Ephesians

6 : 10 and the following verses. Next they showed him the roads leading to N. and other villages where he would have to go and preach the gospel. This second vison lasted for a total of 12 hours. At 10 o'clock the next morning his mother came into the room and found him still sitting on the stool which he had sat down on the previous evening. He got up, had something to eat, and by eleven o'clock was already dressed and walking towards N. His mother, being a little worried about the whole affair, sent some of his brothers and sisters along with him to keep him company.

Philip felt at peace, and began to sing, "I will follow you, that is peace to me." As he passed people walking the other way, he noticed that they were sweating a great deal in the sun. He realized suddenly that he was not sweating himself and that he was walking in the shade. Looking up he saw a cloud in the sky which was following him as he walked and keeping the sun's rays from off his back. This continued until he had reached N.

While he was walking, however, his obedience was tested on a number of occasions. As a group of people approached him once, a voice said, "Stand still and start to pray." Philip protested, "I'm not a Pharisee." The voice persisted, "Stand still and pray." Philip thought to himself, "Well, I can stand still and pray in my heart with my eyes open." "No," said the voice, "pray aloud." He obeyed. His brothers and sisters became extremely embarrassed and stepped a few yards back from him in alarm. Philip, however, was filled with joy as a result of this obedience, and started on his way again singing. During the fifteen mile journey to N. he had to pass the same test on altogether four occasions.

Arriving at a village where one of his uncles lived, just as he was about to enter his house, the Lord stopped him and said, "You must pray before you enter this house." Although his relatives did not understand what he was doing, he began to pray. When he had finished and had sung a hymn concerning the Lord's second coming, he found that the whole village had assembled together around him. He began to preach to them the message he had heard himself preach in his own garden before the crowd in the second vision he had had. Like the sermon in the vision, this message too lasted for five hours, from 5 o'clock in the afternoon till 10 o'clock at night. When he had finished, the people returned to their homes and brought out their fetishes and magic roots and burnt them.

The conversion of the villagers, however, was not the only fruit of his ministry. Philip was amazed to find that while he was actually preaching, blind people began to receive their sight, while those who were lame, started to walk. And yet it had not even entered his head that miracles like this would occur. It was then that he remembered the words of John 14:12 through which he had received his call: "Truly, truly, I say to you, he who believes in me will also do the works that I do; and greater works than these will he do, because I go to my father." Philip remained in the village for a further two days before returning to Soe.

On the 26th September 1965 the Lord showed him that he should start working with another native brother named Saul. On the 27th of the same month, in the morning, they visited the schools in Soe. Wherever they went, the children and the teachers started to cry and to pray and to confess their sins. It became simply impossible to continue with the lessons. Saul proposed that they all go across to the church and hold a revival meeting there. However, when they arrived it was hardly possible to hold a meeting at all, since the spirit of revelation and prophecy came over almost everyone present. Children began to say to children, "There are fetishes in your home. Bring them out and burn them. You've got roots as well, and herbs, and you've a belt which you use for sorcery too." And so it went on. Each person began to uncover the occult sins of his neighbour. Philip was startled, for he remembered that he too had brought some fetishes home from the island of Flores. He wondered if what was taking place was scriptural, but just as he thought this, one of the school children started calling out, "There is someone here who doubts. Read Acts 2:17—21. You will find that the gift of prophecy has been promised by God." Philip knew at once that the words were meant for him, and he was glad in fact that he had not been publicly named in the process.

The spirit of revival affected so many of the people that soon the church became filled and many had to stand outside. As the news of the meeting spread, the two local ministers came to see what was going on. Superintendent Joseph wondered at first whether or not it was the working of God's Spirit. As the thoughts went through his mind though, they too were suddenly revealed through the prophecy of one of the people present. This happened on three occasions until in the end his doubts were assuaged. As he watched the events proceed, it became doubly clear to him that this was the work of the Holy Spirit, and today this brother is one of the leading figures in the whole of the revival movement.

That evening the people simply refused to return to their homes. The meeting which had begun in the morning continued throughout the night. It was during this time that over 20 different evangelistic teams were born. Every leader was chosen personally by the Lord. At 2 o'clock the next morning, 18 hours after the meeting had first begun, Saul urged the people to go to their homes. When Philip himself left at about this time, he could find no peace in his soul. He therefore continued in prayer for the rest of the night. The following morning, after a voice had told him which verses of the Bible to read, he assembled his team together and set out to go to K. His only clothes were a shirt and a pair of trousers. He did not even have a pair of shoes.

For two and a half months he and his team worked in the interior of the island preaching the gospel wherever they went. Having no extra clothes with him, the ones he was actually wearing began to get more and more dirty. He asked the Lord what he should do. "Stroke your shirt and your trousers with your hands," he was told. Obeying, Philip found that his clothes became clean. The miracle continued to occur until the team returned from its mission, but then it stopped and he had to resort to using soap and water again.

Sometimes it could be quite embarrassing to meet Philip for the Lord had given him the gift of knowledge, whereby he often knew what secret sins and impurities a person carried on his conscience. I was once present in Soe with him and another two Christian brothers from overseas, when he turned to the man sitting next to me and said, "When I saw you for the first time in East Java, I saw a flame hovering over your forehead. You have some occult objects in your home. I can even now see the flame above your head. You have some fetishes." My companion replied spontaneously, "Yes, that's true. I brought back some gold fetishes as souvenirs from East Asia which were decorated with precious stones. I never thought they could be dangerous to Christians. I'll write home at once and tell my family to destroy them." I found this little episode of great interest, since for years now I have pointed out to people that a missionary should never take any objects home that have been used in cultic rites as mementoes of the mission field.

On another occasion Philip was attending a meeting at which another native evangelist was present. During the message the evangelist began to suffer from a severe attack of ear-ache. When the man could stand the pain no longer, Philip questioned him about his life. It transpired that the evangelist had in his possession a pair of ear rings which had been made from part of an idol. When he threw the rings into a fire, his ear-ache ceased.

Philip was not always welcomed by the churches he visited. Those who heard him preach, and especially the nominal Christians and the church elders, were often afraid of him. The Lord had given his messenger the ability to lay open the lives of the people to whom he spoke. Closing his eyes he was able to see the secret sins of the people present as if by a spiritual form of photography. When he met a person for the first time, he would quite often have a vision of their whole life of sin, and would subsequently seek an opportunity to speak to that person and to tell him what the Lord had revealed to him.

But his prophetic gift was not a static affair. On account of the anger it often produced in other people, Philip prayed that the Lord would change his method of working, and this He did. Before entering a village, for example, the Lord would show him the sins of the people in the local church. He would then preach against these sins, and through his subsequent ministry a great cleansing movement began to spread through the churches. This in turn was again followed by the healing of many who were sick.

In N. a girl was brought to him whose foot had been badly torn in an accident and was bleeding profusely. Laying his hands on the wound Philip felt power going out from him. The blood stopped flowing. Next day some new skin had already formed over the wound and it was healed.

The name by which Philip's team was usually known, was the Fire Team. We have already heard a little about their work. Sometimes the flames were seen not only by the leader of the team, but also by all the people present at the meeting. The natives feared these flames for they knew that through them their secret sins would be uncovered. Yet even when they fled to their houses, the flames would still follow them and not relent.

Pak Elias once said to me, "This brother is spiritually

one of the most powerful team leaders on the island."
But he too needs our prayers, for the devil is always
seeking a means by which to make such men stumble
into sin. The experience of other revival areas of the
world shows that when a man falls victim to pride, he
soon loses his spiritual authority. One of the team leaders
has already fallen into this trap.

XII. THE CALL OF A HEATHEN PRIEST

In a village some 5 miles from Soe there lived a certain
heathen priest who had many followers. One day in 1963
just after he had arrived at his small temple, he was
suddenly caught in a beam of light, and he heard a voice
saying to him, "Your name shall be no longer called Ham
but Shem. If you do not obey, the judgement of God
will fall upon you." Ham obeyed. That very same day
he spoke to his followers and said to them, "God has
revealed himself to me. We must no longer offer sacrifices
to the sun and the moon and the stars, but must instead
begin to serve the God who made the heavens and the
earth."

Before this time Ham, together with all his followers,
had been a sun-worshiper, and he had often sacrificed
pigs and chickens to the sun and moon respectively.
Following his talk to them, however, 60 of his disciples
accepted the new faith which he had adopted.

Shem, as he now became called, was greatly blessed
following his obedience. Although he is illiterate, the
Lord taught him a certain type of hieroglyphics, and
through a process of direct revelation revealed to him
an account of the story of creation. Later, when he had
come into contact with the Christians and had read his
account to them, it was discovered that the story agreed
with that of the first chapters of the Bible. In addition
to this revelation, the Lord told him that he would one

day be visited by some people who would tell him more about his new faith. The promise came true.

A year after he had received his call from God, some Christians who possessed the gift of healing arrived at the village. Shem, who up till that time had been a leper, was wonderfully healed. Another year passed and then, when some more Christians arrived and spoke to him about Jesus, he surrendered his life to Christ immediately.

He began at once to make regular visits to the church meetings in Soe, as well as starting up meetings of his own for his former heathen followers. I have had the opportunity of meeting this brother in the Lord on two occasions, and he even allowed me to take photographs of the hieroglyphics he had written out. It can also be mentioned here that another brother sent me a drawing of Jesus sitting above the sun illustrating the vision I have already described on page 143.

XIII. THE CALL OF A WOMAN

The ministry of women in the Church has always been a great cause of contention among certain groups of Christians. In the revival area, however, the Lord has answered the problem by even calling women to be the leaders of some of the teams.

Sarai was first called on the 29th September 1965. She was suddenly woken up in the night by the sound of a loud voice. At first she was quite frightened and thought she was in the middle of a thunder storm. It was then that she heard the words, "Read Acts 2:2." When her brother began to read the passage to her, however, she lost consciousness. Then, while she was still unconscious, she heard the voice speak to her again and say, "Read Matthew 10 : 27—28." Later she discovered that her family had also heard the words which had been spoken to her. Finally the voice spoke to her a third time and she was told, "Go out and preach the message I give to you."

This third command was followed by the feeling of a warm force coming upon her head. Putting her hands up to protect herself, she cried out, "Lord, help me." But the force became even hotter and continued to affect her for some time until she had regained consciousness fully. After this, however, Sarai felt as if she had been completely changed.

That same evening at about 6 o'clock she began to preach. Gradually a number of her neighbours and other members of the village collected around her to listen what she had to say. Although she had spent no time at all in preparation she continued to speak of the things that the Lord had given her to say until 3 o'clock the following morning.

During her preaching the spirit of prophecy suddenly came over her, and she began to tell the people present what fetishes they had in their houses, and where they were hidden. Those concerned hurried away and fetching their amulets and charms, they brought them back to the meeting and threw them into a heap. Later that same morning, after all the fetishes had been carried to the church, Superintendent Joseph arranged for them all to be burnt.

Following this eventful commencement of her ministry, Sarai received new commands from the Lord. "Go out and preach," he told her one day. "But Lord," she replied, "I'm not an educated woman." The voice went on, "Read Matthew 10:20." There she found the words, "For it is not you who speak, but the Spirit of your Father speaking through you." Before setting out, the Lord showed her the faces of the other people who were to be the members of her team. They included three young men and another Christian native woman. Just before her first preaching campaign, she was given a fresh vision. She saw two messengers coming towards her dressed in white, who, after they had handed her a key, said to her, "This key is the Word of God, and with it you will be able to open the hearts of men." Wherever the team now went, the words that Sarai spoke began to strike at the consciences of those who came to listen, forcing them to bring their fetishes out and to burn them in the sight of all. This angered one of the people who heard her so much that he secretly decided to try and kill her. Sarai, however, was warned by the Lord of this proposed attempt on her life, and when the man found that he was unable to fulfill his plans, he too repented and gave his fetishes over to be burned.

One of the side effects of this campaign was the healing of many who were sick. Sarai was not aware at first that her preaching was having this effect, but during one of her messages a person who had been ill for many years suddenly sprang up and started shouting out, "I've been healed, I've been healed." There are other examples too.

An old man who had been lame for three years attended one of her meetings. While he was standing listening to the message, he suddenly found that he could walk properly. At once he sought out the nearest church and fell on his knees and gave thanks to God.

On another occasion, among the people who had come to listen was a 27-year-old man who had been blind from birth. Suddenly in the middle of the message he cried out, "I can see light." Coming to the front, he was not only soundly converted but was also completely healed of his blindness.

A fifty-year-old man who had been deaf and dumb since childhood was prayed for by some of the Christians. He was wonderfully healed and later gave his heart to the Lord.

There were in fact many people healed in this way, and yet it was noticed that if a person failed to follow

Christ after his healing, the illness would return and would become worse than it had been before.

After labouring for some time on the island of Timor, Sarai was commanded by God to go to the neighbouring island of Rote and to begin work there. After trying unsuccessfully to obtain a passage on a boat crossing from Timor to Rote, she went down to the sea shore with her team and asked the Lord, "How are we going to get across the sea?" Replying, the Lord said, "Wait another seven days and I will send you a prau (a small sailing boat)." They waited, and just as predicted a prau arrived seven days later which took them to Rote. Sarai began to work now under the leadership of Pastor Gideon, and very soon the spirit of revival which had already swept Timor, came upon Rote as well. When Sarai brought the report of her own work to a close, she added, "If I fail to read my Bible for even a single day, I feel as if the Lord accuses me for my negligence. Yet when I do read a passage from the Scriptures, the Holy Spirit himself interprets the meaning to me verse by verse."

XIV. WHO WAS RIGHT?

When we arrived at Soe, the team that first amazed us was team number 49. Its leader was a simple illiterate woman.

They had been working in the interior of the island for a period of eight months up to our arrival, but then this woman had heard the Lord's voice saying to her, "Go back to Soe. An international team of seven Christian workers is going to visit the island soon." It would have been impossible to have contacted the team by either post or telephone, since these forms of communication hardly exist in the island's interior at all. The team started making their way back to Soe on foot, and when they arrived they went to Superintendent Joseph and asked him, "Has the international team arrived yet, with the seven Christian workers from overseas?" "No," replied Joseph, "they are not here yet, and anyway, Pak Elias has written and said that there would be ten people coming and not seven." "It can't be ten," the team replied, "for the Lord told us there will only be seven coming." A few days later we reached the island. There were seven of us, and not ten! Three of the Japanese Christians who had intended to accompany us on our visit, had been unable to obtain their visas in time. The 'direct communication' which the team had had with the Lord, was therefore more reliable than the postal communication between Pak Elias and Pastor Joseph.

As we talked with the simple native woman who was leader of this team, we were amazed at the way the Lord had worked in the smallest details of her life. Like many others she had received her call as a result of a vision, and as is always the case, the vision had been closely associated with the Scriptures. This is the encouraging thing concerning all these miraculous signs, for invariably the person to whom the vision is given is told to turn to the Bible and to read a certain text. If the person is illiterate, the text is read aloud to him and he has to learn it off by heart.

After her call, Mary continued to be given directions from the Lord through both visions and verses from the Bible. On one occasion she saw an unusually strong light and found herself surrounded by angels. A voice then said to her, "Do not be afraid. At the end of this age the world will be burnt up by this light. You shall be my witness. Go wherever I send you, for the time is very short. The people must repent." Wondering whether or not the voice was genuine, Mary asked, "Who are you?" The voice replied, "The words are mine," and immediately she saw the hands of Jesus appear with the nail prints in the palms. "My hands," the voice continued, "are pierced anew each day by the sins of the whole world." Mary was frightened and replied, "But who will believe me? I'm not even educated." The Lord answered her again and said, "I am giving you five fellow workers." Immediately Mary saw the faces of the five people who were to make up her evangelistic team. The Lord continued, "You shall not speak your own words. I will speak for you, and you will stand behind me."

While Mary was telling Pastor Joseph and our international team the story of her call, she added, "The Lord gave me a song, but I can't understand the words." She then began to sing her song out loud. We were amazed. It was in English, and she sang it without making any mistakes. The words were as follows:

> I hear my Saviour calling,
> I hear my Saviour calling,
> Take the cross and follow me.

The only language that Mary knows is her own Indonesian dialect. She is not even able to speak the official language of the country and can also neither read nor write. Yet here she was singing a song to us in English, a language which no one in the area in which she lives can speak.

It would take too much time to report all the details concerning the work of the different teams. One could write many books on the subject. The situation is similar to that which John the apostle found himself in when he wrote, "I suppose the world itself could not contain the books that could be written" (John 20:25). Jesus is the same today as he was 1,900 years ago.

XV. FROM PERSECUTOR TO DISCIPLE

Andrew is a police officer. While our international team was staying in Soe, we were able to hear him give his own testimony. He told us the following story.

"When the revival originally broke out on Timor, I was one of its chief opponents. I decided to go out of my way to persecute the Christians, and when Saul started preaching in the schools I had him arrested and beaten up at the police station. I even tore off his moustache in the process.

The reason I was so strongly opposed to the Christians was because my own life was deeply involved in occultism. I come from the island of Sumba where a great deal of black magic is still practised. Whenever a person leaves the island, he takes a number of fetishes and charms with him to protect himself wherever he goes. When I myself left, I took 66 of these fetishes with me. Once when a man tried to cut my throat with a bush knife, the knife bounced off my skin and I wasn't even hurt. The black stones I wore as a means of protection were very effective; otherwise I would have been killed. There were altogether 36 of these stones hidden under my skin in various parts of my body. I continued to oppose the revival movement for almost four years until I finally fell ill in February of this year (1969). The doctors could find nothing wrong with me at the time, but they took my appendix out just in case. However, there was no improvement in my condition, for the real cause was not my appendix at all, but rather the unforgiven sin of my occult practices. In the end, because I feared that my disease might be incurable, I went to see a believing brother who showed me the way to Jesus. That night the Lord appeared to me in a wonderful light. When I had surrendered my life to him completely, my body was immediately healed. While I continued in prayer, my skin gradually began to split open and the stones of sorcery that were buried underneath came out. After this the Lord commanded me, "Give your testimony before the whole church or else your illness will return. I have now done what he told me to do."

Our international team was actually present when

Andrew gave his testimony for the first time. I asked him afterwards, "Have all the stones come out yet and did you have to have any of them cut out?" He replied, "No, there's still one of the stones left, it's the mother stone in fact. See, it's here near my collar bone. You can feel it if you want to." I reached my hand out and touched the place he indicated. The stone was about twice the size of a thimble. Andrew went on, "It has taken two weeks for the other 35 stones to come out, but none of them were cut out. We have just had to pray, and as we have done so the skin has broken open and the stones have come out one by one. We'll have to pray a lot more though, before the mother stone is removed, because it's that stone which possesses the greatest occult power."

I have since heard that the last stone has now broken through his skin, and so, by the grace of God, the ban on Andrew's life has been completely broken.

XVI. A SORCERER CAPITULATES

Just before our arrival on Timor, a man who had been much feared by the people in the neighbourhood was converted. We were able to listen to his testimony, too, at the church in Soe. While he was waiting his turn to get into the pulpit and speak, he looked as white as a sheet and was trembling all over at the thought of having to speak before an audience which must have totalled almost a thousand people. By means of an interpreter I was able to take down the following account of what he said.

Titus first called upon Satan for help when he was only 15 years old. "Give me magical powers," he begged. He had been brought up as an animist, and as a result was dominated by an occult view of life. At the time when he first called on the devil, he heard a voice answer him and say, "Come out to the front of your house." He had obeyed and was further commanded, "Hold out your right hand." As he did so an invisible force suddenly cut his hand across the fingers and he saw a small stone being placed into the wound. At once the stone began to travel up his arm and into his heart and then down the other arm, following the blood-stream as it went. He found that as a result of his Satanic gift he was endowed with great power. There was not a person who could stand in his way. Using his powers of evil, he began to steal, to kidnap people, and to seduce the native women, and he was even able to kill. He got a job first working for the local authorities, but they later sacked him on account of his evil practices. Although the police were often after him, he was never caught, his magical belt providing him with the protection he desired. Magical phenomena of this nature exist also in other parts of the world, and in Germany for example the saga of Siegfried is based upon the same idea. In the East, however, these powers are very real, for the prince of darkness is able to endow his servants with the very powers of hell themselves.

In March 1969 Titus finally came to Christ. His conversion resulted from a vision which the Lord gave him of the archangel Gabriel, and yet on the day of his baptism, the 1st April, he had still not been fully delivered from his occult past. But at least the stone had stopped moving, and it was once more back in his right hand where it had originally entered his body.

When I talked with Pak Elias about this and asked him why the stone had not come out at his conversion, he replied, "Perhaps it will act as a thorn in the flesh and serve as a continual reminder to Titus of his former evil ways. The most important thing is that the stone has been robbed of all its power through the blood of Christ." It is still possible for the stone to come out one day, for just as in the case of Andrew, a magician is not always delivered from all the evil influences around him on the day of his conversion.

In June 1969, Titus became very ill. For three days he was unable to eat anything and started suffering from a high fever accompanied with bouts of shivering and stabbing pains in the chest. The illness, however, was used by God to call Titus into His service. On the 1st July at midday he suddenly heard a voice saying to him, "Titus, listen to me. You will not eat for two periods of six hours, for I wish to speak with you. I am giving you a staff to use." Titus asked, "What shall I do with this staff?" The voice replied, "You must use it to destroy the Islamic faith, to destroy Buddhism, to destroy animism, and to destroy Catholicism. These have been the cause of much harm in Indonesia." It was astonishing to hear of Catholicism being mentioned together with the other three religions. It would seem as if the Lord does not approve of the present day ecumenical aims of the churches.

When Titus received his first commission, he was still partly conscious and he was able to hear his wife talking about him and making fun of him while she was doing the cooking. However, when the Lord spoke to him the second time, he was completely unconscious of his surroundings. "I have called you into my service," the Lord began, "Preach the Word. Are you prepared to serve me?" Titus replied, "I'm not the right person for you. I've been one of the worst men in the village." The Lord refused to let him go. "I want you to be mine. Abide in my love. Read Jeremiah 48:10, the first part of the verse, and read John 15:9. As a bird leaves its nest and later returns, so I will lead you to places far away and bring you home again."

During the next stage of his call the angel Gabriel appeared to him and said, "I have been commanded by the Lord to take you into the heavens" (2 Cor. 12:2, 3). Together they arrived at the first heaven. Titus could still see the sun and the moon and the stars. Walking across a bridge they came to a large gate which opened by itself. Gabriel turned to him and said, "This is the second heaven. Here the sun and moon and stars do not exist." When they had entered the gate, Titus found the second heaven to be filled with a marvellous light. They continued on their walk crossing bridge after bridge and passing through one gate after another. Gabriel spoke to Titus again and said, "You are highly favoured to be able to see what your eyes are seeing. Others who have been here have fallen to the ground as if dead" (Rev. 1:17).

Titus became more and more conscious during his journey through the heavens of the tremendous difference that exists between the terrestial and the heavenly spheres. "The reason you have been permitted to see all these glories," the archangel told him, "is that you might proclaim them to the rest of mankind. Do not cast your eyes back to your past life, for if you do you will lose everything."

Gabriel continued to lead him until they had reached the seventh heaven, whereupon he said, "This is the new heaven." Titus was overwhelmed by the glory of this highest of heavens. There before him he saw tables prepared as it were for a great feast, stretching for miles into the distance. The seats were of silver and gold and each was designated for the person for whom it was prepared. The tables themselves were richly decked and laden with heavenly manna. Around the tables ornaments swayed in fan-like motion producing a fragrant and refreshing breeze. At the end of the tables there were two seats prepared for the bride and bridegroom. Gabriel said to Titus, "Tell the people to repent and to follow Jesus so that they will be ready for the marriage feast of the Lamb" (Luk. 14:16—24; Matt. 22:2—24; Rev. 19:6—10).

After this Titus was struck by a beam of light and he sank to the ground as the vision of the seventh heaven disappeared from his sight. Gabriel touched him on the shoulder and lifted him to his feet. He was then led back the way he had come. Stepping out of the last palace, Titus saw on his left a stream flowing with milk and honey, and on his right a stream flowing with gold and silver. The streams flowed through the middle of the paradise of God. As they continued to walk along the wide street that led through this veritable garden of Eden, Titus turned to Gabriel and asked, "Is this the place of the righteous, and if it is, where is the place of the wicked?" Gabriel replied, "The Lord has not allowed you to see the place of hell itself. However, I can show you the roads that lead there." With that Titus had a vision of three broad ways so crowded with men and women that he was unable to see any of their faces. Titus was filled with horror at the sight of these three massive columns of people marching endlessly on to the place of hell. He started calling out, "Go in through the narrow door and you will be saved." But no one heard or heeded his cry.

After his vision of the lost, Titus received the last vision connected with his call. He saw the Lord Jesus amid seven angels, four on his right side and three on his left. Suddenly Jesus fell upon him and immediately Titus felt in his body that he had been healed. His spirit was now on the point of entering the earthly sphere again, and he saw his house and his family come into view once more. His vision then ended with the sight of the angels falling upon his relatives who were also healed in a moment. Among them was his own wife who had previously been ill for a number of years.

At midnight that night Titus was once again fully conscious. The two visions had lasted for exactly six hours each, just as the Lord had predicted. He found that as well as himself, his wife and children had also been completely restored to health and strength after this experience.

Titus now knew assuredly that he had been called into the service of the Lord. He was next told to recount his vision before the assembled church. At first Satan tried to hinder him from doing so, and he received a terrible bite in his leg from a large dog. However, after he had prayed, the wound healed up completely and was better by the following day. When he did finally give his testimony, I was seated in the church listening to him speak.

These visionary experiences pose us many questions. How should we classify them from the point of view of the Scriptures?

1. The revival on Timor is in itself an extraordinary event of which these extraordinary signs are but a part.

2. The visions are a result of the Holy Spirit falling upon these simple native Christians.

3. These miraculous signs have a double purpose: they serve to announce the nearness of the Lord's return, and they act as a fulfillment of the promises in Joel 3:1 and Acts 2:17. Many indeed are the prophecies which announce that the Lord's coming is near. The time is short!

4. The visions are closely associated with the Holy Scriptures.

5. The recipients of these spiritual experiences are ever open to correction from their brothers in the Lord if something amiss is discovered in their lives.

6. The visions are never greater than the One who is their author.

7. Our faith can never be founded upon a visionary experience, only upon the redemptive work of Christ on the cross and upon his resurrection from the dead.

8. God does not always send a vision before he calls a person into his service. The most important thing is obedience to the Word of God.

9. If visions ever become an end in themselves they merely lead to a desire for the sensational and to

pride. If this is the case, instead of being a blessing they can become a curse.

10. We must guard against criticizing these visionary experiences in Indonesia too hastily, without due regard to what the Scriptures have to say on the matter.

XVII. THE WORK OF AN EVANGELIST

Although we have heard the testimony of Pak Elias already in this book, I want now to go on to describe some further stories connected with his work as an evangelist and minister of the Word. I have been able to meet this brother in the Lord on altogether three occasions. The first was in East Java in 1968, the second in Germany when I organized a series of meetings at which both Pak Elias and David Simeon spoke, and the third time was when we were together in Indonesia again at the conference in East Java and then with the international team on Timor. But before going on, let me underline a principle which we can so easily forget. If we were to indulge in the adulation of a man, we would be committing idolatry. We must always remember: the cries of Hosanna in Jerusalem were not intended for the ass, but for the Lord who sat upon it. Today we are often in danger of forgetting the Lord and thinking only of the ass.

A total of sixteen months separates this second section from that which precedes it. In this time I have been able to collect a number of stories which help supplement our first report concerning Pak Elias.

Pak Elias was preaching once on an island in Indonesia, when the Lord sent a revival among the Moslems living there. Seeing that many of his own people were being converted, a deaf Moslem, who as a boy had learnt to read before his illness, began to read the local reports of what was taking place. In the end, coming to Pak Elias, he said, "If the Jesus whom you preach can make me hear, I will believe in him." Pak Elias sensed that his work was being challenged, and so when the Lord gave him the inner freedom to pray, he prayed for the man under the laying on of hands. As he did so, the Moslem suddenly felt a force flowing through his ears. When the prayer was ended, finding he could once again hear, he handed his life over to Christ as he had promised.

While Pak Elias was preaching on the same island, a rich Moslem attended one of the meetings he was holding. Although the man was touched by the message, he subsequently stayed away, for it had made him feel extremely ill at ease. However, with just three evenings to go before the mission ended, the Moslem's chief wife encouraged him to go just one more time. Again the message gripped his heart, and speaking to Pak Elias later he said, "If you can help me, I will give you a new car." The evangelist replied, "God can help you, but you needn't give him a car in return." "Is that really true?" asked the rich man, "I have committed many sins, as the people here well know. I have 16 wives, and have stolen a lot of money, and I have even committed murder." As Pak Elias showed him the way to Christ, both the Moslem and his chief wife were converted. After openly confessing his sins, he gave his other wives money and allowed them to go free, while he and his chief wife went home determined to live a new life for their Lord.

On another island where it was forbidden to preach the Gospel publicly, Pak Elias climbed into a taxi and started to tell the other passengers about the message of Christ. A few months later he heard the joyful news that the actual taxi driver had been converted as a result of his taxi-preaching.

A professor once came to Pak Elias and said to him, "Although I'm a Christian, when I read the Bible I get nothing from it." The evangelist replied, "There are three types of Bible readers:

a) the first type merely tramples over the Scriptures looking for arguments with which to mock their contents;
b) the second type of reader, bowing down to his own intellect, critically examines anything which to him is unreasonable and reduces it to the level of his own human understanding;
c) the third type of Bible reader on the other hand, gives the Scriptures their rightful place, and thereby places himself in subjection to the Word of God."

To this the professor replied, "I can see that I belong to the second group." However, the next morning he came to see Pak Elias again, and after confessing his sins and surrendering his life to Christ, he submitted both himself and his reason once and for all to the authority of the Scriptures.

One of the greatest events during the revival consisted of the missionary campaign which was held in West Irian (New Guinea) in March 1969. When Pak Elias first got up to preach, the rain started to pour down in torrents. There were some thousands of people gathered in the open air at the time. Turning to prayer the evangelist quite simply commanded the rain to stop in the name of Jesus. It ceased immediately. He then prayed that the Lord would keep the whole meeting free of rain, and so it happened. Not until the meeting had drawn to a close, did the rain begin to teem down again. The following evening a very strong wind began to howl around the building in which the meeting was to be held. As the wind increased, the building's corrugated iron roof began to bang and rattle so much that it was impossible to hear a single word of what the evangelist was saying. Again Pak Elias stopped, and turning to the wind he commanded it in the name of Jesus to be still. Before an audience, which again ran into thousands and which included among other people the German missionary Willi Haseloh, the wind ceased.

During this 18 day mission in West Irian almost three thousand people were converted. At the same time some 250 young men dedicated themselves to full-time gospel work. At the close of the mission an offering was taken which was pledged to the support of these young people. In spite of the utter poverty which exists in the country, the sum collected amounted to more than £ 400, and included among other things a gold ring, a gold necklace and a new wrist watch.

God has also honoured the private prayers of his servant. One night Pak Elias saw himself hovering over a distant land, and as the vision ended he suddenly found himself praying in a language he did not understand. Memorizing what he had said, he was amazed to find a few months later when he visited Thailand that the language he had used was that of the Thai people. His experience therefore had not simply been one of speaking in tongues, but rather a miracle similar to that which occurred on the day of Pentecost in Acts 2.

It is an unforgettable experience to be able to accomany this brother in his work for the Lord. And yet, like all other servants of God, he needs our prayers so that the blessing he receives may not result in pride and so rob him of his spiritual power. Above all he needs the gift of being able to discern between spirits to enable him to distinguish between the extreme and the fanatical on the one hand, and the spiritual and charismatical on the other.

XVIII. THE SONGS OF THE REVIVAL

Travelling about as a missionary I have often had the opportunity of listening to Christians express themselves in music and in song. Occasionally in the Western world

I have been able to witness the technical perfection of a professional choir, only to be left untouched by a delivery issuing from unbelieving hearts. What is technique if the Lord himself is missing?

In Barrow in Alaska I was particularly moved by the singing of the Christians in the Presbyterian church. The life and the fervour it possessed compelled me to tape and record it for myself.

I have already described elsewhere the wonderful singing of the Christians in Ambon, Indonesia, which meant so much to me at the time.

However, nothing I have heard before compares with the singing I was enabled to hear in the actual revival centre on Timor. The wealth of songs in the revival churches is indeed amazing.

Although they continue to sing some of the traditional hymns of the Reformed Church, they do so with hearts and voices and spirits renewed by the Holy Spirit. In this way the old tunes are filled with fresh spiritual meaning.

The true songs of the revival, however, are those which have literally been inspired. The teams have not only seen visions and heard voices, but have actually been given songs directly from the Lord. Sometimes these simple but much blessed Christians have had new melodies sung to them up to twenty different times until they have learnt the words and the tune off by heart. What a joy it is to hear them singing these hymns; they have learnt them from the very angels themselves. There is such a surge of joy and feeling moving through the church that one is not only gripped by the music but also transported to the realms of the choirs of heaven. It must have been the same type of singing that captivated the shepherds outside Bethlehem on the night of the Saviour's birth.

Before moving on with our report we will just mention one example, an example which is sure to provoke a lot of criticism from the Western world.

One day a group of children who had been caught up in the revival began to sing about their Lord as they made their way home from school. Walking along, they came across a spot where a number of rocks of various sizes were strewn about over the ground. Suddenly they heard a voice from among the rocks say to them, "You have sung very well. Let me teach you a new song about Jesus. Stay here while I sing to you." Replying, the children said, "We're very hungry. We'll go home first and have something to eat." They hurried on. When they had taken their school things into their homes, they found that their hunger had disappeared. They came out of their huts and met each other again and decided to return to the place of the stones. When they arrived they heard the same voice speaking to them a second time. It then sang a song to them and told them to repeat the words after it. They did so, and after hearing the song through about twenty times, they had both the words and the tune fixed indelibly in their minds. They then returned to the village singing as they went. When the leader of the Bible school heard the song, he wrote it down together with the music, and he later showed them both to me in his notebook.

A psychologist or a parapsychologist would have the gravest of difficulties in attempting to explain the facts behind an experience of this nature, and yet it is not easy to deny the truth of the story, seeing that both the words and the tune are still in existence today.

XIX. PRESENTING A FALSE PICTURE

If a historian from the West were to write a history of the Russian Revolution, his account would no doubt differ a great deal from one which had been written by a 'red author' from an iron curtain country. The alleged objectivity of certain writers is often a very debatable point and depends a great deal on the attitude they adopt.

In this respect I have come across a number of strange and even false reports of the various revivals which have recently taken place in the world, and for this reason I feel it my duty to act in a certain way as a watchman in these matters.

In Germany a Christian member of one of the Pentecostal churches said to me, "You know that the Indonesian revival was brought about by the Pentecostals? In fact they are the only Christians through whom it could have come." In the same way a member of the T. L. Osborn organization declared, "The revival has come as a direct result of our own work in the area."

One would feel quite happy to ignore statements of this nature, were it not for the fact that comments such as these are already finding their way into the various reports of the revival which are currently appearing in the Christian press all over the world.

What I am saying is in no way meant to be an attack on the Pentecostal movement as a whole, for in fact since I became a Christian I have never adopted a narrow denominational attitude. There are false teachers to be found in every confessional group, and the modern theologians who today occupy the pulpits of so many of the established churches of our lands represent a far greater danger to the Christian faith than do those Pentecostal believers who have simply confused that which is carnal with the spiritual.

I have a duty as one who is acquainted with the Indonesian revival of today, to indicate as clearly as I can the actual boundaries of the spiritual events which are taking place there.

First of all something positive. Pak Elias, who is more familiar with the revival than most people, said to me once, "There are some wonderful brethren among the Pentecostals in Indonesia who serve the Lord with all their hearts and who are open to the ministry of the Holy Spirit."

However, on the whole the revival broke out in the Reformed Church rather than in the Pentecostal churches. For example, there was a small Pentecostal church some ten miles from the centre of the revival, and when the members saw the spiritual renewal taking places in the Reformed churches, and realized they themselves were being left untouched by the blessing, they closed their own church and went back and joined the Reformed Church.

There are three Pentecostal groups in K. which have all remained on the outside as far as the revival is concerned. A circular letter called 'God is Marching on', written by one of the leading missionaries in the area, contains an excellent appraisal of this problem. He writes, "It is quite astonishing to see how God is protecting the revival from false and extreme forms of teaching. While I was staying in one of the centres of the revival, some overseas Christians arrived and expressed their desire to preach on the island. Although their views concerning the working of the Holy Spirit were rather strange, they were nevertheless genuine believers. By means of the gift of prophecy, which is frequently found on Timor, the leaders of the churches in the area were warned beforehand that some false teachers would arrive from overseas. And here they now were. The visitors were amazed at the way in which the native Christians stood their ground and refused them permission to speak in their pulpits and before their people. Although I have seen almost all the gifts of the Holy Spirit manifested in these revived Presbyterian fellowships on Timor, not one of these churches has any connection with the Pentecostal movement."

The history of the revival contains many other stories of a similar nature to the one we have just heard. David Wilkerson has spoken in both England and Germany on the invitation of certain groups of Christians in these countries. After visiting the town of Soe in the centre of the revival area for a few hours, he sent some money to the leader of the Bible School there, inviting him to go to America to speak at a series of meetings. The native leader went to Pak Elias and asked him for his advice. After praying together, recognizing that it was not the Lord's will, they sent the money back and declined the invitation. On another occasion Pak Elias was offered about £900 to visit the United States of America. Again though, after prayer, he declined the offer. These experiences seem to show that our Indonesian brothers have a greater gift of discernment than many Christians in both England and Germany.

The following short example also underlines what we have just been saying. As I have already mentioned, Pak Elias and David Simeon spoke at a number of meetings I had arranged for them in April 1969 in Germany. When Pak Elias was calling on the 3,000 people at the Stuttgart meeting to surrender their lives to Christ, as he remained quiet for a few minutes in silent prayer, a man on the platform suddenly stood up and started to pray 'in tongues'. After waiting for just a moment, Pak Elias turned to the man and commanded him in the name of Jesus to be quiet. When I asked him later after the meeting why he had spoken to man in this manner, he replied, "The Lord showed me that the devil was using this interruption to try and disturb the meeting." The other brother from Indonesia then explained to me, "It often happens that when one comes to the point of urging people to repent and to turn their lives over to Christ, the Pentecostals slip into tongues speaking and thereby hinder people from making their decision." A little while after this I found the man who had actually spoken in tongues and asked him what had prompted him to do so. He began at once to apologize and said, "I didn't want to speak in tongues but something inside just made me do it." We should ask ourselves what is happening when the spirit of a prophet is not subject to the prophet!

In Indonesia I was present when a girl started to pray in tongues at one of the meetings. When she had finished, however, no one rose to interpret what she had said. Afterwards one of the leading Indonesian Christians rebuked her saying, "Don't you know your Bible? It's written that a person should keep silent if there is no one to interpret." The Indian evangelist, Bakht Singh, was also present at the time and he said to me later, "Immediately the girl stood up and began to speak in tongues I started praying that she would stop, for I knew that what she was doing wasn't good."

While I was on Timor I asked the leaders of the revival what part tongues speaking was playing in the movement. Their reply was quite astonishing. "Within a space of about 2½ years some 200,000 natives have become Christians. We have at the same time experienced thousands of cases of healing, together with many other miracles of faith, and yet we know of only one single instance of a person speaking in tongues, and even then the person doesn't use his gift in public."

What a crushing blow this statement must be to the numerous fanatic advocates of the present day tongues movement. Among a total of 200,000 new converts and some 30,000 miracles of healing, only one single case of a person speaking in tongues! There may in fact be others who have received this gift, but like all who genuinely possess a gift from God, they will not broadcast the fact but simply use it to praise their Lord in secret. One can see that as Paul the apostle urged in his first letter to the Corinthians, speaking in tongues plays a very insignificant part in the revival in Indonesia, that is if it can be said to play any part at all. Anyone who tries to inject this gift into the revival movement from outside — and this has already been attempted by three misguided brothers from the West — will find that he is labelled as a false teacher by the Lord himself. The Christian leaders in the area are prevented from allowing such people to work with them in any form whatsoever.

XX. FIRE OVER ROTE

While I was on Timor the news reached us that 30 temples had been burnt down on the neighbouring island of Rote. This happened in the summer of 1969. What, we may ask, was the background to the story? It was quite simply that the revival on Timor had spilled over on to Rote with the result that when the natives had been converted, they had straightway burnt down their heathen temples which had been filled with their fetishes and charms, wanting nothing more to do with their former way of life. But this was not the first fire that had, like a torch of God, heralded in a new epoch on the island.

The Place of Sacrifice

On the west coast of Rote a massive shoulder of rock reaches out into the sea. For centuries this site has been used by the natives for the sacrifices they have made to their heathen gods of nature, and many are the mysteries surrounding the caves in the rock.

In the 18th century the island was inhabited by 19 different kings who were continually engaged in wars with one another. Finally one of the kings defeated 16 of his opponents and subsequently the sacrificial site of Tolamanu was named after him. The remaining two kings, Foembura and Ndiihua, decided on a desperate plan. Knowing that the Dutch authorities were located in Batavia (known today as Djakarta), and hoping to receive help from them, they prepared some small sailing boats with the intention of attempting the 1,500 mile journey to what is now the capital of Indonesia. They took as provisions, maize roasted in sugar, intending to supplement their diet with fish and bananas, the latter being found on all the islands in the area. They intended also to obtain their drinking water from these islands when they needed more. And so in 1729 the adventure commenced.

On account of the many adverse currents and ever changing wind conditions the journey lasted altogether six months. Their boats each bore the symbolic name 'Sangga ndolu' which means 'we seek peace and powers'. They were hoping in some way or other that the colonial authorities would be able to supply them with enough magical powers to enable them to withstand their enemy Tolamanu. At the same time they hoped to find rest from the tribal feuds that continually raged on their island.

When they did finally reach Batavia, however, they came face to face with a new problem: the people spoke a different language from that of their own. Had the journey just been a waste of time? The answer was no, for God in his great mercy and wisdom had prepared the way before them. While they were in Batavia, they one day came across a woman who had originally been born on the island of Rote. Recognizing their clothing to be that of her native island, she went up to them and spoke to them. Their faces lit up at once at the sound of someone speaking to them in their native tongue.

But how had their interpreter come to be living so far from her country of birth? While she had been living on Rote she had one day met a sailor who had fallen so much in love with her that he had married her at once and taken her with him on board his ship. And so here she was acting as the advocate and interpreter of the two kings. They were introduced to the Dutch governor but were disappointed to find that the colonial authorities were not in possession of the magical powers they were looking for. However, the governor acted wisely and after contacting a Dutch missionary he placed the strangers under his care.

It was through this that the two kings ultimately found peace, not the type they had originally sought, but one based upon faith in Christ. They were both converted and later baptised, receiving at their baptism the new Christian names of Meshach and Zachariah. When I visited Rote I was overjoyed to find that Christian descendants of these two kings still live there. Pastor Gideon, whose story I have already described on page 117 is in fact himself a descendant of the king who was renamed Zachariah.

The joy that the two kings experienced from their new found faith was so great that when they decided to return to Rote they left a number of their servants behind in Batavia as tokens of their thankfulness. They were accompanied on their homeward voyage by the same missionary through whom they had first heard the gospel message, and he took the opportunity provided him during the journey of acquainting himself with the dialect of Rote. They finally reached home again in 1732, after an absence of altogether three years.

The Sacrificial Fire

For the first time in its existence the heathen fortress on Rote began to come under attack. The returning kings built the first church and Christian school on the island in a village called Ti. It was not long, though, before their work started to meet with the opposition of Tola-manu. Realizing that his influence was declining, he concocted a devilish plan. Arranging a great feast, he invited the two Christian kings and their missionary friend to be his guests. To allay any suspicion of his evil intent, he also invited the governor of K. who sub-sequently arrived at the feast accompanied by his secretary. The climax of the evening came when the five unsuspecting guests were suddenly overpowered and bound with ropes. They were then placed in a circle of heaped leaves and offered up as sacrifices on the now infamous mountain of Tolamanu. This was the first time a fire had burnt on Rote on account of the Christian faith. It took place in 1732, the same year in which the two kings had returned from Batavia.

But if Tolamanu had thought that the new religion would now die a natural death, he was sadly disappointed. In Ti the school and the church continued their work of teaching the islanders the message of Christ, and the fire that had been lit began to spread further. The sacrificial blood of the martyrs bore much fruit. The school was instrumental in the training of many Christian teachers, and as the years passed new schools were built on the neighbouring islands with the result that more and more people heard the teachings of the gospel. In this way Rote became the centre of a great missionary work.

In the Hunting Ground of the Sharks

Today, after a period of more than 200 years, Rote has once more become the spiritual focus of this small cluster of islands in Indonesia. Both Pak Elias and Pastor Gideon, whose testimonies we have already heard, are natives of Rote, and God has been using these two men in a mighty way ever since the revival originally began there in 1964. In fact all the early Christians of the revival have shown and continued to show a remarkable boldness with regard to their faith. The following is a wonderful example of this.

Two ocean currents, one from Australia and the other from the west, meet and clash with one another between the islands of Rote and Timor. The waves can suddenly rise without warning and break over the sides of the small boats which make the perilous journey from Timor to Rote, as we ourselves experienced on a number of occasions on our trips between the two islands. Although I personally was only soaked to the skin, others had to pay for their passage with the tribute people are often forced to give to a troubled sea. For myself, serving in the air force has made me immune to the elements. I watched, though, how perilously the ship would often keel over on its side, and heard from the mayor of B. just how many small sailing ships were lost each year in this troubled stretch of water. The catastrophe which we are about to describe occurred on a similar trip from Timor to Rote. Pastor Gideon, whose own father was aboard the boat when it capsized, related to me the story as it had happened.

A prau or native sailing boat was making its way across this difficult passage when it suddenly capsized just before reaching the island of Rote. Everyone of the 30 people on board was flung into the water which teems with sharks. Included among the passengers were two pastors and many genuine Christians. Gideon's father, however, had been prepared for this calamity, since the Lord had warned him beforehand that he was about to be called home. Three of the thirty, with much boldness and faith, lifted their Bibles to heaven and cried out from the sea, "Lord, you have said that you will be with us in the waters. If it is your will, we ask you to save us." With this the three young men began to swim towards Rote in an attempt to reach the shore. Because of the strong current, however, they were driven away from Rote towards the island Semau. Since the catastrophe had taken place at night, they were unable to see the land at all. For twelve hours they continued to fight the sea and the waves, taking it in turn to pray aloud while they were swimming. Unbelievably, not a shark came near them. It was as if God had shut their mouths even as he had shut the jaws of the lions when Daniel had been thrown into their den. Moreover, none of the swimmers was overcome by exposure or by the rough seas.

The next day they were washed ashore on Semau, but in spite of their terrible ordeal, they at once hired a boat and returned to the scene of the disaster in an attempt to save the people they had left behind. Pastor Gideon's father had actually called to them to bring a boat when they reached land. But there was no one to be found. The remaining 27 had all drowned. The tragedy occurred in 1966 but it was marked by the occasion of a notable miracle. The Bibles in the raised hands of the three young men became symbolic of their salvation, and it was discovered that when they finally reached the shore, they not only still had their Bibles with them, but the Bibles had not been damaged at all by the sea water.

In a Small Village

On Rote I found myself in the company of two native pastors, Pastor Micah, the former minister of the local church, and Pastor Gideon. Micah's church had consisted of a group of 30 Christians, yet many of these had been addicted to the strong alcoholic drink which we have already mentioned, called palm wine. This wine is obtained from the sugar palm, and there are in fact many of these trees dotted around the village. After Pastor Gideon had taken over the pastorate of the church, revival had swept through the village, and today everyone of the villagers belongs to the church, whose membership amounts to some 300 people including the children. Each week they hold a total of six meetings. On Mondays the church workers come together to pray and to talk about their work. In all about 23 of the church members attend this meeting. On Tuesdays a second meeting is held for the 60 or so young people in the village, and on Wednesdays the women meet together for their time of prayer and fellowship. The weekly Bible study is held on Thursdays and this is attended by almost all the adults in the village. Then on Sundays there are the two worship services of the church. When a three months Bible course was started in B. with the aim of training young evangelists, 18 young people volunteered to attend from Pastor Gideon's church alone. Whereas in Europe the missionary societies are crying out for new recruits, the young people on Rote and Timor have to queue up to be accepted, for the simple reason that there are not enough places to go round. In fact I met one young teacher on Rote who had already been praying for a year that she would be accepted by one of the Bible schools for missionary training. This is the difference between tradition and revival.

One event in particular which occurred at the village deserves to be mentioned. A few years ago William Nagenda, who comes from Uganda, visited Indonesia. He spoke to the Christians there on the theme of walking in the light. What does this mean? During the revival in Africa the Christians began to confess their sins openly to one another. William Nagenda's own testimony illustrates this practice well. Before his conversion he had been the director of a tax office, and had regularly taken the opportunity of stealing from his employers. However, when he had become a Christian he went to the police and confessed to them his crime. During the court case which followed, the judge, who had never come across a case like this before where a man had been his own accuser, allowed William Nagenda to go free. Such a confession of sin was a radical course of action to take, yet other Christians began to follow his example and to put their own lives in order.

This story made a deep impression on the Christians in Indonesia and many groups of believers were led of God to bring their own sinful deeds into the light. In the village where I was staying, the Christians had begun to confess their sins openly to one another and to pray for one another that their lives might be ordered aright. In this way the church remained in full control, a thing that would have been impossible in an established church where the sins of an individual would have been gossiped about by all the members. Indeed, the 'pious talk' which occurs so frequently in the Western churches almost cries to heaven. But within the revival fellowships on Rote the sins of others are not bandied about.

A Memorial to Prayer

The doors of Rote have remained wide open to the gospel message ever since the revival came to the island. Wherever one travels one can feel the effect of the spiritual atmosphere. When I first visited the office of the district president who governs the whole of the island, it seemed only natural to spend a short time in prayer together with him. The same was true at the homes of the mayor of B. and the mayor of T., who are both believing Christians. Where could one find a situation like this in the West? There was even an opportunity of having fellowship in prayer at the passport control on the island. It seems as if one is being plunged into an entirely different world, and this was brought home to me particularly by the following experience.

Having hired the only privately owned jeep on the island, I drove out one day to see the site of the new airport. Again I found that one was able to enjoy Christian fellowship not only at the airport, but even on the landing strip itself. I could hardly believe my eyes when I was shown what had taken place there in recent days. Rote is in point of fact very difficult to reach from the surrounding islands, as it has no connections by either ship, plane or rail with the main traffic routes in the area. And the frequent loss of the sailing boats which travel to the island has already been mentioned. For this reason the government sent an extremely capable civil officer to the island to organize the building of an airport there.

The events which followed his arrival are absolutely unique. The airstrip was started on the 7th July 1969, and within the space of three weeks it had almost been completed. How was the work carried out so quickly? The answer lay in the people of Rote themselves. Without receiving any wages they organized the labour forces and completed the task with no outside help at all. During the first week about 3,500 of the islanders, both men and women, volunteered to begin work on the project. In the second week the number of workers rose to 5,000, and in the third week another 3,000 turned up at the site to work. They slept out in the open at night, and for their meals they ate what rice they had brought with them to nourish them during their work. Their first job consisted of felling the trees. Since they had neither saws nor axes, they used their bush knives instead, burning the trees after they had cut them down. Next they cleared away the roots with tools simply made from hard wood, as there were no spades on the island either. The stones were broken in pieces by using harder stones to crack them, and then the complete landing strip, which measures roughly 55 yards by 1,200 yards, was covered with gravel to the depth of some 16 inches. Finally a layer of chalk, obtained from coral, was spread over the top. In this way, without tools or machinery or trucks, and by simply using baskets on poles to carry the chalk to the site, the work was completed by the natives walking barefoot over the sharp coral chalk. It only remained to wait for rain, so that the water would dissolve the chalk which would then cement the stones together.

Every morning before work began a short time of fellowship was held, and every evening the gospel was preached to the people on the landing strip itself. Over a thousand natives were present on each occasion. In spite of having to sleep out in the open, it was noted that not a single person fell sick throughout the whole operation, and when the workers returned to their homes they declared, "Nobody was taken ill because we committed everything to the Lord in prayer." During the three weeks it took to construct the airstrip, over ten thousand different people heard the gospel message. The task of preaching fell on the shoulders of three full-time evangelists, including Pastor Gideon. Although there were another 40 Christian workers present at the time, they were unable to deal with all the people who came to them to be counselled and to confess their sins. The building of the landing strip therefore served a dual purpose in that not only was a site prepared on which planes would land in the future, but the opportunity was taken to preach the gospel in the present. In the field of missionary work this story has no equal. Oh yes, landing strips have been built before on other mission stations throughout the world, but the landing strip at R. is not simply a track just a few hundred yards long with no real foundation. Instead it is a regular runway constructed on a genuine hardcore foundation. Even in Europe or the United States with the help of the latest machinery, a runway of this nature would have taken far longer than three weeks to build. And on top of all this there was no architect present to direct operations. Those who visit the airport are almost lost for words in attempting to describe this 'three week wonder'. As I drove along the length of the runway I thought of how wonderful it would be to be present when this miracle of the prayers and efforts of the natives on Rote is ceremonially opened and the first plane lands on the island.

It was quite characteristic of the Christians there to find that from the day construction began they did not cease to pray that the island would be kept free of tourism and all the evils this modern industry involves. It is quite distressing to see how much these native Christians are fearful of the influence of the West, in spite of the way in which the Lord has been blessing their work.

Although I have already mentioned some of the details of the conversion and life of Pastor Gideon, after having been able to meet and talk with him again following an interval of 16 months, I can now give a continuation of the story I began earlier. The heading of this section is, however, rather misleading as we shall shortly see.

It is quite a spiritual experience to be able to meet this wonderful brother in the Lord. But again I have no intention of setting him up on some kind of pedestal, for whatever a man achieves comes only from the Lord.

The number of fellowships in which he preaches has grown since last I met him from 30 to 52, although he must still travel to each of them by foot. But even if he had a car, he would not be able to use it, for roads suitable for traffic simply do not exist, and although a motor-cycle might enable him to travel along the forest paths more easily, there are none on Rote to be bought. And even if there were one, nobody would have enough money to buy it. Pastor Gideon refused the idea of having a salary, and when the church offered him financial help, he replied, "No, I want to put into practice the words of Matthew 6:33 and be solely dependent upon the Lord." He continues to practise this principle today. The Lord is so generous though, that he receives more than his colleagues who depend on a salary to supply their daily needs, and he sometimes even supports them.

On the question of salaries, I heard of one jungle pastor receiving a monthly income of only £4. Others seem to receive about £6 to £8 per month for their work. The highest paid minister I ever met received only £14 a month. Wages like these should come as a shock to people in the West, although it must be admitted that the daily lives of these brothers of ours in the Lord are much simpler than those of our own. For example, they receive **no** bills for either lighting, water or main drainage.

These amenities just do not exist in the areas where they live. For them even bread and potatoes are luxuries, for rice is the main constituent of all their meals. And their shoes are cheaper too — they walk from village to village on their own leather! One pastor, wanting to talk to me in Sumatra, travelled about 120 miles on foot in the tropical heat in order to meet me there. In the end he had been unable to walk another step, his swollen feet being so painful. The first thing I did when I met him, was to go out and buy him a pair of shoes. Some of my friends on hearing this story have decided to send him a small sum of money regularly in order to supplement the 'huge salary' he receives as a jungle pastor. In eternity the frugality and the sacrifices of these native Christians will overshadow much of the pretended greatness of the servants of God in the West.

Pastor Gideon is a man apart. Through being forced to come face to face with sorcery wherever he goes, in the end he decided to take the bull by the horns. His first mission took him to an ancient sacrificial site which was the subject of many taboos. Within the numerous caves found at the site, card players used to sit day and night practising their terrible art. In many areas card playing grips the natives almost like a disease. At the beginning of this century one particular cave used to be frequented by a notorious card player who was a dwarf. He had been an exceptionally cunning player and when he had died at the age of about 30 he had come to be regarded almost as a kind of god among the other card players. They had placed his coffin in a particularly honoured site in one of the caves, and it later became surrounded by a whole system of taboos. Whenever a person entered the cave, he had to put a small coin into the coffin as an offering. Naturally as time went by, the money mounted up, but the superstitious people were careful not to attempt to steal any of it. When Pastor Gideon arrived at the site, taking the coffin up in his hands in the name of Jesus he smashed it in pieces on the ground, throwing the money he found in it into the sea below. The natives waited, expecting him to die, for he had broken their sacred taboo, but when nothing untoward occurred, they were filled with awe and began to fear the pastor instead.

This active servant of God, however, was not content with a single victory. Entering the house of a man who had in his possession numerous charms and fetishes as well as many breast plates, swords and magic spears, he found that the wife was ill. The sorcerer spoke to Pastor Gideon and said, "I'm not able to heal my wife with my own magical charms. If you can make her better, I'll forsake my sorcery and burn all my fetishes." Gideon replied, "You can't bargain with God. Get rid of your charms and fetishes first, and then maybe God will listen to you and answer your prayer." The sorcerer asked to be given time to think about what he should do, but by the next day he had decided that he was prepared to destroy all his articles of magic. Having completed this task, he prayed together with Pastor Gideon for his wife, and the Lord healed her. When the people in the neighbourhood heard about the story, they began to esteem Pastor Gideon even more highly than before.

One of the main bulwarks of occultism in the area was a much feared sorcerer whose magical powers enabled him to kill people instantly. Magicians like this assert that they can send a flying fox to their victim who dies soon afterwards. The sorcerer our story is concerned with, had built his wife a house beside his own, and although he himself hated Pastor Gideon and all that he stood for, his wife was open to the gospel message. When the pastor visited the woman in her home a very mysterious thing took place. The sorcerer was lying in a trance in his house next door when suddenly his spirit appeared in the room where Pastor Gideon and the woman were talking. When they saw the ghost, the wife began to cough up blood and to roll her eyes as if she were going out of her mind. At the same time Pastor Gideon experienced some terrific pains in his back which continued to trouble him all the following night. In the end he had no other choice than to command the spirit in the name of Jesus to leave. Next day the pains had disappeared completely. The pastor went to visit the sorcerer a second time. In addition to all his fetishes and charms the evil man possessed a box of sugar which he maintained would cause a person to die if he attempted to move it from where it stood. Ordering a fire to be lit, Pastor Gideon, together with a friend, lifted the box up and brought it outside and destroyed it. He told me later that both he and his fellow believer, together with others who had been standing by watching, had seen blood dripping from the box as they had carried it to the fire. Everyone who knew the sorcerer's power was now convinced that Pastor Gideon would die. But again when nothing happened, a fear of the pastor spread throughout the whole neighbourhood. Everyone began to say that he possessed greater powers than the sorcerers, and when the pastor entered the houses of the natives, they would automatically surrender all their fetishes to him and allow them to be destroyed.

And so the 'chief magician' who is feared by all the other sorcerers on the island is none other than a simple believer, who, by the power of Christ, has been able to break down the bulwarks of darkness which once held the people in their grip. As the fetishes within a village are destroyed, the natives become receptive to the gospel message. In fact the revival only advances when the people's charms have been burnt. Again, I thought it very significant to hear Pastor Gideon say that just as on Timor, "The fetishes must not simply be burnt, but a prayer of renunciation must be prayed over them before their spell is really broken." In the West theologians are usually unaware of the reality of such phenomena, and even if they are presented with the facts, they generally find them intellectually indigestible. There are certain things that simply do not fit into the Western 'system', and one finds that the kingdom of God often operates according to an entirely different set of rules to those postulated by the unenlightened rationalists of the West.

But one thing is certain in all these conflicts: Jesus is able to deprive every outpost of sorcery and occultism on Rote of its power. Pastor Gideon is merely the Lord's instrument which He uses to achieve his goal. A Christian never acts in his own name, only in the name and on the authority of the One who bruised the serpent's head on the cross of Calvary.

The Teams

The Christians on Rote use the same method of evangelization as that which developed on Timor itself. In 1969 there were three teams working on the island, the largest of which consisted of a group of 15 believers under the leadership of a brother named Obed. This team, however, has only been able to work on a part-time basis since Obed is still in active government service. Once when the team was preaching in an area where the natives had destroyed and burnt down a number of their heathen temples, as they were about to leave, the villagers came and begged them not to go away. Driven by a spiritual hunger for the Word of God, they took hold of the feet of the team members and cried, "Don't go, don't go. We want to hear more about Jesus." It is almost impossible to imagine the scene. In contrast to the West where the churches use anything from beat music to dancing to lure the young people into their meetings, the natives of Indonesia cling to the feet of the Christians in their desperation to hear more of the Word of God. Since judgement is to begin first with the house of God, Western churches should examine themselves to see whether or not they will stand the test.

The leader of the second team on Rote is Samuel, the brother of Pastor Gideon. Although he has never attended a Bible school in his life, the Lord has equipped him with a great deal of spiritual authority. His gifts are similar to those found among the believers on Timor, and he is able to uncover the hidden sins and fetishes of those to whom he speaks. His ministry has resulted in the conversion of many of the islanders.

The last team is led by Naaman. He has a very moving testimony to tell. He was once a leading member of the Communist party in Indonesia, but after the abortive Communist attempt to take over the country he was arrested and put on the list of those to be executed. The loneliness and despair which overwhelmed him as he waited for the day of his execution finally resulted in bringing him to Christ. He began to pray a great deal in the prison and his heart became at rest. The day arrived on which he was to be shot. The names were called of those who were above him on the list. He waited, knowing he now had only a few more hours to live. But there was a delay, and when night fell he found himself still in his cell. Suddenly at midnight he heard a voice saying, "Get up." Naaman thought to himself, "They must be going to shoot me now." But the voice went on, "Leave the prison." It was only then that he noticed that the guards were all asleep, and he was able to escape unhindered. It was exactly like the experience of the apostle Peter when he too was imprisoned and under sentence of death (Acts 12).

Not knowing what to do now, Naaman fled to the forest and hid. His hair gradually grew until it reached his shoulders, and with only a little fruit from the forest to live on he soon became terribly thin and weak. Finally, driven by hunger, he found his way to a remote village on the island, but when the villagers saw him, he was immediately recognized. They wanted at first to take him along to the nearest police station, but since he had just been bitten by a snake and was hardly able to walk on his swollen foot, they handed him over to the custody of the local mayor until the island's authorities had been informed. That night the Lord spoke to him again and said, "Do not be afraid. I will send a man to you in the morning and he will give you help." The next morning a police lieutenant arrived who was also a believer. Recognizing very quickly that they were both Christians, the lieutenant said to him, "You will be interrogated tomorrow. When they ask you certain questions, answer them in exactly the same way as I tell you, and you will not be harmed. If you don't, they will kill you." Obeying his Christian brother, Naaman soon found himself free. He had hardly recovered from his ordeal, however, when he started to preach the gospel. It was evident that his conversion had not been motivated solely by fear, but that he had genuinely committed his life to the Lord. After working for a time on Timor, the Lord told him to form a team and to travel across to Rote where he was to evangelize further. Pastor Gideon described to me the blessing that had followed Naaman to Rote, and how the Lord had confirmed his ministry with signs following the preaching of his Word.

And so Rote is experiencing a visitation of the Lord as the salvation of God sweeps over the islands of Indonesia.

XXI. THE SPIRITUAL SITUATION IN INDONESIA

Between 1964 and 1970 three distinct groups of people have been touched by the revival in Indonesia. These are: the Moslems, the nominal Christians, and finally the animists or heathen.

When the revival originally began in 1964, it started among the Moslems of southern Sumatra, and in particular, among the poison mixers of whom we have already spoken. There are today some 1,500 converted Moslems in the area, and this includes a number of priests. There has also been a revival among the Moslems in West Java, Sumbawa and in the southern half of Celebes, but this has been on a smaller scale than in Sumatra. Besides the conversion of Moslems in these main areas of the revival, there have also been many cases of individual conversion very similar to that of the apostle Paul outside the walls of Damascus.

Numerically the greatest effect of the revival has been felt among the nominal Christians in the dead and traditional orthodox churches. Before the revival came to the area these Christians were characterized by the way in which they still clung to their former heathen occult practices. If a 'Christian' possesses charms or fetishes, he will always return to them in his hour of need. The spiritual outpouring on Rote and Timor fell upon many people who were in this position, and the same was also true in the smaller revival centres in East and Central Java.

The third group we have mentioned is difficult to fit into a unified picture. It is mainly a matter of governmental decree as to which particular religion a citizen of Indonesia is said to belong. Officially the only recognized religions in the country are Islam, Hinduism, Catholicism and Protestantism. This third group, therefore, can be divided into two sections. It is comprised in part of a number of former nominal or leftwing Moslems who have taken refuge under the flag of Christianity where they find it safer to abide on account of their previous connections with Communism. In addition to these, the group includes the animists from whose ranks the Catholic Church obtains numerous candidates for its mass baptism campaigns. As we have mentioned already the Karo-Batak tribe are included in this number. I have been able to gather some more material since my last visit to the area which helps a great deal in clarifying the picture. There are in front of me at this very moment some reports from a German missionary, together with a number of shorter reports from Christians who have worked in Sumatra and who have followed the history of these mass baptism from their very outset.

When a whole host of people queue up for Christian baptism, it depends to a large extent, if not entirely, on the attitude of the minister and elders present whether or not those who desire to be baptised are simultaneously led to a living knowledge of the Lord Jesus. In many mission fields today the spiritual situation is very similar to that of the churches in the West, where many of the pastors and ministers and workers have no personal knowledge of the Lord. Where this is the case, people desiring baptism can have little hope of being guided aright into faith in Christ. Yet if the church leaders are believing men, as the gospel is preached, genuine New Testament cells are quickly formed and the wind of revival begins to blow. In the Karo-Batak revival these cells have developed among the majority of those who have come forward for baptism. This is partly the result of evangelistic teams coming into the area from outside. For example, the Christian students in Bandung, after forming a team, went to the district of Karo-Batak and became responsible for a number of genuine conversions in answer to their faithfulness in prayer. The Lord has also revealed himself in the districts where believing missionaries have been working, but these revival groups are in the minority, and on the whole the vast majority of those who have supposedly become 'new Christians' through the campaigns of mass baptism, have been left completely untouched by the revival. But it would be a small thing for the Lord who has been working in such a wonderful way in Indonesia, to light His fire among the Karo-Batak, if that were also his will.

XXII. ASIA'S GREAT OPPORTUNITY

It is time to bring our report to an end. If the Lord will, we shall include further reports in later editions of this book. The revival continues in its state of flux. Every new day brings some fresh revelation from the Lord. In spite of the dangers which threaten, the blessing is plain for all to see.

Every revival is encompassed by a night of darkness which seeks to drown the work of God under a curse of sin. In Indonesia, the danger which threatens the Christians most stems from the many visions, miracles and voices which the believers are allowed to receive. We must always remember that our faith can never be built upon supernatural events like this, but only upon the Word of God and the Lord Jesus himself. Up till now these spiritual revelations have continued to retain their biblical form and divine characteristics, but if these are one day lost and a desire for miracles as an end in themselves, together with the sin of pride, creep in, then the days of the revival will be numbered. At the moment, though, we can praise God that he continues to guard the work which he has begun.

The true blessing of the revival lies in this: it is utterly dependent upon the written Word of God. The spiritual outpouring is a wonderful expression of the power and glory of the Lord Jesus Christ and of the Holy Spirit of God. This revival in Indonesia is a twentieth century Acts of the Holy Spirit. The flood of spiritual power which our brothers and sisters in the Lord are experiencing there gives us a glimpse of the Kingdom of God in all its might, and is God's open door in Asia today.

PART THREE

THE REVIVAL IN ASBURY

I. GOD WILL PROVIDE THE ANSWER

The following chapters originated in the United States of America. During the course of my ministry I have crossed this great continent on 13 different occasions and have preached the gospel of Christ in several hundred churches, colleges and seminaries. In this way I have gradually become aware of the actual conditions prevailing in this land.

The scope of the problems there, however, is so wide that one cannot even begin to describe them in any detail. Let me simply quote therefore from the daily newspapers lying beside me at the moment. The articles are dated the 13th and 14th May 1970.

The first report I see describes a fresh confrontation between the blacks and the whites in the State of Georgia. A 16-year-old negro boy has been beaten to death. The whites maintain that the blacks are responsible for his death while the blacks retort, "He was killed by the whites." The result of the conflict which followed was: 6 dead and 63 admitted to hospital, not to mention those suffering from minor injuries. At the same time 50 fires were reported in the area, and 300 National Guardsmen had to be flown in by helicopter to help the local police contain the opposing groups.

We are faced here with the ever increasing problem of black versus white. As a result of the increased organization among the negroes, the so-called Black Power movement has come into being. The most radical members of this movement form a kind of élite among the negroes called the Black Panthers. They make no secret of their aims and openly declare, "Within the next few years we will start a nation-wide revolution designed to repay the whites for the way they have treated us."

What are the forces behind the ever increasing intensity of these confrontations? It is not possible to place all the contributary factors over a common denominator.

First of all there are those who say that America is being presented today with the bill for the slavery she has fostered in past centuries. As history progresses injustices are balanced out.

Another factor which contributes a great deal to the problem is the question of colour and the discrimination against the negroes. The oppressed classes always rebel against those who rule over them. No matter what the continent or what the century, this problem has always existed.

Then again, one of the most important factors is the world-wide political confrontation between Communism and the Free World. Communist ideologists find this racial conflict extremely useful, and they are for ever trying to stir up more trouble in order to bring the struggle for power to a head. Even as I write these words, the walls and buildings of the United States are plastered with the slogan — Revolution Now! What does this mean?

There are about 16 million negroes living in the U.S.A., mainly in the Southern States. The aim, which is continually being fostered by the Communist agitators, is: the expropriation of the white landlords. The blacks must inherit the land on which they have been forced to work for centuries. The 'black belt' must leave the Union of States and become an independent State in its own right. The cry which went up between the First and Second World Wars of 'selfdetermination' has changed now to one of 'national freedom'. What some of the Communists have in mind is nothing less than a 'negro-soviet' republic — an expression which was first coined as far back as in 1928 by the international Communist, John Pepper. Politically speaking, a break-away Southern State would be a heavy blow to America, but a great boon to the Communists.

Yet the struggle is not only racial. The Communist ideologists have very decided aims, one of which is to win over the youth of the country, particularly the young intellectuals. On the 14th May 1970 the newspapers contained the following reports.

As a result of the events taking place in Vietnam and Cambodia, students from 192 colleges and universities demonstrated against the Nixon administration. In the University of Los Angeles alone some 8,500 students took part in a protest march. The main roads of the city were blocked. In other towns and cities the police were pelted with stones, public buildings were demolished, and college property smashed. In Columbus, Ohio, four students were shot dead in clashes with the police.

What inspires these demonstrations? One could think of many answers. Many people claim that the students are being stirred up by minority left-wing elements. Yet these rebellious young people will be occupying the country's key positions within the next 10 to 15 years. Those who mold their political outlook today will reap the profits tomorrow. The Communists often realize this fact far better than the worn out liberal government officials and authorities of our day.

The world situation is extremely confused. In the West students march under the Red flag holding the Mao Bible in their hands, while in the East the nations under Communism form one great concentration camp where freedom has long since ceased to exist. Peking's slogan, 'Red or Dead', contains much truth. If students in Moscow or Peking dared to protest like their counterparts do in the West, the Communist crematoriums would soon be working overtime.

Again and again I have heard Christians in the Far East ask, "Why aren't the Western stone-, egg-, and tomato-throwing students given the chance to take an active part in the construction of the Red paradise? They would have no time to protest during their 10 to 12 hours of 'voluntary' labour each day, and although they would get every tenth day off in Russia they would still have to spend some of their free time in attending classes for political indoctrination. And in Red China the only free day they would get each year would be the Chinese New Year's Day. Having to work solidly for 364 days of each year might make them appreciate the freedoms they have in the West, and it might stop the smear campaign they are engaged in against Western democracy."

If one were to believe, however, that the only factors behind these protests were of a political or a social or a racial nature, one should apply for a stronger pair of spiritual glasses. The Scriptures are quite explicit about the situation of the world today. In 2 Timothy 3 : 1—4 we read, "In the last days there will come times of stress. For men will be lovers of self, lovers of money, proud, arrogant, abusive, disobedient to their parents, ungrateful, unholy, inhuman, implacable, slanderers, profligates, fierce, haters of good, treacherous, reckless, swollen with conceit, and lovers of pleasure rather than lovers of God."

We are living close to the end of the age. The chaos is growing and manifesting itself more clearly every day. Law and order is crumbling before the onslaught of the powers of darkness. Today's revolutionaries hang like puppets from the hand of the arch-enemy of our souls, completely unaware of his true designs. But how could they know? They neither read the Bible nor are open to the illumination of the Holy Spirit. As Goethe himself once said, "Even when the devil takes them by the collar, people still remain oblivious to his presence."

The end is fast approaching. The world can no longer be saved. No matter what the false prophets of optimism say, nothing will divert the world from its present course.

The columns of the newspapers I have already mentioned describe a small attempt to solve the racial struggle. A church decided to use all its capital resources, which amounted to something in the region of 3 million dollars, in an attempt to alleviate the suffering of part of the poor negro population. The result was that the church became filled on Sundays with a coloured congregation. The pastor, although white, will have nothing to fear now from the blacks in any future racial strife, yet one wonders whether the day may come when he is struck by a white man's bullet. To take sides is to become the enemy of the opposing party.

The result is the same whether the bullet which kills us was fired by a black or a white hand.

The world is like a great train which is rushing with ever increasing speed towards its final goal. It is impossible to jump off for the train will only finally halt at the STOP sign at the end of the age.

God himself has fixed the sign ahead. In Acts 17 : 31 we read:

God has appointed a day.
God has ordained a man.
God's judgement is ready at hand.

Our earth is passing away. The solar system in which we live will not abide for ever. In Matthew 24 : 35 Jesus says, "Heaven and earth will pass away." Only one thing will remain: the Word of the Lord.

We are standing at the threshold of some of this world's greatest events. Those who have eyes to see, let them see! Those who have ears to hear, let them hear! God is going to provide the answer. His silence to date is simply a sign of his patience. His forbearance speaks of his mercy. Yet the spotlights are already focussing upon the One who is to come.

II. GOD'S PREPARATORY WORK

This century, in which the final accounts of the world will almost certainly be presented, has already seen the windows of heaven open on several occasions. In 1905 Western Europe was richly blessed through the revival in Wales. Then Korea experienced her prayer revival, the spirit of which continues to be effective even today. The German book 'Koreas Beter' describes this. Next came Uganda in Africa, where God stirred up a great movement of repentance and confession of sin among the people. It was there that the Christians learned to practise the habit of 'walking in the light'. In 1945 a missionary revival sprang up among the Tayal mountain tribes on Formosa. Then in the autumn of 1965 the glorified Lord lit a fire on the island of Timor in Indonesia, and a revival of an almost apostolic nature began.

And today the Lord is still at work shedding his light in the darkness around us in order to show us the way. The most recent glimpse of his light can be seen in the revival at Asbury College in Wilmore, Kentucky, U.S.A. But before we go on to describe this movement of the Spirit of God one important question must be answered:

Are we right to write about a revival?

Many people will answer almost spontaneously, "But of course. Why not?" Yet the question is justified, for after the original publication of this book in Germany, two missionaries opposed its distribution. They maintained that it would have a damaging effect on the course of the revival. One of them went so far as to try to actively hinder the distribution of some free copies in his area. They lay idle in his home for months before the people they were intended for finally managed to get him to hand them out.

Is it right, therefore, to publish a report of this nature? First of all let me say by way of a personal confession: not one of my books is written without a lot of 'knee-work' beforehand. The prayer is ever on my lips, "Lord, fill these books with your Holy Spirit and use them for the salvation of those for whom you died."

Let us look at the pros and cons quite objectively. It is definitely wrong to blow something up out of all proportions. Sensationalism, exaggeration, and the describing of miracles for miracles' sake, presents a danger to the healthy course of any revival.

Moreover, there is the problem of the devil attacking those involved in the revival whose stories are published abroad. Every genuine missionary and evangelist knows how easy it is for believers to backslide and to become proud when reports of their spiritual histories are made known publicly.

In Moslem countries too, there are further sources of danger. Christians are often exposed in these places to the terrorization of the fanatical followers of Mohammed, and for this reason it is often best to avoid the use of personal names and geographical locations — as we have sometimes done so in this book — when speaking about the movement of God's Spirit in these areas.

In the light of these three arguments against the writing of a report on a revival, what reasons are there for publicizing such events?

Basically there are three important reasons why one should inform the Church of Christ at large when a revival has broken out.

Had Matthew, Mark and John been over-anxious about writing their reports, their Gospels would not have existed today. Had Luke closed his eyes to the revival which occurred during his lifetime, neither his Gospel nor the Acts would have found their way into our hands. The history of the Christian Church would have taken a very different course had these reports never been published, and what a blessing would have been lost to mankind.

Somehow a short circuit has taken place if Christians who are called to intercede for mission fields and to donate richly towards their work are later refused the blessing of being able to share in a written report.

But the problem is even greater than this, and it leads us to the very front line of the work of God in this world. Mankind today is passing through a time of great suffering. In Vietnam some 300,000 children have been orphaned since the conflict began there. In Nigeria we have heard of the millions of Ibos who have died of starvation. We are shocked to hear of the cruel tortures which Christians are forced to suffer in Chinese and Russian prisons. Such sorrows as these are almost too much for those who sometimes pray for nights on end for the world in which we live. There is a need to tell these lonely children of God within whose hearts the suffering of their fellow creatures burns, the wonderful miracles which God is doing in the revival areas of our day. Such reports are like balm for their wounds. Is it wrong for those who weep with those who weep, to be given the opportunity in a similar way of rejoicing with those who rejoice in an outpouring of the Spirit of God?

It cannot be considererd right when certain Christians out of a concern for the treasures of a revival shut out the rest of the Body of Christ. When God pours out the oil of gladness on a part of his Church, it is meant to be enjoyed not only by those who stand in the actual course of the stream, but by the Church of Christ as a whole.

Not least we should remember as one of the chief arguments the scriptural fact that the Body of Christ is a unity. Paul writes in 1 Corinthians 12 : 26, "If one member suffers, all suffer together; if one member is honoured, all rejoice together." And 'all' does not only mean those who live in a certain geographical location near to where God's outpouring has taken place.

We are therefore more than justified in informing the Church about the revival in Asbury. What a terrific blessing would have been lost by other colleges and universities in the United States if the revival in Asbury had been kept to itself. But the teachers and the students have testified, sometimes even on the radio, to the American people of what God is doing in their midst. What matters is not the pleasing of people but the building up of the kingdom of God.

The revival, however, is significant in another way. Thousands of Christians in America have been horrified by the hopeless moral, political and spiritual depths to which their country has sunk over the last few decades. And now at last, in answer to their prayers, God has sent revival. This is proof that God has not finally given up the Western world. So are we to keep quiet? Are we to remain silent about the answer that God has given to the cry of these Christians' hearts?

Yet this is not all. Do the students of Asbury realize that in Korean prayer meetings, and in the simple huts of Timor and other Indonesian islands, native Christians have been praying for years for a revival to come to the United States? Have these American students, who have been called to carry the torch of the gospel still further, realized that Christians in Communist prisons too, have been praying for a spiritual awakening of their land?

The Asbury revival may well be called a prayer revival. There are countless thousands of Christians the world over whose prayers form the backbone of this spiritual outbreak in the U.S.A. The East has not only brought the Red and murderous terror of Communism to America, but it has brought something far better — the prayers of those tortured for Christ in Communist prisons.

I was deeply moved to hear of the testimony of Richard Wurmbrand when he described how Christians with 50 pound chains at their feet pray every night for their brothers living in the freedom of the West, who, although they are not bound by chains of iron, are bound with fetters of a different sort.

The revival in Asbury is a miracle of God. The praying Church in the East has found her brothers in prayer in the West. A chain of prayer has encircled the world. The Church of Christ is being prepared through the Holy Spirit for the coming great day of the Lord's return. But this is running on ahead. Let us see how the course of events took place.

III. GOD'S GLORY REVEALED

Asbury College is situated in the small town of Wilmore in the State of Kentucky, U.S.A.

On Tuesday the 3rd February 1970, the regular morning meeting was held as usual at 10 o'clock. It was scheduled to last for a quarter of an hour. However, although the preacher kept to the time allotted to him, God had other thoughts in mind. As the minister challenged the congregation to decide to follow Christ, several of the students responded and began to make their way to the front.

As the minutes passed, however, more and more decided to surrender their lives to Christ. Recognizing what was happening, the school authorities cancelled the lessons for the morning. The Holy Spirit had begun to work in the hearts and lives of the students. "Not in the wind, not in the earthquake, not in the fire, but in a still small voice" (1 Kings 19 : 11—12).

The movement continued on into the afternoon with the students remaining in the chapel kneeling around the altar. Gradually more and more people found themselves joining in the prayers, and the number of those praying in the Hughes auditorium grew to 1,200. On this first day of the revival several hundred people committed their lives to Christ.

For many, the thought of eating had left their minds completely, and the huge prayer meeting continued on into the evening. By midnight, although the number of those who were praying had fallen by half, many remained to pray the whole night through. On Wednesday morning at 6 o'clock 75 students were still praying in the hall.

IV. THE PRAYER REVIVAL

That Wednesday normal classes were still impossible. The students simply knelt on the floor of the great auditorium all day and prayed.

On these first two days no sermon was preached, but instead the time was filled with praying, singing, brief confessions of sin, and testimonies of personal blessing.

News of the event spread quickly through the neighbourhood. Friends of the school, together with many spiritually hungry people, soon arrived hoping to share in the blessing. On Wednesday the number of visitors rose to 1,300. Yet there was still no evangelistic message given. The only people who spoke were those students who had been converted in the first two days and who now wanted to tell how God had dealt with them.

Yet even at such times there were still usually over a hundred students on their knees in silent prayer. One particular student who had been present when the revival had begun, did not leave the hall for a total of 48 hours. The power of the Holy Spirit had overcome him.

Within a few days visitors had arrived at the college from all over Kentucky. Indeed they came from all over the United States. And every one of them was able to share in the stream of blessing. A wave of cleansing and a spirit of prayer gripped all those who joined in the large prayer meetings which ensued.

Even people who were unable to be present began to share in the blessing. Requests for prayer and intercession arrived by letter and over the phone. As a result the whole of North America was soon covered with a network of intensive prayer. But this would never have happened if the teachers at Asbury College had jealously guarded the blessing of revival and kept it to themselves.

Other colleges and theological seminaries started to send messages of greetings and requests for prayer, as they sought to share in the spiritual renewal which the students at Asbury had experienced.

The spiritual discernment and wisdom of the teachers at the college is underlined by the fact that normal lessons were not restarted until a week after the initial outbreak. On top of this the sports meetings were cancelled at the request of the students themselves.

The theological seminary situated nearby was also engulfed by the wave of prayer.

V. HE SENT THEM OUT TWO BY TWO

In Luke 10 : 1 we read of how Jesus sent the seventy out two by two. At Asbury the revival developed in the same way. After three days and three nights of prayer two of the students rose to their feet and declared that they felt a responsibility towards other colleges in the land. While Mark Davis went to Greenville College, Wayne Anthony felt called to visit Azusa College — a college in which I have also preached only a few years ago.

And so the missionary work of Asbury College had begun. The college's own report described quite clearly how the students decided after 72 hours of prayer that they should spread the blessing further for the sake of the kingdom of heaven.

The messengers who subsequently left the college were supported by the unceasing prayers of those who remained. In the meantime requests for prayer were coming in not only from all over North America but also from other places throughout the world.

Soon after the departure of the first two messengers of the gospel, other teams followed. On their return, like Paul and Barnabas in Acts 15 : 4, "They declared all that God had done through them."

Colleges visited by the teams reported revivals among their own students similar to that experienced at Asbury College itself.

VI. MORE AND MORE BELIEVERS WERE ADDED

In Acts 5 : 14 we read, "And more than ever believers were added to the Lord." By the evening of the fourth day some 1,600 people were gathered together in the great auditorium at Asbury. There were students there from many other universities and colleges. But it was not curiosity which had drawn them. Each one had been driven by a desire to meet with God. Like myself, they had felt compelled to come and share in the blessing which God was pouring out.

The college staff appointed one of their members to act as public relations officer between themselves and other institutes of further education. On top of this reporters began to arrive from various newspapers and above all from Christian magazines. Dr. Kinlaw, the college president, reminded the newsmen that theirs was not the only college to have experienced revival. Dartmouth, Princeton and Yale had all been scenes of God's outpouring in the past.

There were the critics too, who sought to uncover some extreme or psychical movement at Asbury. But they were disappointed. There was no sensationalism, no noising abroad of spiritual experiences, and no speaking in tongues either.

The special characteristics of the revival were all on the same plane: a spirit of worship, song and prayer; thanksgiving; supplication and intercession. Every one of these involved communion with God. The intensity of their prayers was the key to the answers they received from heaven. "The prayer of a righteous man has great power in its effects" (James 5 : 16).

One of the ministers present begged the students to intercede on behalf of his son who had been paralysed since birth. When a number of the students began to pray for the boy the Lord answered them and he was healed.

VII. THE WORD OF GOD INCREASED

When the shepherds of Bethlehem were honoured by God with the news of the Saviour's birth, instead of adopting a legalistic and pious attitude of secrecy, these simple men felt compelled to spread the story abroad.

In Asbury, instead of shepherds or craftsmen, it was students. But what the shepherds and the students had in common was a mighty revelation of the grace of God. And like the shepherds, the students could not help but pass on the blessing that God had poured into their hearts.

On the Sunday following the commencement of the revival, instead of attending their usual places of worship, many of the inhabitants of Wilmore went to the college's auditorium. They were irresistibly drawn to this fresh fountain of the blessing of God.

What an experience it was for the visitors when they heard the students testifying of the manner in which the Lord had saved them. In America, even more so than in either England or Germany, students have the reputation of being just 'undiciplined, critical demonstrators'. It is true that such a label only fits one section of the student population, but the negative picture always seems to overshadow the positive one. This, however, only served to increase the astonishment of those who heard the reports as they spread throughout the United States.

Invitations were received from all over the country. It would have been impossible to answer them all, had not many of the students been ready to carry the torch of the gospel further.

One of the teachers told the students of all the requests they had received. The response was enormous. Of the one thousand students at the college, some four to five hundred volunteered to go out and work on the teams.

To keep track of the overall picture, the teams' movements were traced with coloured pins on a map of the United States. Yet, unusual as it may seem for Americans who love to quote impressive figures, the number of those converted was not recorded. This was an amazing sign of the moderation and reserve of the Christians concerned.

Instead, they gave themselves to a far more rewarding task. The college, by means of the radio, brought into being a great network of prayer. Their program is broadcast each afternoon at 5 o'clock on shortwave at 14325 kc. By the end of the first week 16 other colleges had joined in the scheme. By now, however, as I write these words the number has increased fivefold.

Such a rate of growth within a single week is almost impossible to grasp. Just think of the number of thousands of people who were caught up in the streams of blessing issuing from the world's most recent revival through the gospel broadcasts and the missions of the teams! Our brothers in America did the exact opposite to the two Indonesian missionaries who tried to hinder the spreading of the news of the revival on Timor and the surrounding islands.

Of course, it would be easy for the European in his

arrogance to retort, "Well, what can you expect of the Americans?" But this is unfair. If there exists the possibility of reaching a million people instead of a thousand, then surely it is more scriptural to make use of the greater opportunity in furthering the work of the Lord. Those who only have one talent should not endeavour to hinder those who have had five talents entrusted to them. And in any case, it is not a matter of either our own 'shortsightedness' or 'longsightedness', but of the command which we receive from the Lord. God is judge, and not the brother who seeks to measure us according to his own standards.

VIII. THE NEW SPIRIT

By the end of the first week some 12,000 people had come from all over the country to visit the college in order to share in the outpouring of God's Holy Spirit. The students themselves had continued in prayer for a total of 168 hours. One of them had remained at prayer in the chapel for the whole of the seven days. What physical resources this must have required! Yet he was able to draw from the same fountain from which Elisha fed during his 40 days journey to Mount Horeb.

Classes had been discontinued during this time, and they only began again on the Wednesday of the week following the first outpouring. Yet the spirit of prayer at the college was not quenched, and whenever the students were free, they would make their way to the chapel to pray.

The first wave of blessing was carried into 16 different States through the work of the missionary teams in this first week. And several thousands of people were converted as a result of their labours.

Even the reporters were amazed at the miraculous new spirit among the students. In an article from which I will quote, one of them wrote, "What is wrong with these students? . . . . All of a sudden they have adopted a different attitude towards the opposite sex. A wave of inner cleanliness has swept away the sexual licentiousness. The militant spirit is gone. Instead of charging through our towns like wild animals, throwing petrol bombs and assaulting our citizens and police, here in the small town of Wilmore a quiet spirit of prayer and communion with God reigns. While the peace of the nation is being disturbed by political and social unrest, here in this student revival the atmosphere has been cleared as if by the presence of God. Up till now I had thought myself to be a Christian. Here in this college, however, doubts have been raised concerning the whole of my Christian life."

A minister from Pennsylvania who invited me to hold a mission in his town, wrote a letter to me describing how he and his own church had been gripped by the spirit of the revival in Asbury. His life and his ministry had been utterly changed.

IX. DAILY WITH ONE ACCORD IN THE TEMPLE

In Acts 2 : 46 Luke wrote these words, "And day by day, attending the temple together and breaking bread in their homes, they partook of food with glad and generous hearts." To live day by day under the Word of God! Today those of us who call ourselves Christians hardly do this week by week!

Every revival is characterized by believers meeting together daily to pray and to hear the Word of God preached. As it was in Korea, so it is in Indonesia, and also in the Asbury revival.

After three weeks the students were still meeting together every day to pray. Throughout the day hundreds of students could be found on their knees in intercession and prayer. Each evening visitors from all over the United

States crowded into the large auditorium which, in spite of its 1,500 seats, was unable to contain all who came.

These meetings illustrate the unity of the Church of Christ. Irrespective of their denomination everyone shared in this new manifestation of the Holy Spirit. Among those present were Lutherans, Baptists, Nazarenes, Methodists, Episcopalians and Independents, as well as members of various missionary societies.

Questions of doctrine and theological disputes and liturgical differences no longer mattered. Only one thing was important: getting right with God and conforming to His will. — Theology only creates churches. The Holy Spirit creates the Church of Jesus Christ.

X. THEY DID NOT CEASE

The ministry of the Early Church was one of almost 'non-stop' evangelism. In Acts 5:42 we read, "And every day in the temple and at home they did not cease teaching and preaching Jesus as the Christ."

The revival in Asbury has developed along similar lines. In the first few months, as a result of the evangelistic work of the teams, 35 other universities and colleges experienced similar movements of God's Spirit. During the same period the effects of the revival became visible in 25 other States. Large numbers of people were converted through reading the reports in the newspapers, and through radio and television programs. Why should these modern means of communication be used exclusively as weapons of the prince of darkness?

The following examples illustrate the growth of the spiritual movement. A Christian business man in Anderson, Indiana, hired the local town hall and invited students from Asbury to come and speak there. A number of prayer meetings were held and the hall was crowded with people. Each lunch time the students, together with office workers, business men and manual labourers met together under the Word of God. The spark of revival spread from the town hall to a local church and from there to the nearby college.

On another occasion a team of three Asbury students, Mark Davis, Janie Wiley and David Nesselroade, accepted an invitation to visit Denver, Colorado. On a Sunday evening some 3,000 people gathered together in the beautiful Calvary Church to hear the Word of God preached.

At the time of writing, meetings of this nature are spreading all over the United States in the wake of the Asbury revival. At the close of these meetings when the audience is invited to surrender their lives to Christ, hundreds of people come out to the front. There is hardly ever enough room for all those who wish to register their decision, and sometimes the area before the altar is filled more than three or four times by inquirers desiring counselling and intercession.

The spiritual wave of repentance and soul-searching is gradually filling the whole country. It was seeing these results for myself which caused me to write this report.

Genuine revivals always seek to spread to areas as yet untouched by the Spirit of God. The apostle Paul felt compelled to travel from Asia Minor to Europe and to Spain. Thomas was called by God to go to India. Nommensen was drawn to preach to the Batak. Hudson Taylor felt the call of the Chinese people. It is not a love of adventure or of travel which grips the heart of every true missionary of God, but rather the urge contained in the command of our Lord Jesus when he said, "Go into all the world and preach the gospel to the whole creation" (Mark 16 : 15).

The Asbury revival has been led along this same pathway by the Lord. The first call the students received was to visit Canada, and there they were instrumental in carrying the flame of this new fire further.

The next request came from Columbia, a country in which remarkable changes have been taking place in recent years. Only 20 years ago Protestant missionaries and churches were being brutally persecuted and opposed. The stamping out of religious freedom had taken on such terrible forms that other countries throughout the world began to voice their disapproval. But the time of persecution was followed by a period of much blessing. Today Columbia is hungry for the gospel.

A friend of mine is currently sending thousands of Spanish editions of the New Testament into Columbia and other Latin American countries. The gifts of German and Swiss Christians have made it possible to send 5,000 Spanish New Testaments and several hundred copies of my own books printed in Spanish into these South American countries. And the fruit of this work is already being seen. As I write, another shipment of some 40,000 New Testaments is again on its way. The doors of Latin America are opening to the gospel and to the work of the Holy Spirit. A time of great opportunity faces these countries so shaken by social problems and revolution. There is no human answer to these troubles; only the gospel can help.

While we are on the subject of the Catholic countries in South America, there is one wonderful spiritual event that just cannot be left unmentioned. Only a year ago a Catholic archbishop was converted, and one of the first things he did was to order some thousands of New Testaments for his country. His aim was to supply every Catholic in his archbishopric with one of these New Testaments.

I am aware that there will be much scepticism about a report like this. For example, when the author of the book 'Koreas Beter' described two of Pope Paul's religious experiences, the publishers asked him to leave the stories out of his book. Yet since then I have met a minister in Canada who actually heard Pope Paul describe these experiences himself during an audience at the Vatican. The truth of the report was therefore confirmed.

There are many strange events taking place today. While Protestant bishops are becoming modernists and are denying the sonship of the Lord Jesus Christ, high Catholic dignitaries are opening their hearts to the gospel of Christ. And I write this as a Protestant myself. God's Spirit blows where he wills.

In Columbia, however, the door has opened to the gospel message among the Protestant population. The visiting Asbury students came face to face with this new situation. It is absolutely essential that the missionaries and evangelists who go to this land take with them a healthy and sober attitude towards the Word of God, for these Spanish countries are in grave danger of being swamped by the extremism of certain Christians and by the tongues movement.

The missionary venture of the Asbury students in Columbia was climaxed by a ten-day missionary campaign. The campaign was financed by the home churches of the students concerned. Neither Asbury College nor the students would have been able to finance this work themselves. Through actions of this nature tired and weary churches have sometimes been stirred to share in the blessing of the Asbury revival.

Looking back over the first six weeks of the revival, which began on the 3rd February 1970, the results are astonishing. The man in charge of public relations, Arthur Lindsay, says in his report, "More than a thousand evangelistic teams have already gone out. On top of this the neighbouring theological seminary has also given birth to several hundred teams."

One is simply lost for words and compelled to worship the Lord who has wrought such a wonder as this. All the honour is due to his name. In an already chaotic world the exulted Lord has erected a sure sign of his imminent return before our very eyes.

And still certain over-anxious brethren attempt to hinder the reporting of these events. Yet the whole of Christendom longs to be able to share in the workings of God's Spirit today. For this reason therefore, it is essential to publish the story of the revival at Asbury as it actually took place.

XI. GOD HAS ANSWERED

Several years ago Billy Graham said that he could see no hope for America in the future if it failed to find its way back to God.

Anyone who has travelled widely — and the Lord has granted this privilege to me — will realize that America is a country which is bleeding from many wounds.

A college lecturer told one of my friends, the Rev. Plaum in Chicago, that 60 % of the students at his college were on drugs. It is impossible to imagine what the future holds for a nation whose youth is destroying itself in such a way. America, having freed herself from the grip of the slave-trade, is now gripped by a far worse form of slavery — drug addiction.

I was told in Los Angeles of a new sect that had just been founded called the 'New Heaven'. Their meetings consist of the teaching, demonstrating and practice of all sorts of sexual perversity. They are the slaves of sex.

In Chicago I listened once to a discussion concerning the late Dr. Martin Luther King. European Christians usually have a much more optimistic opinion of him than Christians in America where he is accused by many of having been orientated more around racialism than around Christ. This, they claim, is what led to his assasination. But let us avoid discussions of this nature. I simply wanted to point out that his death was basically due to the old evil of racial hatred. The colour problem, which has had a long history in the U.S.A., is like an ulcer which cannot be healed.

While I was in New York I talked with the pilot of an American air line who was a genuine Christian. He told me that for the past two years he had been watching the acts of sabotage which had been taking place under the instigation of the Communistically orientated transport workers. When he had informed his superiors, they had merely told him to keep quiet about it and to tell no one of what was taking place, or else he would lose his job. When he found it impossible to live with his conscience any longer, after having seen for example expensive pieces of electronic equipment being destroyed, he reported the matter again. The result was that he was immediately sacked. I asked him why this had happened. He replied, "Many important posts in our country are undermined by the Communists." This amounts to Americans stabbing their own government in its back. They betray their own country in the cause of Russian and Chinese 'imperialism'.

During my most recent visit to the United States I heard a lot about the latest student demonstrations. We will mention just one instance as an example. A son of one of the astronauts was beaten up quite unmercifully for the simple reason that the radical left-wing students regard the astronauts as representatives of a form of society they seek to oppose. And so the son had to suffer for the successful mission of his own father. Students who accept without gratitude the benefits of their Western colleges and universities spend their time rebelling against all authority.

We have only mentioned five of the wounds from which the American nation is suffering: drug addiction, sex, racialism, political extremism, and the overthrowing of past traditions and authority.

Neither the State nor the Church, neither force nor reason, have succeeded in dealing with these ever growing problems. Humanly speaking there is no answer to these questions.

Yet God has given his reply. What men found impossible to do in spite of their good intentions, He has wrought. He sent his Spirit among the student population which many had already given up as lost. And so America's youth, part of which is recognized for its rioting and malicious radicalism, is becoming the bearer of the glad tidings which are able to heal every wound. God has begun to work through this movement at Asbury College, and he continues to work today.

In a Western world in which prayer is almost unknown, He has sent a prayer revival. Instead of the rioting, the protesting, the criticism, and the demonstrations of the past, there is prayer: a praying motivated by the Holy Spirit in answer to the disasters which have almost overwhelmed the Western world.

Forgive me for having the audacity to ask, but I appeal to all those students who have been gripped by the spirit of this revival, to pray for me too. I need your prayers.

DATE DUE